IS IT JUST ME?

IS IT JUST ME?

Miranda Hart

791. 45028092

WINDSOR

PARAGON

First published 2012
by Hodder & Stoughton
This Large Print edition published 2013
by AudioGO Ltd
by arrangement with
Hodder & Stoughton

Hardcover   ISBN: 978 1 4713 3457 3
Softcover   ISBN: 978 1 4713 3458 0

British Library Cataloguing in Publication Data available

Printed and bound in Great Britain by
MPG Books Group Limited

To my dear reader chum

ACKNOWLEDGEMENTS

This book would not have come into existence without the help of some very lovely and kind people. Many thanks firstly to my agent Gordon Wise at Curtis Brown and Hannah Black at Hodder, for their wisdom and patience in guiding me through the process and for the encouragement to accept the task to write a book. And most importantly, for the laughs along the way.

Also thanks to Rowena Webb and all at Hodder for their support and generally being a wonderful bunch. Would any other publishing house gallop a mile for Sport Relief in my honour I wonder?

My Mum and Dad deserve a big thank you for allowing me to treat their house like a hotel and putting up with me regressing to a teenage like state when I retreated homeward to get the book written.

And finally, for their advice, comment and input Rose Heiney, Paul Powell, and my sister Alice, who remains patiently at the end of the phone to be asked the constant question 'Is this funny?' for anything I do.

Right, that's enough about you all, back to me and my book . . .

CONTENTS

1

LIFE, EH . . .?

My Dear Reader Chum, a very hearty hello to you. What an honour and privilege it is to have you perusing my written word. It is nothing short of tremendous to have you to chat to and, I hope, now that we're on sentence three, you are sitting comfortably. Or maybe you're lying. Lying, perhaps, on a beach, or snuggled in your bed; perhaps you've constructed a small fort out of cushions, in which case I applaud you. Or maybe you've thrown caution to the wind, and you're lying on the bookshop floor having a little breather (if that's the case, I'm not being rude, but you're a bit weird). Maybe you're standing on a commuter train, using this book as a filter between you and a repellent armpit. If so, I'm terribly sorry. That's no way to start the day, is it? Face in a pit. Commuter trains are the only place you'd not question standing what in any other social scenario would be freakishly and embarrassingly close to a friend, let alone a stranger. But, I welcome all readers standing. Maybe there are others kneeling? Perhaps you're in church; maybe you're at a wedding, with this book tucked surreptitiously into the Order of Service.

Whatever position you find yourself in, I hope you are ensconced and comfortable, for we are—can you believe it?—already on our second paragraph, and well in to this little literary journey together. Should you wish to continue, I suggest that you take this opportunity to arm yourself with a cup of tea and a biscuit, or a bucket of cappuccino and a bollard-sized muffin, or a nourishing soup or, if you're so inclined, just break all the rules and grab yourself a full-on roast. For we've got a book, yes, a whole *book*, to romp through together, and I wouldn't want you going hungry as we begin a-romping (now stop it, cheeky: you're making up your own jokes).

What I'd most like to say up front and with all the love that I can muster is that you are very welcome indeed. Whoever you are, however you've chosen to arrange yourself, and whatever snack you've selected, I clasp you firmly to my writerly bosom. Let there be no confusion about that. You are a much-loved guest in my storybook castle. I applaud you for choosing—and I say this with absolutely no impartiality or objectivity of any kind—such a marvellous book. Of all the books on the shelf, just look what you've gone and bought. Give yourself a round of applause, even if you're in public. I dare you. Actually I tell you what, as this would make me very happy: if you're in public and see someone else reading this book, why don't you applaud each other? What a lovely moment that would be. I advocate that as much as I advocate adults galloping, or people randomly wandering into an optician to try on the most unflattering and amusing glasses for no good reason. It's what I call 'making your own fun'. Because you have to, really, don't you? As, let's face it; life does have a tendency to throw up difficulties, depressions, moments of boredom, loneliness or grind. I don't know. Life, eh?

*   *   *

'Life, eh?' It's a phrase I've heard myself and others say over the years, many times. It's often only just audible, thrown away over a sigh, or comes at the end of a laugh. A phrase, or tic, or jerk, or (and I beg your pardon) ejaculation reserved for significant moments. Times when you just can't put into words the emotions and happenings of this weird and wonderful journey of existence. I recently said it on holiday with my friend, Nicky, looking out at a sunset over the sea, when she and I realised we'd known each other ten years to the week. We looked back at all we had wanted then, and all we had achieved. It was a lovely moment, and I heard myself punctuating the conversation with, 'Life, eh?' When my little sister had a daughter, we sat with my newborn niece in our parent's garden, where she and I had often sat as young girls thirty years before. We said together, wistfully, 'Life, eh?' It says everything without having to say anything: that we all experience moments of joyful or painful reflection, sometimes alone, sometimes sharing laughs and tears with others; that we all know and appreciate that however wonderful and precious life is, it can equally be a terribly confusing and mysterious beast. 'Life, eh?'

Those kinds of moments—the big ones, the meaty ones, the births, the deaths, the reminiscences—I can handle. Those kinds of moments I enjoy or endure, much as we all do. There's usually a sort of road map for them. Traditions. Procedure. But . . . where I feel alone and unprepared is with the less serious but

3

undeniably discombobulating and embarrassing hiccups, nuances and foibles of just . . . being a person.

Let me furnish you with a recent example: has anyone else, whilst negotiating a slippery prawn in a smart restaurant, catapulted said prawn over their shoulder so it hit their next-door diner in the eye? Now it is, of course, at times like this that one should remain very serious. Stand. Go over. Perhaps say to the poor lady, 'Are you alright? I'm terribly sorry. Could I get you another coffee?' (the prawn landed in her cappuccino and sank delicately through the foam), and generally make all the right social noises. But in that sort of situation, I get stuck in a helpless state of giggles and can't communicate at all. I couldn't help it: it was the *noise* of the prawn when it whacked her in the eye. A sort of dull splat. Of *course* I exploded into giggles and called her a bit of a name: Mrs Prawn Eye, to be precise. And to her face. Which didn't help. Nor did my trying to make her see the funny side by saying, 'I wouldn't drink that coffee, it looks a bit fishy, ha ha.'

Her stern look would normally have warned me off, but on seeing a prawn whisker on her lash, again there was nothing to do but laugh.

So, I changed tack and regrettably, as sometimes happens, embarrassment tipped me into rage directed at the unfortunate waiter: 'Excuse me, good sir. Thank you very much, to you. Now can I just say, on behalf of both myself and poor Mrs Prawn Eye—nay, Whisker Lash, here—that if I order prawns I want them ready to put straight into my mouth, yes? Why should I have to remove the inedible bits and do all the prawn-administration,

4

the "prawn-min", if you will? What's that you say? "It's all part and parcel of eating prawns?" Well, I tell you this, good sir, thank you to you: I quite firmly believe that any activity that is messy enough for a restaurant to provide me with a finger bowl should be carried out by the kitchen staff. Sorry, could you come back, please? What? No, I won't leave. I've paid for these prawns and I'm damned well going to finish them. No, YOU calm down.'

I'm sure you can imagine how the rest of the evening panned out (if you can't, it involved a security guard, ten minutes hiding behind a wheelie-bin, and an illegally sourced chicken korma). In the grand scheme of things, I can see this experience is not so huge, but in the moment it feels like the toughest thing one will ever experience. I suppose what I'm trying to say is does anyone else have trouble negotiating these sorts of life hiccups: smart restaurants and all the accompanying etiquette or . . . is it just me?

Worse still, is it just me or has anyone else been on a date, thought it was going quite well, gone to the loo to have a breather, looked in the mirror and said, 'Not too shabby, missus,' then walked confidently back to the dining area not realising that loo roll was unwinding behind you from where it's stuck in the back of your tights and swirling over other diners' heads, adorning the restaurant like a streamer? Then wondered, how on earth does one deal with this?

Where's the flipping guidebook? There are thousands of years of writing devoted to dealing with birth, death, ageing, love and the meaning of it all; but absolutely nothing to tell me how to handle the indignity of briefly turning oneself into a human party popper, to the immediate detriment of one's romantic prospects.

Excuse me?

Yes, hello? Who's rudely interrupting my tome, please?

It's me. Me. Your eighteen-year-old self, Miranda. Don't you recognise me? Six feet tall, thin as a rail, school-issue straw boater, one red, one green sock, and a lacrosse stick slung over my shoulder?

Oh, well, hello. My dear gangly young self. How absolutely lovely to see you in all your *Malory Towers* finery. Why, I was just—

This isn't a social call.

Oh?

I'm just a bit freaked right now, as I don't particularly like the way you're talking, actually . . .

I think I'm talking jolly good sense, thank you very much.

No, you're not. So **ner.** *For starters, you're saying we went on a date and got loo roll stuck in our pants. Please say that's not true . . . please . . .*

Of course it's not true. (It's true, reader, true.)

PHEW. Because talk about total mortificato; I mean, I might as well just give up . . .

OK, let's drop it now . . .

No, but seriously, massivo dweeb alert.

All *right.*

And telling people in a book—not that many people will read this rubbish.

Rude. Can you leave, please?

One mo-mo. You're basically saying life is a series of embarrassing moments which leave you feeling alone in your confusion and shame. I am not sure I like that.

Well, I'm hoping that by sharing our discomfort with the way life sometimes goes, others will relate to us and we'll all feel a little bit less alone.

OK, but please DON'T tell anyone that in Maths

yesterday when Mr Beckett asked me to define Pi I said, 'It depends on the filling.'

I think you'll find you've just told them.

Oh . . . bog off.

You bog off.

*Consider me bogged . . . *runs away embarrassed, trips over a lacrosse boot and falls into a laundry basket* Meant to do that.*

Sorry about her, where were we? Oh yes, messing up romantic prospects . . . Has anyone else ever drunkenly addressed a post box as 'darling', certain that it was their stout, red-jumper-clad then-boyfriend? And gone in for a kiss, fully embracing the post box? The real boyfriend was ten feet away, silently looking on at this crazy woman and her post box cuddling antics. Are these—the loo roll, the prawn and, worryingly, many more besides— common occurrences or, well . . . *is it just me*?

This is the nub of life, isn't it, dear reader? (Good word, 'nub'. Say it loud, say it proud; wherever you are, one, two, three . . . *NUB*. Lovely, very satisfying.) Yes, the nub of life is surely negotiating and avoiding idiocy. Doing your best to hit the pillow at night without, for once, having to go over the day in your head for its one excruciating moment. Last night, I lay on my bed in what I can only describe as my 'foetal-cringe-ball' position, as I re-lived my opening gambit to an important man at a formal work do.

I'll set the scene: a drinks party. I am standing in a group of people I feel relatively comfortable with, no drink has been spilt, I am conversationally fluent, no nibble has landed on clothing causing an embarrassing stain: so far so good. Then my agent comes over to introduce me to an important head honcho who is apparently keen to meet and perhaps work with me. Clearly a risk taker.

AGENT: Miranda, this is Bob.
BOB: Hello Miranda, very nice to meet you.
ME: You too.

I go in for the handshake. He goes in for the kiss. But don't worry; as he leans in I quickly move my hand before it ends up anywhere inappropriate. I further save the moment by aiming for the correct side of the cheek for the kiss, avoiding that, 'Oh, we nearly snogged, ha ha' hideousness. Tick, well done me.

But then here it comes, the hateful post-introductory conversational hiatus. Who's going to start the formalities and break the ice? Surely my agent will say something? I start to panic: it's me, *I've* got to say something. Quick.

'So, Bob . . . how do you pronounce "Bob"?'

'Ummm . . . *Bob*,' said Bob, looking perplexed.

'Right, good, no, I thought so, I just . . . good.'

My agent has never stared at anyone with such disappointment. Bob looks confused, very confused . . . And, of course, I've created another conversational pause. We're back where we started.

My agent quickly says, 'Bob has just come back from Australia.' Brilliant save, now we can all say, 'Oooh, lovely,' and ask inane questions about his trip, bore ourselves silly with small talk and feel socially comfortable.

So there I am on my bed in foetal-cringe-ball position replaying: 'HOW DO YOU PRONOUNCE BOB?' 'HOW DO YOU PRONOUNCE BOB?' It wasn't even as though it was written down to have to ask; somebody had already introduced him as 'Bob': that's how you pronounce it. But even if it WAS written down, it's Bob. B. O. B. How could you possibly and in any conceivable way mispronounce BOB? 'HOW DO YOU PRONOUNCE BOB?'

*   *   *

When I was eighteen I was certain that it was just me who regularly came a cropper in life. Any little embarrassment I'd quickly cover up, so as to

10

convince people that I wasn't really 'that idiot'. Do a little trip in the street on a jagged bit of pavement, and before anyone could laugh and point the finger, I'd quickly turn it into: 'Actually, I meant to do that. I'm practising for the triple jump. Olympic triple jump.' Then follow it with a demonstration. I might even do another triple jump demonstration after a minute or so, to prove it *really* wasn't a trip. I was quite the triple jumper, with Olympic ambitions, and practise I must.

I was certain—absolutely certain—that everyone else just *breezed* through life. For example, I'd walk past a neighbour's BBQ, hear the familiar, jolly, incoherent hum of a social occasion from afar and hope that *someone* at that event had sat down to eat a sausage bap and felt the chair sinking into the lawn. Is it just me that regularly experiences the sinking-chair-into-grass scenario? Always awkward. You hope people don't notice but you invariably slip so far down, and at such an angle, that the chair often tips you up on the lawn as if to say, 'Don't sit on me, fatty.' Rude al fresco chairs.

The trouble was that if at the age of eighteen I *had* braved the BBQ, I wouldn't have seen others failing, stumbling, muddling through. I never did. I just looked on with envy, miserable in the assumption that everyone else was happy and uninhibited. That everyone else *wanted* to be there, and anticipated absolutely no awkwardness with the experience. I would never have imagined that anyone else was harbouring that most devastating secret of all: that they felt a bit self-conscious, and just wanted to be at home watching telly in their pants.

11

Then, there was the joyous moment in my teenage years when I saw the film *Dirty Dancing* for the first time, and witnessed the initial meeting of Patrick Swayze and Jennifer Grey. If you don't know the scene I'm about to refer to, then you must watch the film, but for now let me explain. Jennifer Grey's opening gambit, in a brief conversational pause when she is totally over-awed by Patrick Swayze's handsomeness, is: 'I carried a watermelon,' whilst no longer in possession of it. The Swayz didn't know that she'd been carrying one, so telling him she carried a watermelon was possibly the weirdest thing she could have said. 'Yes' I thought. 'There's another idiot. It's me and Jennifer Grey versus the world.'

That's why I love watching *You've Been Framed*. Not because it's the funniest programme on television ever (which it is, closely followed by *The Planet's Funniest Animals*—cat falling in a loo, anyone?), but because I secretly play *You've Been Framed* bingo. If I've done five of the things on the programme that night, Bingo, and reward with a glass of wine.

I remember in my teenage years thinking, 'I wish I could do things in life *my* way.' I wished I could negotiate the intricacies of this life with a confidence that meant I could subvert conventions, break the rules and get rid of the need to be 'acceptable', which had been stamped on me by my very British upbringing. But a maverick I wasn't.

At eighteen I thought, 'Never mind. I shouldn't worry that Jennifer Grey and I are the only idiots in the world.' Because hope told me that as I got older I would gain the elegance and confidence to breeze over the speed bumps of life in my own special style. But the fact is (and thank heavens that eighteen-year-old Miranda isn't around to hear this), I am still an idiot. Life still throws up an almost daily, certainly weekly, moment that seems impossible to navigate with grace. I might deal with it better these days . . . The other day, for example, in a café, I leaned forwards to push my chair back before getting up and the inevitable occurred. A really quite significant fart. But I didn't cover it up: I admitted it, I laughed it off. I coped. We've all done it, right? It's the pushing back motion of the chair, with the slight bend in the leaning forwards . . .? We've all done it, yes? Reader? Hello? Moving on . . .

I also used to think that fame might bring confidence. 'Perhaps fame's the ticket to freedom,' I thought: any weird or wrong moments could just be passed off as part of your eccentric famous persona, and thus be beyond judgement. 'What's that? Miranda's got her head in the bin and can't get it out again? Oh, well. That's famous people for you. Probably some sort of meditation technique she picked up from Sting.' You can be whatever you want to be when you are famous, can't you?

What I'd say to Little Miranda—lying in her dormitory at her all-girls boarding school, dreaming of the bright lights—I'd say, firstly, I am now a tiny weeny bit famous. I know: life, eh? But I also feel duty-bound to say that fame doesn't bring you freedom from self-consciousness: not a bit of it. Quite the opposite. Recently, I was checking in at an airport and was asked to put my hand luggage in what I elegantly refer to as the 'hand-luggage-size-measurer-does-your-bag-fit-in-here-hole-cage-bracket-

13

prison' thing. My bag was a touch on the large side, but it fit; well, more or less. The woman in charge of the desk, a creature so dollishly well-put-together that her only career options must have been 'air hostess' or 'Lady Penelope from *Thunderbirds*' said, in her most cloying, annoying, sibilant hiss, 'No, sorry, it has to fit fully in. All the way, please.' So I did as any mildly offended Englishwoman would have done under the circumstances, and gave my bag a defiant shove. It now fit very nicely—too nicely. It was stuck. My hand luggage was stuck in the 'hand-luggage-size-measurer-does-your-bag-fit-in-here-hole-cage-bracket-prison' thing. I asked a burly stranger—always my first port of call—to give it a yank. He did so, and the bracket fell over with a clatter. I was now, officially, 'causing a kerfuffle'. (Great word, kerfuffle—it keeps on giving. Almost worth causing one just so you can use it.) Then, the *thing* happened: the 'getting recognised' thing. All of a sudden, I wasn't just a bolshy lady accidentally making a fuss—I was Miranda off the telly making a fuss. A small crowd gathered, then a larger crowd and, before I knew it, my shame was being held up before a gang of tittering holidaymakers, all muttering things like: 'Is it?' and 'Who's she?' or 'Is she the one who—?' with 'No, it's not, is it?' and 'Was she on *Grand Designs*?' followed by 'Doesn't she look *cross*?' and 'I hope her trousers fall down. I think they might be about to fall down.' A phone was whipped out. I feared becoming a YouTube sensation, one of the day's 'Top Hits' alongside a video of a fat panda eating a Yorkie bar. Far from easing the pain, the tiniest bit of well-known-ness only magnifies it. You shift from curiosity to

14

accidental freak show.

eighteen-year-old Miranda charges in, panting, in a green pleated skirt and fetching Aertex shirt Hiya. What have I missed? What have you been talking about?*

Oh, hello you. Aren't you meant to be playing lacrosse or something?

Nope. Match got rained off.

It didn't, though, did it? You actually got sent off for putting sweets and cigarettes on the half-time plate instead of oranges.

Who wants an orange when there are Wham bars in the world? So, what's been going on?

I've been continuing to explain to my lovely reader that I've often found life rather . . . tricky. As you know, we're a bit awkward, aren't we?

Yeah. But don't worry, we're going to grow out of that by the time we're twenty-eight. Life will be sorted by then. I'll be nearly thirty. That's REALLY old. By the time I am twenty-eight, I'll have the love and support of a confident husband, achieved my career goals and be poised for a graceful old age. Hang on, why are you laughing?

Well, it's not going to be quite like that. It's still going to be interesting and jolly good, just . . . bumpier. A bit bumpier.

Oh.

And may I also point out that thirty is very young. Very young, indeed. As indeed is thirty-eight, which I happen to be. In fact, I would say thirty-eight is probably the age when a woman is only just reaching her *lowers voice* sexual *normal voice* prime.

Urh, urh, urh.

Moving on. I have a hunch that life is a bit bumpy, not just for us, but for everyone, so I've been sharing our little foibles with my dear reader. I told them about Jennifer Grey carrying the watermelon, and how much we loved that—

We LOVED that.

Exactly. It made us feel that we weren't alone. And I'm hoping that maybe this book can serve the same purpose. Can help someone feel that they're not the only one who always sweats the small stuff.

Yeah. That would be quite a cool thing to do.

getting a bit grand, politician-style Maybe, just maybe, this book can be . . . someone's watermelon. Because *even grander now* life isn't always about the big things, but the little things. The little things we encounter over the years that go to make up the big part of life—

Now you've gone too far. You've ruined it.

16

Soz. But I hope that it'll give *you*, eighteen-year-old-Miranda, a glimpse of what's to come. A few pointers because, just to warn you, life might take some unexpected twists and turns.

So, I have chosen eighteen vital subjects to reflect upon: one for each year of your life so far—I know, clever, isn't it? We weren't given a rulebook at birth about this whole how-to-manage-life business (there really should be some kind of manual, methinks), but I can at least show you what I've learned since childhood. Call it your own personal Miran-ual. Ooh, don't you love that? A Miran-ual. I am very pleased with that.

Show off.

But come on—*Miran-ual*.

Yes, all right. Now, I've gotta dash. Me, Bella and Clare-Bear are watching **The Breakfast Club** *in the common room. For the thousandth time. Don't you just love it? 'Eat. My. Shorts.'*

What?

It's a quote from **The Breakfast Club,** *you dweeb. Bella's got a new Swatch watch just like one Molly Ringwald wears. She'll be showing it off. Bella's so annoying. Laters. *vanishes**

Bye, Little Miranda.

So, My Dear Reader Chum, whoever you are . . . Whether you are a bit famous or not famous, young or old, tall or short, dark or fair, beanpole

17

or Rubenesque, soprano, alto, tenor or bass—I am hoping you might relate to my tales, rants and musings. I'm hoping it's *not* just me. So, let us for now park life's big issues. You may say to me, 'But, Miranda, each of your chosen subjects is an innocuous, trouble-free issue—there's surely nothing to discuss?' Well, I will say to you this: there is many a muddy, murky, lurk behind my carefully chosen chapter headings. Let's forget the economy, forget war, forget births and deaths and big, deep, serious gubbins. Let's buckle down to the nuance-y nub of life on our literary romp. I'm talking the different stages we go through in life. I'm talking dating; I'm talking holidays and all that blooming beach etiquette. I'm talking how to cope with being mistaken for a pregnant lady on the bus when all you're really carrying is a second-helping-of-pie-and-mash baby. Not that that has ever happened to me. (It has.) I'm talking not feeling awkward having a massage; I'm talking how to use chopsticks with grace. The real coalface of life.

I'm not sure I'll have all the answers to these conundrums (or is it conundra?). But I'm practically an expert having made every mistake going, and it will be a pleasure simply to get these weighty issues off my chest. (Or issues off my weighty chest. Either works.)

Now, let's enjoy a brief fanfare, drum roll, excited cheer and a replenished cup of tea or second roast dinner as we turn the page, proceed to chapter two, and confront head-on our first issue ... MUSIC.

2

MUSIC

Now, are you settled? Lovely. For it is time you and I have a little chat on the subject of Music. You may be wondering, My Dear Reader Chum—actually, hold on, this is going to get a bit cumbersome as we proceed, My Dear Reader Chum, isn't it? How about an abbreviation; how about I call you 'MDRC'? OK with you? Good. So, whenever you read the letters MDRC, in that order, please know that you, My Dear Reader Chum, are being directly addressed with all the love and affection that you deserve.

So, MDRC, I don't know whether you're a 'muso'? Have you always had an ear for the latest sounds? (a ponytailed Status Quo fan would ask, 'Are you down with the rhythm?'). Are you in your late thirties or beyond, and still aware of what the current Number 1 is? Can you *really* be that age and stick with Radio 1 and not be drawn solely to Radio 4; or if when feeling 'a little bit groovy', Radio 2? Do you actively seek out new bands, or perhaps collect vintage vinyl, whilst keeping cheerfully abreast of the mainstream? If so, I applaud you; because ever since I can remember, I have always wanted to be . . . well, you. You literally and figuratively rock.

I love music, I do, but for some reason I have never really found my groove. Forgot to pay it enough attention, I suppose. And now—and I do hope this isn't just me—I could blithely walk past most of the world's pop stars and have absolutely no idea who they are. Though I might assume that any boy aged around sixteen with very, very neat, blown-forward, invisibly gelled hair was some kind of pop force to be reckoned with. What *is* it with the hair-brushed-forwards-over-forehead-and-cheeks thing? Have you chaps got cheek shame? Or is that where you keep your sweets? Are you hiding something? And if not, why would you *choose* to have hat hair? Confusing.

I imagine that by now you don't need much more convincing that I'm old before my time as regards the world of music. And, I confess, this never-finding-my-music groove has led to some awkward social hiccups. Recently, I found myself at a party, and an on-trend muso type approached me. (This was confusing enough.)

'I really like this DJ,' he said.

Confidently, I replied, 'Yup, oh, tremendous. He has some smashing beats.'

'Do you know Kanye West?' he went on.

'Oh, isn't that near Cockfosters?'

'What?'

'Kanye West—I think it's on the Piccadilly Line. Would you like a tube map?'

'No,' said terrifyingly trendy man with a mix of bewilderment and pity. 'Kanye West—the musician.'

'Oh, of course, the *musician*. What am I like?' (By now I'm nervously doing my over-the-top laughing.) 'I thought you were looking for a tube stop.'

I hoped this might be endearing until I remembered that my over-the-top laughter to disguise feeling at sea at a social event makes me look like a cross between a horse, a goldfish and

Princess Anne. (No offence, ma'am, your good sir-ladyship—well, she is bound to be reading.)

Strangely, the young man scurried away, pronto.

I then got myself terribly muddled in a conversation about Tinchy Stryder. I'd always assumed—and I have a horrible feeling this *will* just be me—that Tinchy Stryder was some sort of toddler's walking boot. Come on, don't laugh, be fair; it does sound a bit like it might be one. So when my friend's new 'I've achieved everything at twenty-five' manager said, 'I really like Tinchy Stryder,' I said, 'Oh, yes, lovely—how old are your children?' Which, of course, would have come across as a totally random segue. Bemused by her scary, blank face, I blindly continued, 'Are they good for kids' feet?' An equally confusing statement. (For my non-muso readers, Tinchy Stryder is a 'rap artist', innit.)

'Sorry, I'm confused,' she said. 'I was talking about Tinchy Stryder.'

'Yes, me too,' I replied. 'I think they must look so cute. Nothing sweeter than a grown-up shoe on a toddler.' We both stared blankly at one another for a few seconds, before moving slowly off, aware that we'd somehow come a serious conversational cropper. Later, I realised my error and rushed over to her, shouting, 'Rap artist. Not small walking boot.' Cue the horse, goldfish, Princess Anne laugh.

I tried to claw back some cool by casually sauntering off saying I was going to listen to Kanye West: 'Yes, that's right, I'll be *listening* to Kanye West, not getting off at him on the Piccadilly Line.' Which would, of course, have sounded desperately weird, as she wasn't privy to my previous Kanye mishap. Every single thing I had said to that professional groovester made me look, at best, crazy. I left it there. The evening could not be salvaged.

With all this embarrassment in mind, I think it only fair that I take a moment to give my younger self her first life lesson. It is time to warn her just how things are going to turn out on the music front. So please, bear with, MDRC.

Dear Eighteen-Year-Old Miranda.

Oh, hello. So you've deigned to address me. At last. From your big throne in the sky.

I'm not in the sky. I'm on earth. Like you; just twenty years on in the future. It is a tad confusing, I admit, but it's hardly *The Lord of The Rings.*

I just assumed that twenty years into the future I'd be dead. From being so old and dweeby and everything.

I told you, thirty-eight is VERY YOUNG. It still very much falls under the 'late twenties' bracket in my literal and metaphorical book. And I am very much alive and thriving, thanking you. Which is lucky for you, because I think it's time we had a little chat. About music, specifically. From my current vantage-point—twenty years your senior (but still young and fresh), looking fondly back at you and eager to spout a few home truths, I can see that you're in need of some help.

No, I'm not. I know heaps about music. Actually, I've just—

22

holds up hand, regally I'll stop you there. I know what you've just done. You're going through a brief and, I hate to have to tell you this, wholly unique period of being 'musically cool'. The reason being you've just returned to boarding school after the holidays, carrying a cassette of music by a band (or group, or troupe, or 'combo'—to be honest, you're not entirely sure what you should call them) named Talking Heads.

Yeah, I know. Talking Heads. I love them. Well cool. They're kind of punk rock . . .

Yes, I know. They were of the New Wave musical style and combine elements of punk rock, avant-garde, pop, funk, world music and art rock.

Well, you sound musically cool. I'm not sure we should be fretting about this.

Ah, no, but you see, I just googled them.

Googled . . .?

Oh, yes . . . Umm, it's like a library on a laptop . . .

Like a what on a what?

It doesn't matter; I'll explain later. You have to admit, you don't really like Talking Heads, do you?

I do. I really do.

No, you don't. When cool cousin Steve gave it to you, you had to work very, very hard to summon up even the tiniest bit of enthusiasm for this noisy popular music quartet. And you're rewarding yourself by swaggering round the dormitory loudly saying things like, 'Yeah, I'm just gonna put some Talking Heads on, OK? What, you don't know Talking Heads? I'll just put the Talking Heads on now.' You're saying these things in a confident, nay, arrogant fashion, but deep down you're hobbled by a sense of fraudulence. Crippled with it. Because in your heart, you know that you're not a music person.

How dare you? I like LOTS of music. I like T'Pau *sings* 'China in your haaand ...'

Please, don't . . .

And, and, I like . . .

Kylie and Jason? I can't help but notice there's a Jason Donovan poster on your wall.

He's gorge.

You might briefly think he's gorgeous, but he's not musically cutting edge. Admit it, Little Miranda, you know absolutely nothing about music. It's official: you lack the muso gene.

You are totally rude. And wrong. So stop bugging me.

Well, let's look at the record (PUN. MDRC, pun. Just saying—at ease). You recently participated in what a newspaper report would describe as a 'horrifically botched sing-along'.

I don't know what you're talking about.

Oh, I think you do. A merry band of sixth-formers were on the bus to a lacrosse match (rock and roll). You were all singing 'Do They Know It's Christmas?'. After a chorus or two, the others became distracted and piped down. You, unaware of this, ploughed on through the chorus, revealing to the assembled crowd that you'd been singing the lyrics as 'feed the birds' instead of 'feed the world'.

Yeah, maybe. That might have happened.

It did happen. And it happened, I think, because you'd got the song muddled up with 'Feed the Birds' from *Mary Poppins*. I mean, think about it: why on earth would Bob Geldof have been getting so het-up about feeding the *birds*? What birds would he have been talking about? He's staging a massive campaign, Band Aid, for starving birds? What birds? You should be ashamed of yourself.

All right, fine. Why are you reminding me of all this?

It's for your own good. I want you to know and accept a certain fact about yourself, Little Miranda. You will never, ever, be a music person. You will forge a strong attachment to three songs by Billy Joel, four or five hit Broadway musicals, one song by Dolly Parton ('9 to 5', obviously), one album by ABBA and a sort of jolly thing, which may or may not be by Stevie Wonder. And that's

25

it. You'll spend the next two decades listening to those same songs on a loop, and you'll waste barrels of your time and energy feeling vaguely guilty about this.

No. Negativo. This I will not accept. My whole life is going to be like this moment, this Talking Heads moment at school. I'll forge a niche as a curator of edgy, interesting music, discovering new bands, perhaps trawling obscure gig venues scouting for talent. I'll be a John Peel figure. A cowboy. A well-informed musical cowboy with the legs of a goddess.

Oh, bless you. No, that won't happen. Your musical tastes will fossilise, and your record collection will forever be that of a Berkshire schoolgirl in 1991. Sorry.

But won't I meet bands at gigs?

You won't go to gigs.

What? Everyone goes to gigs.

Not you, I'm afraid. Actually, I tell a lie. You will attend the *Smash Hits* Poll Winners Party at the age of twenty-six.

Twenty-six. But that's untrendy now. At eighteen.

I know, I know. But, my little one, you will go. At twenty-six. And you'll have quite a nice time in the brief bits where you're not worried about being arrested. Not because you'd had any reason

26

to be arrested. But because the presence of a policeman there makes you look and feel guilty. (In fact, MDRC, I usually go red in the presence of a policeman and do a kind of bob and say 'Evening', whatever time of the day it is. Why, *why* does that happen?) I also have to warn you, Little Miranda, that you stick out like a giant in a sea of nine-year-old pop fans at the Poll Winners Party. In fact, at one point, when you stand up to dance in a moment of excitement as the boy band A1 do a rendition of A-Ha, you are tapped on the shoulder by a tiny pre-teenage girl behind you, who asks you to sit down because she can't see.

But don't worry, gigs-wise, things aren't *that* bad. In your thirties you'll come very close to booking a ticket to see Michael Ball live.

Who's Michael Ball? Is he alt rock, post-punk or

New Wave?

Um . . . sort of.

But won't I stalk bands? Won't I be a groupie? I always thought I'd quite like to be a groupie. That's very me. Loud, wild parties that go on till dawn. Dancing with leather-clad rockers.

I'm going to have to stop you there. That's not you. You *will* be a groupie, just not of musicians. All of your stalker-ish energy will be channelled into the aggressive stage-dooring of comedy actors and actresses. And the odd tennis player. (By the way, Goran Ivanisevic is still not our husband. I KNOW. Don't worry, there's time . . .) Maybe if Noel Coward had been around in our twenties and thirties, you would have gone to one of his 'gigs'. Possibly even bought the tour T-shirt and slipped into his dressing room with a flagon of Pimms. But no. No gigs.

Why not?

Oh, lots of reasons. Most of them fear-based. Fear of crowds, fear of loud noise, fear of sweat. Fear of a festival. You've got to have a muso gene to want to spend four days in mud in June in England. Then there's fear of 'cool'. Fear of being coerced into dancing, or of dancing when it's not appropriate to dance. If you have the muso gene, you can just get up and dance wherever. You can be in a slightly arty café at night, no one else is dancing but there's a bit of room, you're feeling it, so you get up and off you go. How can anyone

28

be so liberated and un-British, yet still technically British? Unfathomable.

Big Miranda, please tell me I get better at dancing.

Afraid not. Largely because of the fact that you are going to remain tall. And dancing when you're as tall as we are goes beyond indignity and strays into the territory of health and safety risk. Once at a wedding, I attempted to 'mosh', and I got a bit carried away . . . and . . . well, let's just say that marquee structure clearly wasn't stable if me clinging on to one of its poles in a brief moment of misplaced exuberance brought the whole thing down.

Oh, Big Miranda, that's appalls-balls . . .

Can you not call me 'Big Miranda', please? And 'appalls-balls' . . . ?

'Appalling'. Bella made it up at school last term. She's so cool.

Right. Well, yes, it was a bit appalls-balls. But I must say, it was very amusing. Aunts swept off chairs by a marquee ceiling swooping down and forcing them into a flowerbed. Much flailing to escape from the billowing, sail-like covering. A swearing vicar. All the stuff that makes life worth living. But, because you have basically decent manners and dislike being the cause of physical injury in others, you'll never be truly free on the dance floor.

I'll never dance?

Oh, you'll dance. But you'll settle for ironic dancing, which is really where you just dance the finale of *Grease*, enthusiastically and badly, to whatever music is playing. Over the years you will dance the finale of *Grease* to everything from hardcore drum'n'bass (no, I don't know, either) to the Blue Danube waltz. You'll become known for it. Ironic dancing is, I think I can confirm, the solution to the dancing problem. It's all very knowing, you get to have a nice time making fun of your five left feet and your limby-ness, but underneath it all you can actually have a jolly good bop. Terrific.

One thing we do get excellent at as regards dance, and that's watching it. One of our favourite television programmes in our thirties is focused around the art of ballroom dancing.

Granny alert. Were you born in 1912? What about 'jamming'? Will I ever turn into the person who whips out a guitar at the end of a party like crazy cousin Steve? Make sweet music?

Oh, come on. Firstly, you're not the person who can stay awake long enough to see the end of a party. Admit it, even now with your insatiable appetite and the lure of a Penguin you can't stay awake for a midnight feast. Staying up all night has always been a chore and just gets worse as the years go on. (NB: tips for staying up all night: throw a glass of water in your face, rub ice cubes in your eyes, eat coffee granules, do cola shots and lick a 9-volt battery.)

Secondly, you do *not* want to be that guitar jamming person. Everyone hates that person. The person in the dirty T-shirt who breaks up the party by dragging out a guitar and performing their innovative, minor-key acoustic version of 'Eleanor Rigby'. (Please note—cool, crazy cousin Steve can now be found working in Greggs on the Waterlooville High Street.) That's not how an evening should end. An evening should end at 10.45 p.m. sharp with 'I'm in the Mood for Dancing', enjoyed whilst throwing a few shapes, eating pizza with one hand, before falling over sideways onto a bean bag (simultaneously crushing the person whose rendition of 'Eleanor Rigby' you've just interrupted).

Oh. Actually, that does sound sort of amaze-balls.

If you mean amazing, it is. It really is. It's the kind of fun you were born to have. Other people may be born to sit around in smoky rooms listening to Radiohead and not washing their hair for six months because apparently it eventually cleans itself but, for you, music's not meant to be a downer, a conversation-starter or a status symbol. For you, it's just a reassuring sugar-rush. A bag of Flumps. A choc-ice. Something to enhance . . . *jollity*.

'JOLLITY'? It's sounding dweeby again.

Embrace your inner music dweeb. For by telling you this, and any readers who might also lack the muso gene, you can learn that jollity is every bit as worthwhile as cool. More so, in fact. You'll defend jollity until you fall exhausted to the floor.

31

You'll stop trying to join a club that you weren't born to be a member of. You'll stop wondering why dancing to Billy Joel is some kind of guilty pleasure, while an undernourished student smoking a spliff to Pink Floyd is somehow acceptable. It's one area where you're able to just be who you are, not caring one jot whether or not your neighbours can hear you singing along to *Annie*. *sings in an embarrassing American accent* 'The sun'll come out tomorrowww . . .'

whispers That does sound more me.

We are all about the musical, Little M. Now put down that Guns N' Roses tape you were about to put on (and pretend to love).

I will. And do you know what I am going to do? There's still time to go to the music block for Miss Everett's The Sound of Music *auditions . . .*

Well done. Go, girl.

Yeah. Because knowing all this, I must be in with a good chance of scooping a lead role.

Right, don't get your hopes up . . . Hello? She's gone. Oh, dear. We only get the part of 'Waltzing Man in Ballroom scene'. I am *not* bitter. It's fine. No really, I'm over it . . . (it could have least have been 'Waltzing Woman'). As I say, over it . . .

3

HOBBIES

As I officially lack the muso gene, music isn't something I could ever legitimately put down as a hobby. (That is, until the musical genre of 'cheese' becomes formally recognised.) In fact, announcing what my hobbies are, whether socially, at interviews or on CVs, has always caused more anxiety than it should have in my life. So MDRC (My Dear Reader Chum, lest you forget), together we embrace our second subject and begin another chapter. Are you with tea or some equally reassuring beverage? My current choice is the drinking chocolate sachet. Just add some boiling water and a-yummy-yum-yum—chocolate in liquid form. In fact I might just replenish. Excuse me, as I sashay up to my sachet. *whistles from kitchen whilst sashaying so you don't get lonely*

I'm back, and Mr Mug is replenished (occasionally I find it a bit o' fun to preface an object with a title: please forgive, and back to Miss Book). It's time for a bracing discussion on the world of hobbies.

You might be thinking—really? What can *possibly* be said about hobbies? Can they really be included in the list of life's perils where we might come a cropper and feel all at sea? I am afraid I firmly believe they can.

One of the very *worst* questions you can ask an adult—over and above, 'When are you going to do something about your hair?' and 'In a typical

33

week, what do you eat?'—is 'What are your hobbies?' *What are your hobbies?* It should be an easy one. You should be able to spring gratefully forth and say: 'What are my hobbies? Oh, I'm so glad you asked. I'm actually taking my grade 8 bassoon exam at the weekend; it's been terribly hard to fit it in around all the rock climbing, and it's going to be a nightmare getting it and the potter's wheel into the back of the Volvo, but I must cram it all in before I head off with the choir on a chapel tour of Dieppe. Honestly, I'm a slave to my hobbies. Well, when you're as thrilled by life as I am, who wouldn't be?' At this point, you would shriek with laughter, your flailing arms displacing a beautifully alphabetised archive of graphic novels and a bag of snorkelling equipment.

But, no. Who among us—and *please* say this isn't just me—when asked that question, doesn't simply shrug, stare at their shoes and mumble 'Uh—cinema?' Only then they remember that they haven't actually been to the cinema for eight months, and even then they got the wrong time for the film so just wandered into Nando's and queued there for half an hour before shuffling home with a chicken wing to watch telly. And, no, telly doesn't count as a hobby, any more than 'sleeping' or 'washing' or 'sitting quietly on cushions' (unless you claim that 'sitting quietly on cushions' is meditation, in which case you're very sneaky indeed).

There are some people born with certain passions, which they've happily and confidently carried forwards into adulthood. I envy them because for me, the question of hobbies is a troubling one. As a child, it was easy. Aged ten, you could unashamedly reel off a list of much-loved recreational activities, all of which you enjoyed regularly, and many of which involved some kind of natty uniform and an elaborate badge system. Cubs, Rainbows, gymnastics, roller-skating, kiddie disco, ballet, swimming, trampolining or, in my case, an unwavering passion for the Brownies (hello, Brown Owl, if you're reading this). If you were a bit more left field, so much the better. You'd have hobbies that marked you out as an 'imaginative' child. These might include: playing horses, being a medieval knight in a turret, playing with trains, *being* a train, climbing trees, *being* a tree, hosting elaborate tea-parties for one's stuffed animals (hands up, I was all about that), or putting on matching C&A tracksuits with your friends, pretending to be an army and going to war—which I assure you I never did. (I did.) If the imaginative side of things wasn't for you, you could be one of the sticker collectors. That was a highly regarded and specialised hobby, aged ten. As an aside, I will share with you this: I was a collector of, wait for it, National Trust bookmarks. Oh yes, rock and roll. I was sixty before I was sixteen. But I could still put that down as a hobby, thank you very much. Whatever your bent, these were all joyous, clearly identifiable and legitimate pastimes. And we made space for them in our lives, sandwiching them in between homework and tea. They were, simply, things we did. As necessary as washing or eating.

Then you become a teenager, and that terrible concept of 'cool' makes its way into your life. Suddenly, you're only able to do hobbies if you're actually good at them. If you want to be in an orchestra, you have to be able to actually play an instrument: you can no longer get away with screeching blue murder into a recorder and waiting for the grown-ups to clap. Or, in my case, randomly plucking at the double bass: I disregarded the bow, thinking I was instinctively Jazz (and whilst we're on it, was it really necessary to give people instruments proportionate to their size? I think it would be have been far funnier for tiny Twig Smythson to struggle with a double bass and me to have the piccolo, but there you have it.)

Excuse me, but do you really need to tell everyone about the double bass?

Yes, alas, Little Miranda, I think I do. If only to exorcise its terrible demons from our soul. I thought you were auditioning?

I have been told to go and ask Miss Everett what a basic waltz step is . . . Not sure why . . . Maybe Liesl had to do the waltz . . .

Don't get your hopes up.

*Oh, and if you **are** telling them about the double bass, at least mention lax. I'm VERY good at lacrosse.*

You most certainly are. But that's why you do so much of it. You wouldn't do it if you were rubbish, would you? Just do it for fun?

*Defo not. That would be so square. *goes off singing 'I am sixteen, going on seventeen . . .'**

36

Point made. As a teenager, we suddenly had to get serious about hobbies (which, incidentally, doesn't include walking around shopping centres in feral packs, buying tops). So, no more gymnastics unless your forward roll is good enough to represent the school at the county championships.

And, *by the way*, at what age does it suddenly become impossible and terrifying to attempt a forward roll? I don't know about you, but I always used to be forward rolling. If I wanted to jump on a friend's bed, I might casually forward roll my way on. I was like a piece of teenage elastic, throwing myself everywhere. We all were, weren't we? Then, suddenly, in your later years, you might be faced with the prospect of doing a forward roll only to hear yourself saying: 'I can't do it. Seriously, oh my goodness, it's really scary, I can't, I'll break my neck, won't I? My head's going to fall off. No, I can't. How did I ever do this?' Ditto handstands. There was a stage in my life when I was never *not* doing a handstand of a summer month. There I'd be, walking along; I'd see some open grass, up with a quick handstand, and keep walking. No one would think it odd. *Now* if I attempted a handstand, firstly everyone would assume I was deranged but secondly, I would assume my arms would break underneath me. Also, it looks an awfully long way down, that grass. What happens if I do a good one, a really marvellous perky handstand, but can't get down? Or what if I lose control and flip over? That would be truly terrifying.

I'd like to apologise to any older readers who haven't considered this handstand/forward roll issue, and are now tempted to try one or both.

Good luck to you, I say. If you're reading this in bed, try the forward roll now. Go on. Particularly if you're with a partner who's lying next to you. Don't tell them what you're about to do. Just get up, stand at the end of the bed and do a forward roll. Wait for the reaction. What pre-sleep larks you'll have. I'm now imagining couples in various parts of the British Isles, coaxing each other into a forward roll on their bed. It's a smashing image. Makes me feel I've made a real difference.

*   *   *

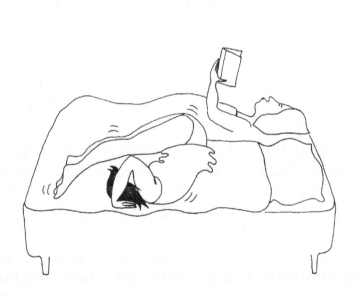

Now I've done what can only be described, in literary terms, as a Big Old Fat digression. So, a Big Old Fat apology needed—sorry, soz, soz buckets, a bucket full of soz to you. Let's resume.

Yes, so—you're in your teens. Hobbies can't be just for fun any more: you have to be good at them. There's no more lolloping around in a leotard and tights for you, missus. No more collecting stickers. And no more swapping. At the age of ten you'll swap your last ever sticker at a swapping party: the next time swapping will be even vaguely acceptable is when you're fifty-five, divorced and exchanging pressed flowers with the ladies from the local Nature Club. Or, if male, when you're fifty-five, divorced and a member of a very serious Stamp Collectors' Society of Great Britain (unless, of course, you're into sci-fi memorabilia. Here, new rules apply—I believe there's a natty underground scene revolving around the exchange of latex Spock masks and *Star Trek* phasers. I don't understand what I've just said, let alone what this involves, but each to their own. And if this appeals to you, then may God bless you, and I hope you find a girlfriend soon so you can move out of your mum's utility room).

The worst thing for me about the teenage loss of hobbies was *NO MORE BALLET*. It was a sad moment in my life to discover that a six-foot fifteen year old was no longer welcome in the ballet class. Suddenly, it was all about being proficient and ambitious. There was talk of certain members of the class 'going to college' and 'turning professional'.

'Balls to that,' I said, as me and my very small, very round friend galumphed on for a few rounds of 'I'm a little teapot.' It was going fine until we got to 'Here's my handle, here's my spout . . .' (the rest of the class were dancing *The Nutcracker*, by the way). I lost my balance, jarred into my friend, whose excellently placed spout nudged into one of the dancers when she was *en pointe*, who then fell into the girl next to her, causing a domino effect of collapsing ballerinas. I thought it was the funniest thing I'd ever seen, but we were, shall we say, 'not welcome back'.

How rude is that? What if I—perhaps at age seventeen or eighteen—had suddenly passed through the clunky teapot phase and really come into my own as a ballerina? What if I had suddenly blossomed? What if my gawkiness had fallen away to reveal a truly major dance talent? I could have been Darcey Bussell. That could have been *me*. I could have re-invented modern ballet with my elongated strides. I now regularly re-invent modern ballet in the privacy of my kitchen and, in my humble opinion, believe it's a crying shame others don't get to pay to witness it on a grand stage. But the English National Ballet will never know because between the ages of thirteen and nineteen, you're not allowed to do *anything* fun unless you're immediately and conventionally good at it. 'Harrumph,' I say to that. *Harrumph*.

The abandonment of hobbies in your teens means that by the time you're in your twenties, the extra-curricular cupboard is bare. You're doing nothing. And, by some terrible twist of fate, this is also the time of your life when you have to start applying for jobs, and applying for jobs involves putting together a CV, and a CV inevitably involves a Hobbies section. The one time you need hobbies, you are hobby-less. You stare at the blank page, and panic. What do I like? Do I like anything? What are my hobbies? You ask your friends—what do I like? What do I do? What do I like to do? Well, your helpful friends respond, you like drinking pints, you like impersonating certain television presenters like Roy Walker from *Catchphrase*, and occasionally you like ordering a pizza. Last night you thought it would be fun to see how long it would take you to eat a bowl of popcorn with boxing gloves on. And last week you thought you liked putting the takeaway container on your head and pretending you were a spaceman (but the next morning you changed your mind about that because your hair smelt of korma). You turn forlornly back to the CV and type 'HOBBIES: Swimming, reading and travelling': the holy trinity of boringly acceptable things everyone likes. Or no one would admit to not liking, at any rate ('Travelling? No, hate it. I'm an enormous fan of staying put, actually. I'm happiest within a three-foot radius of my toaster and my pillow. I don't want my horizons broadened, thank you').

You arrive at the job interview, your CV in hand. Everything's going surprisingly well. You've got through the strengths and weaknesses section (although I'm not sure 'height' does technically count as a strength). You've dealt with work experience and now you are at ' . . . and finally—hobbies': you're practically out of the door, until the interviewer's eye falls on 'Swimming'. It turns out he swims at county level and is very eager to quiz you on your sporting habits.

This is where things can all go very, very wrong, as they once did for me.

'So, what's your stroke?' the interviewer enquired.

Lovely, safe swimming. Now not so safe.

Of course, I panicked. Because basically I only really swim when on holiday. And even then it's mostly just splashing about in a rubber ring, and actually I get a bit frightened when the water goes

on my face. Stalling, I tried a thoughtful 'Umm
...', rolling back my wheelie-chair reflectively. I was
going for smooth, measured and authoritative. And
I said, 'Uh—butterfly . . . Butterfly is . . . my stroke.'

I could have left it there. I *should* have left
it there: silently suggesting that butterfly is so
important to me that I couldn't possibly address my
passion for it in the brief time we had left. I could
have been enigmatic.

I wasn't.

I was nervous. And nerves lend themselves to
the babble. I babbled, 'Well, it's not MY stroke, ha
ha—I didn't invent it, and if I did let me tell you
this, I'd have called it "The Miranda". What would
The Miranda look like, do you think? Probably
something like this—' At which point I gave a very
weird, ferocious demonstration involving flapping
chicken arms and thrashing legs.

The panel of interviewers looked a bit confused.
I began to worry that this wasn't going terribly well
for me. Bravely, I decide to remedy the situation
by offering—unsolicited—my views on body-hair
removal for streamlining purposes: 'You'd probably
need to shave your legs, though, to get a good head
of steam going with The Miranda. I mean, I'm
blessed with very little hair; I'm not hairy, no, no,
siree, I'm smooth as a billiard ball. But someone
like you'—pointing aggressively at the slightly
boggle-eyed county-level swimmer—'might need to
. . . Sorry, not that you're hairy—I mean, most men
have hairy backs. Do you have a hairy back? None
of my business, obviously, but if you do, then—'

Luckily, at that point, the main interviewer
concluded the interview. 'Phew,' I thought, 'I'm out
of here.' Not an unmitigated triumph, but it could

have been worse.

I stood up and things did, indeed, get considerably worse. It turned out my long skirt had got trapped under the wheels of the wheelie-chair, and so as I rose, said skirt shot down, revealing my pants and legs.

Now, this is one of those situations—isn't it, MDRC?—when you think, 'Right, where is the pamphlet on what to do next? Why is there no rulebook?'

I think a lot of people would have quickly gathered their skirt about them and dashed out. Instead, I thought the following would be appropriate: 'Oh, good. I'm glad that's happened, actually. I meant to show you my lovely smooth legs. Just what you need to have a go at The Miranda. Might be useful for you to have a look, in case you want to try it for your next swimming race.

43

Go on, have a feel.'

Was it really necessary to get insistent and a little cross? Time passed; a lot of time, it seemed, until the door discreetly opened and I was ushered firmly from the building. The security guard didn't *feel* necessary, I must say. I was just a babbling imbecile, not an actual threat to anyone's security. Maybe The Miranda demo looked hostile. Strangely enough, I didn't get the job. Your loss, retail section of the Welcome Break service station on the A3 near Waterlooville. I could now be manager there, with a lovely proud grinning photo of me on the staff board, welcoming drivers in for their very welcome break. Your loss, my friends, your loss.

*   *   *

At least in your twenties your need for a hobby is only purely CV-motivated. Your thirties mark another, more worrying shift. Suddenly, you're going out a bit less, you're a bit calmer, you've settled into yourself. You aren't necessarily with husband or children yet; in fact most weekends you never leave the house—you have no need, for there is Dominos on speed-dial—then the moment comes, when you're embarking on your second chicken wing, and the question hits you: 'What AM I doing with my life? I don't have a *thing*. I need a THING that I DO. Something which will make people think of me and go "Oh, yes, Miranda. Did you know, she's a wonderful diver? Yes, she's up at five every morning, bouncing about on the diving board. Can't fathom it myself, but she flies like a swallow, hardly makes a ripple on the pool when she goes in. She says it centres her and gives her perspective. Yes,

Miranda's inspirational. She's got an incredible work–life balance."' Suddenly, just as you've given up on ever really having one, it would be good to have a hobby again.

You panic. 'My life is meaningless,' you think. 'I'm just a shallow little pizza-eating wage-slave.' So you begin to cast around for a hobby. You suddenly appear—for a fleeting moment—at a hula-hooping class. You phone the Martial Arts School then hang up in fear as soon as they answer. You start to pay a little more attention to yellowing cards in newsagents' windows inviting you to join Nigel and Ceri and their group of aspiring vegan cooks for a demonstration at the community centre, Tuesdays at 7.30 p.m. (no classes on Wiccan holidays).

Then, after a short period spent anxiously hovering on the fringes of hobby-land, you take the plunge. You put in a phone call, and before you know it, you've joined a book group.

Your evening at Book Group will, inevitably, go something like this:

A few THIRTYSOMETHING WOMEN in a living room, sitting on chairs, drinking cups of herbal tea. They are all a little uncomfortable, but pretending not to be. They've just had a faux-jokey exchange about herbal tea, including lines such as 'Oh, I'm a herbal tea-aholic. Ha ha!' and 'Careful, you don't want to end up in rehab!' with 'Yes, never mix peppermint and fennel, the hangover's a nightmare! HA HA HA!'

They're now sitting in awkward silence, each of them holding a copy of *THE TIME TRAVELER'S WIFE*. They're awaiting the arrival of the final member of their group.

Right on cue, MIRANDA enters. She is also holding a copy of *THE TIME TRAVELER'S WIFE*. It appears to be well thumbed. This is because on the train on the way there, Miranda has sat on it, bent it out of shape and put a few pages down as bookmarkers. She hasn't read it.

MIRANDA:
Well, hello! We're all looking very serious, aren't we?

The THIRTYSOMETHING women are, indeed, looking very serious. This is because none of them really wants to be there.

THIRTYSOMETHING WOMAN:
Miranda. Have a seat. Would you like a herbal tea?

MIRANDA
Yuck—no, thanks. I bought a bottle. Who else would like da vino? Da vino de campo? A little joke on Gino D'Acampo, the chef off *This Morning*. No?

The THIRTYSOMETHING women all stare at her.

THIRTYSOMETHING WOMAN:
Shall we begin?

No one really wants to begin. They all nod.

THIRTYSOMETHING WOMAN:
So *The Time Traveler's Wife* . . . Well, what a book
. . .

General mumbles of approval.

MIRANDA:
Oh, what a book . . . what a book . . . well, what
a book . . .

THIRTYSOMETHING WOMAN:
What would you say its main themes are then,
Miranda?

MIRANDA:
Me? Well, I would say to you this. *The Time
Traveler's Wife*—its main theme, well . . . its
main theme is that it was about a wife, whose
husband time travelled . . . *downs some wine*

THIRTYSOMETHING WOMAN:
Well, yes, but what issues did it make you
consider?

MIRANDA:
I put that to the floor.

Nervous silence.

THIRTYSOMETHING WOMAN:
Well, the book really moved me to consider
issues of love, loss and free will . . .

MIRANDA downs some more wine and knows
she has to get out of there. It is ghastly. The

47

woman is scary. She has a sudden, potentially inspiring, thought. MIRANDA creeps to the kitchen, dials her mobile phone number from the THIRTYSOMETHING WOMAN's landline. Her mobile rings, she rushes back.

MIRANDA:
Hello? What has happened? Say that again, please? Oh my goodness! Are you serious? That's awful. I must come immediately. I am at a book group. I know, it will be a total shame to miss it, particularly as I was enjoying it so very very much—(MIRANDA starts to leave)— *The Time Traveler's Wife*. I know, it's an amazing book about love, loss and free will, but this is an emergency of the highest proportions, so I am coming now . . .

THIRTYSOMETHING WOMAN:
(From her landline) Goodbye then, lovely to meet you.

MIRANDA:
SCREAMS as she hears the voice on the end of the line. Exits tripping over and into the hummus dip as she leaves.

Still, at least those quests for a hobby are motivated by something essentially noble, some sort of desire to expand one's horizons and better oneself. But in one's thirties another, slightly more sinister, gang of new-hobby-ists emerges: *the Man-Finders*. These are the women who take up traditionally masculine activities in order to find a mate. They will feign interest in Indoor Rock Climbing, Car Mechanics,

Boxing. Or for the less out-and-out Man-Finder, they will attempt to meet their future Mr Right through the hallowed dancing classes of salsa. Actually, I highly recommend you attend one. Not because you're likely to meet an available man, but because there's nothing in the world funnier than twenty-five single women dancing in pairs with one another, each in the throes of a devastating existential crisis, while a perky instructor shouts out, 'Hips, ladies, hips! Feel the rhythm!' (Note to anyone considering joining a class: there is no need to turn up in full *Strictly Come Dancing* salsa outfit including fake tan. Everyone just wears jeans. Briefly awkward.)

Eighteen-year-old Miranda sulkily stomps in We got WALTZING MAN IN BALLROOM SCENE.

Talking of dancing in all-female pairs . . .

Don't laugh . . . I am in a total bate about this . . .

I am not laughing: I still feel your pain, Little M . . .

I don't think I will ever get over this.

Don't worry, you don't.

It could at least have been Waltzing WOMAN.

I know, I know.

I hate being tall. Dire strait pants. And now—as if my life couldn't get any more hideola—I've got to go

49

and pretend to be interested in watching Bella try on her new pixie boots. She's the first one in the school to have a pair—typical. Last term she laughed at my bat wing jumper because it was BHS.

Could I please get back to my Mrs Chapter?

Mrs Chapter? Weirdo.

I'll give you Mrs Chapter and raise you 'Dire strait pants' . . . Off you trot, Waltzing Man in Ballroom Scene.

Meanie. At least I'll be on stage . . . Bet you can't say that about your old thirty-eight-year-old self. *shuffles off victorious*

Ummm . . .
And let Mrs Chapter resume . . . What I know for *sure* isn't just me, and spans all generations, is the New Year's Resolution Hobby Syndrome. At the stroke of midnight on December 31st, anything is possible. The sun has got his hat on, the world is your oyster and whatever you pledge to do, you'll do. Very often, people will pledge to learn a language: 'I'll learn Italian, I am definitely going to learn Italian. And then I'll rent a villa in Tuscany this summer, and probably take a lover, because I'll be fluent by then. I'll be swishing around the markets speaking fluent Italian looking gorgeous, because by then I'll also have lost three stone.'
In January, you'll attend one Italian class and only then remember the horror of reading out loud with a terrible accent in front of classmates, let alone thirtysomething strangers, and decide that

50

classes 'aren't really the way to go. Bit restrictive.' So you'll buy the relevant Linguaphone material at vast expense; you'll try it once, and decide that it's really much too much for you to be getting on with at this very busy stage of your life. Honestly, who's going to get home after a long day at work, put on a pair of headphones and say 'Where is the station?' in Italian, over and over again? That would be the act of a mad person. No, forget languages.

By now it's March, and it's too late to start another new year's resolution: you'll simply have to wait until December 31st again. Everybody knows you can't start something new in March. That would be ridiculous. Similar to starting a diet on a Thursday. Madness. (All diets start on a Monday, as on the Thursday before you start you *have* to eat everything out of your fridge and cupboards for the following Monday. It's a marvellous system.)

But before you know it, it's December 31st again. This year, because you're a little tipsy, your new year's resolution will be something more exciting. This will be the year you finally express your creativity. 'This year,' you announce, 'is going to be The Year I Get Really Into Hats. Ladies and gents, I am going to be a milliner.'

'HOORAH,' everyone shouts. 'You'd be marvellous at that, marvellous.'

'Yes, I'm definitely a hat person.'

'Oh, you are *such* a hat person.'

'I'm going to design hats. Maybe I'll turn professional, maybe I'll do the hats for the Royal Wedding.' (I am presuming that Prince Harry and Pippa Middleton are getting married soon-ish.) And you really believe—not just in that tipsy moment, but for a good while afterwards—that you're going to design hats. The thought sustains you through the grim early weeks of January. But then the year dribbles on into February, and you've not yet booked any classes and, to be honest, your friends don't seem as convinced or supportive as they were last year, and maybe you'll learn Spanish—it was just Italian that wasn't right. But not right now. You've got far too much on. (You haven't.)

Still, there's always gardening. Anyone can make merry with a patch of soil and a happy desire to grow carrots, or so you'd think. But can they? Really? In your twenties—no. There's still the hangover from those teenage notions of cool. In your forties, I think you're allowed an allotment, but only if married/partnered or professionally wildly successful. In your fifties and sixties, if you're still single then fine, go nuts: get sixteen cats, move to Cumbria and spend the rest of your life talking about fennel. Give into eccentric spinsterhood. But in your thirties . . . well, it's a muddy (pun intended) area.

I think you can only justify gardening if a) you blather on loudly about how you're growing your own organic vegetables to save the environment and control what you put in your body or b) if you've always been the 'wacky one' in your friendship group. The one who wore a headscarf at twenty-two, made patterned tights look marvellous and nearly had a professional career as a cartoonist. To truly enjoy and inhabit the odder hobbies, you need to have already sown the seeds (pun still absolutely intended and I am thrilled with myself) of eccentricity.

The only acceptable hobby, throughout all stages of life, is cookery. As a child: adorable baked items.

Twenties: much appreciated spag bol and fry-ups. Thirties and forties: lovely stuff with butternut squash and chorizo from the *Guardian* food section. Fifties and sixties: beef wellington from the *Sunday Telegraph* magazine. Seventies and eighties: back to the adorable baked items. Perfect. The only teeny tiny downside of this hobby is that I HATE COOKING.

Don't get me wrong; I absolutely adore the eating of the food. It's just the awful boring, frightening putting together of it that makes me want to shove my own fists in my mouth. It's a lovely idea: follow the recipe and you'll end up with something exactly like the pretty picture in the book, only even more delicious. But the reality's rather different. Within fifteen minutes of embarking on a dish I generally find myself in tears in the middle of what appears to be a bombsite, looking like a mentally unstable art teacher in a butter-splattered apron, wondering a) just how I am supposed to get hold of a thimble and a half of FairTrade hazelnut oil (why is there *always* the one impossible-to-find recipe ingredient? Sesame paste, anyone?) and b) just how I managed to get flour through two closed doors onto the living-room curtains, when I don't recall having used any flour and oh-this-is-terrible-let's-just-go-out-and-get-a-Wagamama's-and-to-hell-with-the-cost, dammit.

Enough from me on this subject. My Dear Reader Chum, what are your hobbies? What sets your heart on fire? Do you find this whole business a conundrum as well? It's not just me, is it? Why don't you write in and let me know? (Except, obviously, don't actually write in, unless 'Writing in to things' is your hobby; in which case, I don't mean to be rude but that's dull and maybe you should try collecting stickers.) Hopefully, I'll run into you one day at Book Group. Or Cookery. Or Flower Arranging. Or Welding. Or Warhammer Society. Or—here's a thought—a special Ballet Class for 'Oddly Shaped Socially Awkward People Who Have No Talent For Ballet'. Oh yes, let's do that please. Come on, you know you want to. We might sustain the odd injury, but we'll put on one hell of an end-of-term show. *The Nutcracker*, anybody? I'll play the furious crackers; who's up for the enigmatic nut? What do you mean that's not *exactly* what it's about?

4

OFFICE LIFE

One wholly legitimate reason for not maintaining hobbies in one's twenties and early thirties would, of course, be that our jobs are so all-consuming, so important, that we simply don't have time to waste on arts and crafts and hurling ourselves off diving-boards, thank you very much. Yes, we all hopped onto the career ladder moments after leaving school or university, and began slowly and confidently to clamber up within an industry. An industry that suited us perfectly and we felt passionately about. Not to mention a big fat juicy wage packet, which meant we could afford to go on classy, European city breaks at the weekend, shuffling around Florence in a pair of Ugg boots like a true professional. No sitting around in our pants on the sofa, with a tub of Maltesers, wondering if 'taking up sewing in a big way' would give our lives a little purpose. (Just a random example—nothing to do with my evening last night.)

Let's be honest, that's *not* how it happens, or at least I for one certainly didn't get the whole career thing sorted out for a fair while. I spent nearly a decade in low-key office jobs looking forward to tea-breaks, idly wondering if any of my dreams would ever come true, and partaking in what I call 'merry prankage'. (May I point out for those readers who are familiar with my televisual mother and her hallowed phrase, that I just made correct use of the term, 'what I call'. I followed it with a phrase unique to me, something that only *I* call, not what we *all* call. Now, onwards with my, what I call, book. Which is an example of the phrase being used incorrectly. We all call it a book. All of us. Point made.)

Throughout the office job years I was The Great Directionless Wonder. And oh, what a shock that was. At eighteen, one has such grand plans for oneself. World domination hardly begins to cover them. Allow me to demonstrate by means of a little, if I may be so bold, scene-ette:

INT. SCHOOL CAREERS OFFICE. 1991.
EIGHTEEN-YEAR-OLD MIRANDA sits across from a rotund, stern-looking and fairly morose CAREERS ADVISOR, MRS TIMBLE. For someone in such a position, MIRANDA is oddly confident. She speaks in the manner of one who can see clearly into the future, and who likes what she sees.

MIRANDA:
Yeah, I mean, I need to get going by twenty-two, really, if I'm going to have children at twenty-five. So I guess I'll just start up a business straight away—maybe selling jewellery or art or something? Maybe a Notting-Hill boutique that will then go international. That will then give me loads of money for having kids. And then I've got the option of marrying an arty, hippy type with less money. You know: if I decide I'd prefer that to an architect or lawyer or world-famous tennis player or something. Anyway, when I

56

go back to work at twenty-seven, I imagine I'll go straight into government. I *have* always wanted to get into comedy but that's a bit of a juvenile dream, really. And they all seem quite weird as well, those comedians. And there are important issues in the world to address, yeah?

So government feels more worthwhile. More me. For all we know, if I was in politics now, the Gulf War may not have happened. Just saying. And it won't be hard to segue into politics if I'm already a successful businesswoman, will it? Seems like a natural leap. I mean, I want to be realistic—I know that I can't be prime minister until I'm at least thirty. And I'll want to keep some time free to coach international lacrosse.

MRS TIMBLE pretends to take this seriously, but smirks and writes down: 'Will temp until a man finally takes pity' in the box next to MIRANDA's name.

I had all sorts of rollicking professional plans when I left school, and my eighteen-year-old self would be horrified by the years I spent as an office junior.

But what about you, MDRC? Did you whoosh (good word) straight out of education into an absolutely slap-bang-perfect career? What's that? 'No, absolutely not, you giant moron, that happens to almost NO ONE, so stop making us feel worse about it?' Yes, good. Excellent. Then it isn't just me. We're on the same page (figuratively speaking, of course—obviously we've been *literally* on the same page ever since you started reading the book. Do you see? Hello? Anyone there? Oh, come on, it was mildly amusing).

Personally, I think on leaving school we aren't prepared to deal with the seriousness the work place presents. Indeed, the formality of the real world, full stop. School was seven glorious years of anarchy. Rules were there to be broken. Surely anything 'serious' was just a blank canvas onto which we could project our jolly japery?

In fact—and here I digress a little, please indulge me, do—I still find that a formal scenario provokes an odd, childish response. Is it just me who finds they want something inappropriate to happen when presented with one? I can't walk past a vicar without passionately willing him to shout 'Bollocks!' and kick over a traffic cone. Whenever I see a nun I want her to pull up her habit and start dancing the can-can, just for the sheer heck of it. Something, anything, to break the spell. I should add I have nothing against nuns and vicars and good godly folk; it's just the outfits, and the systems, and the baggage of formality and respect. Oh my goodness, here I go . . . *has panic attack at the notion of 'seriousness', runs off to find custard pie, throws pie in own face, sits back, relieved*

This dramatic response to seriousness seems to run in my family: my dear grandmother once attended a very formal Foreign Office dinner in the 1950s. At some point during the evening, she found herself face-to-face with a white-tie-wearing army general. At which point, she suddenly and to everyone's astonishment (including, probably, her own), hurled a glass of red wine over the poor man. And I can absolutely understand why she did it. I'm 90 per cent certain that should I ever find myself standing alongside a formally dressed military leader, it won't be long before I grab a vol-au-vent and ram it onto his nose. (You can get a great purchase on a nose with a vol-au-vent. Try it.) Senior Services Personnel, you have been warned.

Eighteen-year-old Miranda rushes in, giggling hysterically Oh my gosh, listen to this. Mrs Scott the housemistress is about to do an inspection of all the dorms. Dolly's dorm got ready early coz they've got choir practice, so we've just gone and got a sheep from the field and led it in to their dorm. An actual sheep! So when they get back from practice, just before Mrs Scott inspects, they'll have a sheep in their dorm. I think I am about to literally die laughing. I've got to go and see what happens. Last time, Mrs Scott exploded when she found a Jilly Cooper hidden inside Bella's hot water bottle cover . . . *rushes out, hysterical*

I think that proves my point very nicely. Being naughty has always come out in situations that demand decorum. Which made for a rude awakening when it came to embracing the systems of adult life.

On my first day in my first ever office job as a data in-putter, I returned to my desk after lunch and accidentally knocked an open bottle of Lucozade into my bag. At that moment, my new boss approached my desk. I stood up, orange liquid dripping gently to the floor at just about crotch-height, and, of course, I did what I would've done if I'd been in class at school. I made a big jokey thing of it, shouting, 'HA. It looks like I'm weeing myself. But I'm not. It's Lucozade. I know.

59

Why don't we pour Lucozade into someone else's bag, so it'll look like *they're* weeing themselves. That would be HILAIRE! Let's do it to Penny in HR; then we can call her Pissy Penny Piss Pot. Pissy Penny. No?' My boss simply shook her head, put some papers on my desk for filing, and strode off.

I sensed then that this was not going to be a world that welcomed my jolly japes.

Nor is it the sort of thing that parents ever sit down and tell you, is it? That, 'Life might not always be quite as fun as it was in the fifth form, so best start practising your serious-face now.'

OH MY GOD, THE SHEEP HAS BEEN POOING IN BELLA'S NEW PIXIE BOOTS. SO funny. She was screaming! And Bella nearly hit Beady coz she joked the sheep had fashion taste and then Twig nearly choked on her Black Jack for laughing—

Can I briefly interrupt you, Little M, to apologise to MDRC for the Malory Towers-esque nicknames. And explain: Bella (Annabelle, the cool one, good at everything), Twig (naturally thin, enjoyed reminding us all of her 'fast, lucky metabolism'), Beady (big eyes, tiny head). Then there was Milly (Camilla went red every time she spoke, or was passed a ball in sport), Clare-Bear (obsessed with her teddy but in a funny way, not a weird way, top of the list to be in a dorm with), Billy (had a beard,—unfortunate at 12), Pussy (loved cats and had t-shirts with pictures of hers on), Bridgey (what else do you do with Bridget?), Puddles (no idea) and Podge (liked sweets, hated Twig). My dearest friends at school, and harmless nicknames then, but embarrassing when you find yourself

60

shouting 'Pussy!' excitedly across Centre Court at Wimbledon during a quiet match point fifteen years later. Carry on . . .

So, Mrs Scott came in and was so thrown by finding herself face to face with a large farm animal that she simply said, 'Come on, who put a sheep in here?' I have never found anything funnier.

And in fact, Little M, this might be the right time to tell you that you probably never will.

What? How do you mean? Isn't this . . . life? Sheep in dormitories, water-balloon fights, super-gluing Miss Jenvey to her chair when she's having an afternoon snooze in the common room, flashing your bum in the coach?

Well . . . as you get older, you're expected to put a lid on these things. A bit. Certainly the flashing bit. And, be honest, that was never really your bag. I mean, you know, nudity and all that. Remember, we were the one who would always change in the dorms under a kind of what I call 'dome towel tent' (please note *another* correct 'what I call' usage).

Are we over that shyness now and all cool and free and stuff, like Twig when she paraded her first M&S bra?

Umm . . . no. We remain unable to deal with any kind of nudity when it's not in a *lowers voice* sexual *back to normal voice* context.

You can't even SAY 'sexual'.

I just don't like it as a word. It's a weird, serpent-y word. It sounds completely the opposite of what it actually means. And not liking the word doesn't mean I'm not *lowers voice* sexual. It's just, well, I'm a bit British about the whole being-naked-in-front-of-strange-people business. That's all.

In fact, MDRC, it's not just *being* naked. Even feeling a bit more naked than usual can send me into a huge, mad, neurotic tailspin of desperate innuendo and red-faced-ness. Is it just me who finds the whole business of going commando completely, overwhelmingly horrendous? It's only happened to me once or twice—usually due to some kind of laundry 'malfunction'—but my goodness, it's ruined my day. I simply couldn't handle the fact that I was naked underneath a pair of jeans.

But if you've got your jeans on, you're not *naked*.

It feels naked because one is used to another layer between a jean and a bottom.

Oh. My. God.

A woman from mainland Europe probably regularly goes commando to feel sexy or give the day a bit of edge. I just wanted to go up to strangers and shout, 'Hello, yes, excuse me, you're probably thinking that I've got a weird expression on my face because I'm not wearing any pants. Well, that's true, I am pant-less. But I'm not doing it for kicks. Absolutely not. It was a laundry crisis. It was either this or cycling shorts. I am not dirty or weird. Thank you, as you were.'

You are officially a loser from Planet Loser. Can we please get back to the subject in hand before I decide to jack it all in and never become you.

Sure. So, yes, as you get older, Little M, you are going to spend a good deal of time in places where you'll not be able to engage in quite so much unbridled jollity as you are used to.

What? Do you mean like church? Because you can be very jolly in church. All it takes is for one person to do a giant, echo-y fart and you're away.

Not quite. I'm talking specifically about office life.

'Office life'? Do you mean life in government office?

Umm . . .

Or having a whole office full of staff working for you?

Not quite. In fact—here's the thing—we spend the vast majority of our twenties and early thirties doing basic administration in a series of offices.

What? But, but, aren't we in charge? We're meant to be in charge by twenty-five.

Well, we're not. Mostly, we're the very opposite of in charge. In fact, we're quite often a temp.

'Temp'?

A temporary assistant, performing roles for a short period of time, in the absence of a full-time member of staff.

You mean, the person who comes in and does the stuff no one else wants to do?

That's one way to look at it. I always preferred to think of myself as being very much like Superman, magically appearing when most needed and saving the day. Just without a cape.

Humph.

Oh, cheer up. At one point we do so well we're promoted. *picks up imaginary phone* Hello, Miranda Hart, OFFICE MANAGER speaking.

Office manager? Do we get to boss people around?

Not really. It's more organising and ordering stationery. But we do get to boss paperclips around. And we get our own swivel chair. MDRC, aren't swivel chairs wonderful things? Are you on a swivel chair right now? (Are you cheekily reading this at work?) If so, let's all swivel together. One—two— trois (French for three)—*SWIVEL* . . .

Stop it. This is horrendous . . . you're SO square. You're like someone in a novel. A really depressing novel, set during the war, about a lonely secretary who lives in a bed-sit and eventually turns to drink after her boyfriend in the army dies. This is terrible.

Don't worry, little one, I know it sounds unexciting, and a bit like we are betraying our dreams. Life post-school was, admittedly, a bit of a shock. It was all a bit . . . grey. A bit worky. But you realised pretty quickly that you'd get sectioned if you put a sheep in someone's office.

That would be funny, though.

It would. Oh, I agree, it really would. And I've come to realise that it's because we're the kind of person who finds the putting of sheep in offices funny that we *need* a bit of time at the bottom of the professional food chain. I know it sounds boring, but you really don't want a highly pressured job in your twenties. You need time to work out the world, gain confidence, make friends, go through some rubbish times and get stronger. And I tell you what: some of my happiest, funniest times have been spent in offices. Perhaps because the work was mundane, even the tiniest of distractions become wildly hilarious and wonderful. Actually, I'd say that 90 per cent of my doubled-over-gasping-with-laughter-laughing-so-much-that-you-can't-breathe-and-think-you-might-die laughing has occurred during slow days in offices.

It sounds pretty lame to me.

Right, I'm going to drop this conciliatory tone right now. I am going to draw myself up to my full and magnificent height, and I'm going to defend the gloriousness of office life. You need to know that even as life develops in superficially disappointing ways, *there is still fun to be had.*

65

The joy of the office would be best illustrated with a short list, so, MDRC, please re-charge your teacup, plump up that cushion behind you, and settle down nicely for . . . (and cue applause) . . .

MIRANDA'S FIVE FAVOURITE THINGS ABOUT OFFICE LIFE!

1. Stationery

Having read the word 'stationery', I predict that right now you'll either be punching the air in recognition and delight, or scratching your head in bafflement as to why on earth anyone would get excited by such a thing. If it's the former, please read on—you're in for a treat. And if it's the latter, then please read on—because you're sorely in need of re-education.

As far as I'm concerned, *nothing* is as exciting as a giant cupboard full of bulldog clips, Post-it notes, marker pens, pencils, A3 pads, A4 pads, Jiffy bags—oh, the Jiffy bag, with its internal bubble wrap . . . I'm too excited to go on. Reading a large office-stationery-order list is, for me, like reading the menu for a fine and rare banquet. If you like your job and are proud to serve your company, then furnishing the office with the relevant stationery is a satisfying and noble task. And if you're . . . well, if you're perhaps a teeny tiny bit less keen, then the stationery cupboard is basically a safe arena to engage in victimless petty theft. It's *not* just me that has righted many a grudge by the tucking of a booty of Post-it note pads into a bra (men, please feel free to use your pant area instead),

66

and a highlighter pen into a shoe, is it? 'Ha ha, I've got mine,' you think, as you look nervously around you, an inch away from the scene of the crime. It definitely represents MIRANDA: 1 CRUEL WORLD: 0.

Even if you're not criminally inclined, then stationery offers ample opportunity for impromptu, mid-afternoon sessions of arts and crafts. Have you ever made a miniature Eiffel Tower out of bulldog clips, MDRC? Ever challenged yourself to eat a tub of Coronation Chicken using only paperclips? No? Get to it at once. There are larks to be had, I tell you. *Larks.* Not spectacular larks, I grant you, but ones that have saved many a young office drone from falling into a slough of despond. (If only bulldog-clip towers could be considered a suitable hobby for someone in their thirties).

Of course, the more 'extreme' the stationery, the greater the possibility for upbeat creative carnage. During my stint as office manager, I once accidentally ordered the wrong size package of bubble-wrap. Six enormous rolls—the size of those Swedish exercise balls—arrived. And it wasn't long before I'd enticed all my colleagues—even dreary 'It's all about Health & Safety' Debbie—to spend the rest of the afternoon rolling around the office on them. Including (for one misguided moment) using them to bounce down the stairs. For our final foray, perilously close to when the boss was due to return, we decided to place all six in a row and take a diving roll along the top of them. I went first (naturally). As I did so, the rolling effect took my loose top with it, up over my head, as I finished my spectacular manoeuvre with a professional gymnast pose.

Upon which, the boss returned.

My dear colleagues all naturally scarpered, though I wasn't to know this as I still had my top over my head. The boss was greeted by the vision of me standing in my bra proudly doing a 'gymnast finish' in front of a lot of rolls of bubble-wrap as colleagues beavered away dutifully around me. No real way to recover from that one. Another of life's hideous hiccups.

Yes, wholesale quantities of stationery can create an adventure playground for the irresponsible. Which leads me to number two on the list of my very favourite things about office life . . .

2. The Stationery Cupboard
Definitely deserving of its own category, if only because the stationery cupboard provides the

most wonderful refuge from the occasional ravages of office life—indeed, from life itself. In one office I worked in, the stationery cupboard was large and well appointed enough to house at least four people for up to five hours before anyone started running out of oxygen. A bunch of us—when we were hung over and meant to be mail-merging for a big event—used to pretend we were going in there for a 'very important mail-merge-based meeting'. We would then bed down for the morning—lying on the bubble-wrap, heads resting on Manila envelopes—and snooze peacefully, like monkeys in a cage.

Even when you're fighting fit, the stationery cupboard can provide a welcome bolthole. There's nothing like breezily declaring, 'Just popping in for some printer cartridges', only to lock the door behind you and lie back in the restorative darkness or, in my case, begin early attempts to write comedy sketches by torchlight.

Also, if you're any kind of amateur photographer, it's an excellent makeshift darkroom. All hail the stationery cupboard.

3. Complicated Intra-Office Communication Systems

Enjoyable mainly because of the potential for disaster when they get into the wrong hands (my hands). As office manager, I had to set up and maintain a new and rather complicated phone-pager system. After a week of vast confusion and fun teaching people how to page each other, the system went live. Unfortunately, it took a while for the novelty to wear off, and my peers still saw it as an hilarious tool of ridiculousness and joy, rather than a legitimate means of transmitting information. Which led to one particular episode, where I sat at my desk having a serious face to face chat with my boss, while a friend paged me and spent a full five minutes making animal noises at me down the phone. I later paged this friend back and loudly let her know that, 'I've just done a poo so big it won't flush.' Unfortunately, I'd pressed the button which conveyed my message efficiently to all offices, including all desks and meeting rooms. My career at that company was relatively short-lived.

I've had similar troubles with email. When I first started temping, it was still quite new and wildly exciting.

What's email?

What? Oh . . . umm . . . it's a kind of letter, but sent through a telephone line—

WHAT?

Look, can we come back to that later, please? It's going to be a bit of a big explain. Sorry, MDRC. So, once, the CEO's PA sent a round-robin email asking if anyone wanted to go the Millennium Dome (the CEO had a stall there, and was a huge fan). I replied, 'I'd rather have sex with Robin Cook, but thanks, anyway. P.S. I had that sexy dream again last night, the one about Bill in Accounts. This time he was dressed as a knight, but with Speedos. Weird!'

70

I then realised I'd hit Reply to All, including all staff, trustees and all offices in England, Wales and Scotland. I had to formally email all staff, trustees, and all offices in England, Wales and Scotland to apologise, and to let them know that having sex with Robin Cook was absolutely not something I was particularly keen to do, and ditto with Big Fat Bill in Accounts. I then had to immediately send another email, to all, apologising for calling Bill both Big and Fat, and that I was sure there were many people who found him very attractive. Robin Cook, perhaps. I then had to send another email, to all, apologising for suggesting Bill was gay, which I knew he wasn't and apologies to his wife and daughter (who, I understood, worked in the Sussex branch) . . .

Quick, let's move on to number four.

4. Lunch

When I worked in an office, meals took on an almost mythical status. I, and all those around me, became completely, unashamedly and noisily obsessed with lunch. Lunch was no longer a simple refuelling exercise: it was the glittering oasis in the middle of what could sometimes be a dreary day.

At around 10.30 a.m., the lunch-rumblings would start up:

'What are you having? Pret or the Italian sandwich place?'

'I want a meatball sandwich.'

'Ooh, no, *I* couldn't possibly, I had a meaty breakfast.'

'Apple or yoghurt for afters?'

'I've bought a Twix to have at half past three.'

'Maybe you should have half for pudding.'

'Oh, no, I couldn't—it wouldn't go with my yoghurt.'

'Oh, yes. Good point.'

'What time is it?'

'10:45.'

'Oh, well, not long to go now.'

'Is 11.30 too early to have lunch?'

And so on.

I remember when wraps first came in—that was a turning point in office lunch history. 'Do you know, I think I might brave a WRAP?' you'd say. Then you'd come back into the office with your wrap, and everyone would crowd round for a look at your wrap. They'd ask concerned questions like, 'Does it fill you up, your wrap? Does the wrap fill you up as much as the sandwich?' All very important wrap-based questions, because heaven forbid you had a disappointing lunch.

Then sushi came onto the scene, and we all thought ourselves incredibly cosmopolitan and chic. We'd spend £7 a day on sixteen grains of rice wrapped in a piece of green tarpaulin, which over the course of a year added up to the value of a small house on the South Coast. But we didn't care. We were at the very cutting edge of lunch.

Then, at around 4 p.m., the conversation would turn to dinner—what was everyone having?

'Anyone going Chinese?'

'I might get one of those curry banquets in a box from Tesco.'

'I'm going scrambled eggs.'

'Is that all?'

'Don't worry, I'll have chips at the pub first.'

'I was going to say . . .'

It was boredom, pure and simple, which brought about this obsession with the next feed. I was occasionally nostalgic for a richer time, when meals were the boring things you had to do between interesting activities. It was to be a bitter realisation that the older you got, the more vital meals were to alleviate the boredom or pressures of the day.

But, being in our mid-twenties and in an office, we were happy with our daily food convos. And the joy—the total, unadulterated *joy*—brought by the occasional Friday McDonald's. That was big news. At about eleven o'clock, someone would say, 'I feel it today—today's the day, I know it's naughty, but I just feel the need . . . I'm going *McDonald's.*' Audible gasps from the surrounding desks. Then a half-hour conversation about what you get if you go McDonald's.

'Six nuggets.'

'Oh no, I wouldn't waste McDonald's calories on nuggets; I'd go straight for the quarter pounder with cheese.'

'I'd do a small cheeseburger and leave room for the apple pie.'

'Careful, the filling's hot,' some card would shout and oh, how we'd laugh.

'Oh no, if I'm going to do it, I'm going big, I'm going Big Mac Meal, *and* apple pie. There, I said it.'

'Well, I'd go Filet-O-Fish.' Silence. Stares. Who said that? Who on earth would suggest such a freaky, revolting thing?

Um, hello?

Oh, hello, Little M. What's up? Is it urgent? Because, you know, I haven't quite finished my list—

It's just, I don't mean to be rude, except that I do. I was hoping the office list would be a bit less rubbish than this. I mean, making bulldog clip towers and hiding in the stationery cupboard? Making a damned fool of yourself over an intercom? Becoming weirdly obsessed with sandwiches? This seems neither fun nor fulfilling.

Ah, but wait until you hear my fifth and final reason why office life is a little bit splendid. You're going to love it . . . Little Miranda, and My Dear Reader Chum; my fifth, final and far and away most vital reason why office life is absolutely marvellous is . . .

5. It's Sort Of Like School!

What? Really?!

Yes, it most certainly is. Or it can be, if you put in the effort. You see, MDRC, this is the twist in my tale. Over-indulgence in boarding-school jollity made office life very hard for me at first. But then—hey presto—the varied fun-having skills I perfected at school went on to make the whole damned thing that bit more enjoyable. And, what's more, for me, office life very often brought to mind the best bits of school: the day was nicely structured; the job was low pressure

74

but interesting enough; you could switch off at the weekends; all your friends were right there in one big open-plan office; you could steal and hoard people's sweets; you could subtly, cheekily indulge your dislike of authority via artfully placed Post-it note cartoons and delightful slacking off; and every day at five you could shoot out of the door and leave the day behind. Even though I didn't always realise it at the time, it suited me down to a tee. And remember, as the saying goes: 'You spend your youth working eight hours a day so that when you become boss you have the privilege of working twenty hours a day.' Being the office junior has many a perk.

You will enjoy it, Little M, I promise. It's a very positive interlude in our life.

Does that mean you do something different now? Something more exciting, more part of the plan?

Ah, now. That would be telling. You'll know, soon enough.

Ooh, are we an MP? Did we actually become prime minister? Or maybe we're married . . .

spits tea out Sorry about that . . .

Because I suppose the good thing about the low-pressure job is . . .

starts to take another sip of tea

. . . that we have time to go on loads of dates . . .

75

spits tea out again Sorry. Could we perhaps maybe talk about the whole dating/husband issue at a later (pun coming) date. (Good one, Hart, good one.)

Well, MDRC, I hope that if you work in an office in a stimulating but junior role (or even if you're the CEO, dammit), then I've given you some ideas for how best to pass your time. If you've any suggestions for other ways to have good, clean fun in an office environment, then please do page or email me (remembering to cc in all staff, trustees and offices in England, Wales and Scotland). Kindest regards, M Hart, Office Manager.

Hang on . . .

Do you mind? I've just brought the chapter to a rather magnificent close—

You never explained the email thing. Did you mean post? Because if so, how could you accidentally post something to lots of people? Surely you'd notice that you were doing it as you put the notes in all the envelopes and licked the hundreds of stamps. Unless you did it in your sleep . . .

Oh, dear. Well, email is . . . goodness. Email is . . . No. I think we'll need to have a separate chapter on this.

MDRC, please turn the page, and give yourself a round of applause for doing so (although I appreciate you can't do both at once, so you'll have to turn the page, put the book down, then applaud—but please do your best). And off we trot into the next chapter where we shall discuss ... Technology. Exciting, isn't it?

5

TECHNOLOGY

One thing that has most definitely changed since I was eighteen, apart from the fact that I can't now wave without a flap of bingo-wing arm-flesh hitting me in the eye, or the fact that I can't freely sneeze or trampoline without the risk of doing a bit of wee, or my inability to receive an evening invitation without exclaiming, 'Oh, no can do. There's a *Morse* marathon on telly that night, are you mad?' or . . . no, I should stop, I'm depressing myself. And what's that I hear you say? 'Enough of this bingo-wing wee talk, Miranda. The title suggested that this was to be a chapter about Technology, not the indignities of the ageing process. So hop to it.' Fair enough, MDRC, fair enough. My point was to be this—that what has most definitely changed since I was a young 'un is, of course, the marvellous, mysterious world of Technology.

It's extraordinary, isn't it, to think of the unequivocally wonderful and life-affirming changes that have come about as the result of technological progress? How strange to think that at nineteen, I headed to Australia for five months, just me and Clare-Bear, without even a mobile phone for company—

What do you mean? Why would you take the portable phone with you?

What?

Well, I presume by 'mobile phone' you meant portable phone? You know, the cordless one that Mum has? That is AMAZE-BALLS. Yesterday, I talked to Clare-Bear for an hour on my own in my room and walked about when talking, too. Didn't have to sit by where the phone's plugged in with Mum listening to our conversation about who Clare-Bear snogged the night before. It's so cool.

Right . . . No, I meant a mobile phone. It's new to you. It's totally mobile. You can make a call from anywhere.

You mean I could be right at the end of the garden, and still make a call? Because Mum's cuts out when you're just outside the kitchen. It goes 'Pfffffhhht' and stops.

You could be absolutely anywhere and still make a call. You could be at the top of Ben Nevis, the Australian Outback, anywhere. It's a mobile phone. *Mobile.*

Don't be stupid! Where's it plugged in?

It's a MOBILE! IT HAS BATTERIES AND DOESN'T HAVE TO BE PLUGGED IN! IT'S *MOBILE.* YOU TAKE IT WITH YOU. IT'S MOBILE—YOU CAN CALL FROM ANYWHERE. *MOBILE* PHONE! And, breathe. (MDRC, I fear this chapter might test my patience. We'll simply have to bear with our eighteen-year-old chum on this one.)

Are you making this up?

79

No. And you can send people written messages on them as well.

What, like a telegram? Where does it print out?

The telephone has a screen on it.

A bit like a calculator? I wrote 'Boobless' to Beady on mine in Chemistry class yesterday (SO funny).

These messages aren't just limited to 'Boobless', 'ShellOil' and 'Esso'. You can write anything. They're called 'texts'.

Texts? Why don't you just call them, if it's a phone?

Because sometimes you can't be bothered to call. If you're running a bit late you can send a quick note saying: 'Will be there in 5.'

What's the point in doing a 'text' to say that? You're going to be 'there in 5' anyway.

It's polite. It's what we do. Sometimes we text a full conversation . . .

You press buttons for words to come up on a phone instead of just calling someone when it's a phone anyway? One word—WHY?

BECAUSE . . . Well . . . because . . . ummm . . . no, hang on . . . because sometimes conversations are more amusing in text form. And it's good for quickly making plans.

80

But that could just be a VERY QUICK PHONE CALL. BECAUSE IT'S A PHONE!

Look, FORGET TEXTS! Get this—you can even send photos to someone else's phone screen, if you want.

Don't be stupid. How can you send a photo through a PHONE? Are you also driving cars in the sky? How does it all even work?

Ummm . . . well . . . there's a satellite in the sky that . . . uh . . . bounces rays of information on a . . . a superhighway.

So there ARE highways in the sky? Can you drive cars on them?

They're not literal highways. There's sort of . . . an invisible energy and there are . . . waves of air . . . oh, I DON'T KNOW!

I knew you were talking rubbish. Photos on phones. Absurd.

It's not rubbish. It's just an advance on digital cameras.

What are they?

AAAAAHHHH! OK. They're cameras, and you can see the photo as soon as you take it.

Impossible! Even in Boots in Waterlooville the quickest development time is three days.

Please shut your face.

RUDE.

This is just getting more complicated than I'd hoped. Bear with. So the photo immediately comes up on the screen on the camera and you take a photo and if you don't like it, you can just get rid of it and take another one.

OK, so you're looking at a view, and you take a photo. Do you then have to look at the photo of what you are ALREADY LOOKING AT, and decide if you like the photo?

Yes. Then take another photo if we don't like it.

Then presumably look at it to see if you like that one?

Yeah. See, if it's a fun photo, whether your friends look good, if you're showing your best side—

How vain. You're standing around looking at the photos on your camera instead of actually looking at the view. You IDIOT! Why don't you stop looking at photos of what you're experiencing, and just get on with . . . EXPERIENCING it?

We *are* experiencing it!

You're not: you're looking at photos of the thing you should be looking at. You all sound mad. One of the best things is getting photos developed and remembering what we took. Like that time we got the photos back a week after the Isle of Wight school trip and found that photo we'd forgotten about of Bella putting a hotdog in Miss Everett's anorak hood.

Oh, I give up. Just wait and see. You'll enjoy it, you really will.

No, don't you dare give up. You still haven't explained this 'email' thing to me yet.

collective deep breath Oh, MDRC, I'm exhausted. Are you keeping up? But I suppose we'd better do this.

An email is an 'electronic mail'. You know when you type a letter on a computer?

I don't have a computer. Why would I have a computer? What am I—a City banker?

Calm down. Right, you know when you type a letter on your electronic typewriter?

I can't believe that thing. You press the delete button and Tipp-Ex is automatically in the machine, and it rubs the letter out. It's total genius.

Yes, amazing. Anyway, imagine this—you type a letter on that, and it comes up on the paper. Except instead of coming up on the paper, it comes up on a computer screen. And then you can send it to another person's screen. Anywhere in the world.

How does THAT work? Does it go on the invisible

83

electric highway in the sky, too?

I DON'T KNOW HOW IT WORKS. I DON'T KNOW HOW ANYTHING WORKS! IT JUST DOES. IT JUST HAPPENS!

*Now, **YOU** **CALM DOWN!** What about pens and paper? Do people still use them?*

A bit. But we don't really send letters any more.

*Oh, but I **LOVE** getting letters. I love rushing to the door when the postman's just been in the hope I'll have a letter addressed to me to open. Then rush away to see what new writing paper the girls might have used to tell me their holiday gossip. I would really miss that. Not to mention the exotic French handwriting from pen pal Pierre in Perpignan.*

But emails mean that you can do work absolutely anywhere. You can be on a train, and it can be exactly like you're in the office. It's great.

*Seriously, **HOW** is that great? You are really bugging me now. Trains are **NOT** for working on. One of our very favourite things is looking at the lovely views, watching the world go by, having a pack lunch and getting excited about wherever it is you're going.*

I admit I had forgotten that.

Why don't you try life without your mobile phone? Turn it off. Put it away.

WHAT? But I get into a panic in that brief

moment I'm rummaging in the depths of my bag thinking I've lost my phone until I remember it's in the special safe pouch at the front of it.

Oh, grow up! It'd just be for a week.

A WEEK! No, thanks. I'd feel abandoned. Alone. Isolated. Terrified. Weak. Constantly thinking that I might be missing something.

Where do you live? Central Sahara? Oh gosh, we don't live in a remote desert do we?

No, in London.

Do we? Without Mum and Dad? That's well cool, but hardly a place to be isolated, you—I will say it again—IDIOT. I think you'll find that if someone really needs and wants to get in touch with you they will leave an answer phone message telling you to call them back like we do in 1991—THANK YOU VERY MUCH! And there's always a pay phone.

A pay phone?

Don't they still exist?

Do you know—I have no idea. OK, well, how about this invention . . . You are quite a big fan of 'optional silliness', aren't you, Little M?

I most certainly am. In fact, I'd go so far as to say that 'optional silliness' is what makes life worth living.

Then might I introduce you to the most wonderful thing about modern life? We call it . . . The Internet. And before you say 'WHAT?' again, the internet is the whole world on your computer. I can just go to my computer, type in whatever I want to find out about (which we call 'googling') and immediately I receive a vast mass of information.

That sounds very good, actually. I approve.

At last. Also, if you've got the internet, you can watch little video clips of funny things—like *You've Been Framed*, but on your computer, whenever you like. Yesterday I watched a penguin sneezing, a cat eating a cheeseburger, and some ducklings being blown over in the wind. (For seven hours, MDRC, but let's not tell Little Miranda.)

OK. That is a bit brilliant.

And then you get this thing called Facebook, where basically all your friends have pages, and you have a page, and the pages say who you are, what you do . . .

But your friends know who you are and what you

86

do.

No, wait, you can message each other little notes—

But you've got your mobile phones for that.

Yes, but these can be longer messages, if you want.

Isn't that what emails are for?

Well, the messages are about different things to the sort of things you'd text or email. It might be about something you've just seen, a comment about what's going on in the world, what you are up to . . .

Can't you just tell your friends when you next see them?

You don't need to see them—you tell them immediately online.

But then you don't see your friends . . .?

Well, it's good for, say . . . you could post pictures up there of your holiday and stuff for your friends to look at. But sometimes people other than your friends look at them. Which you know they're going to do, and that's sort of half the fun.

I wouldn't let Milly's friend, Minnie, look at MY holiday photos. She's creepy. She sleeps in gloves.

Yeah, but you don't know whether or not they've

looked at your photos.

Oh, great. That's not weird at all.

And if someone wants to get in touch but doesn't know you that well, then they'll just poke you or something.

They'll POKE you?!

Forget it. I don't actually do Facebook that much, anyway. I prefer Twitter, which is just messages, and people choose to follow you and what you're saying.

What kind of things are you saying?

OK, let me look at my last thing I tweeted . . .

Tweeted? What are you, a bird? YOU ARE OFFICIALLY INSANE!

I AM NOT! It's called social media. Loads of people tweet.

OK, what did you last tweet on Twitter, you twerp-er?

I said: 'My cat has rolled in the compost—disgusting.' That's not necessarily the best example. I also said afterwards: 'Is it OK to Febreze a cat?' which I thought was quite funny.

long pause How many people are reading this groundbreaking news?

Well, I have around half a million followers.

OH MY GOD, ARE YOU A CULT LEADER? 500,000 followers! You must be the worst cult leader ever if you're asking whether or not you can Febreze a cat. I don't want to turn into you. I really don't.

That's it. I've had enough. Little M, it's the future and it's going to happen, whether you like it or not. Feel free to call up your friends on your big metal plugged-in phone and tell them all about it. I'm exhausted, and I am going for a bath. MDRC, feel free to join me (but in your own bath, in your own home—our relationship isn't quite ready for bath sharing. I don't think any relationship's ready for that actually: I find the idea confusing, both for reasons of logistics and hygiene). So, to MY bath. Where I shall be taking my laptop—

What's a laptop?

Oh, no . . . it's a computer. Now go away.

WHY ON EARTH WOULD YOU PUT A COMPUTER IN THE BATH?

Give me a break! I might just want to listen to the radio—

HOW THE HELL DO YOU LISTEN TO THE RADIO ON A COMPUTER?

AAAAAAAHHH! Enough. This is over. Over, I tell you. OV-AH (as you can imagine, MDRC, with that spelling I said that in a very aggressive, 'street'

89

way. Ov-ah, innit).

What does innit mean?

I think it means 'isn't it'. But I couldn't be 100 per cent sure. Now leave me alone for I am to bath
. . .

No, you listen to me, granny-pants. I may only be eighteen, but I'm VERY worried about you and what this 'technology' is doing to you. Might I politely suggest that you're so obsessed with screens, keeping up with trends, tweeting with thousands of unknown 'followers' on a computer and getting over-excited about your gadgets that you aren't actually living a life? It seems to me that if you have a bath, you should just have a bath; if you go on a train journey, you should just go on a train journey; and when you go for walk, just be in the moment and walk, not chat on a 'mobile' phone. Don't you remember we would sometimes go for a walk making up songs and little plays?

There's no need to share that . . .

Don't interrupt me, you mad digi-loon. You need to hear this. Do you remember what our life used to be like? Do you remember spending hours alone, just playing and being present and losing yourself in whatever you were doing? I think with all your gadgetry you are never really present, never really focused on making an effort to meet people and talk, because you can communicate so easily and quickly. But it's not real communication, is it? Do you remember being with your friends? Nobody obsessed with whether or

90

not they've just been 'texted' a picture of a pavement on their 'mobile phone'. Do you remember any of this? You probably don't, actually, because your brain's so bloody scrambled from all the animal videos you've been watching.

Twig isn't popular any more because all she ever does is play on her Game Boy and we can't get a conversation out of her. And when Milly got addicted to her Pac-Man for a term, she missed out on the inter-house dance competition. She'll never get back the joy of doing a routine to Yazz's 'The Only Way Is Up'. If you in the future are anything like that, you need to hear Milly's loss.

You used to have good, happy, playful times you could really appreciate. You could really communicate with people, deeply, honestly and happily. I don't want to be thirty-eight and so obsessed with twittering at my followers (whom I have NEVER MET) and getting poked at that I lose the ability to really LIVE.

Please remember that you were very happy before you got into all this techno-business. You may bang on about how I need to learn things from the future, but you'd do very well to learn a few things from the past. And if you really want some kind of technology, what's wrong with the Rubik's cube? That is HARD. *punches air, collapses exhausted to the floor* Phew! Gosh, that was a jolly good bit of public speaking, wasn't it? I'm very talented. I am clearly wasted as an office manager and should defo-pants be prime minister.

'You can learn from the past.' I like that.

I am pleased with that and I am glad I have made my point.

91

'We must remember to also learn from the past.' Yes, that's great. I'm going to tweet that . . .

PIT STOP!

Well, I don't know about you MDRC, but I'm *exhausted* after that. I now declare it time for a literary pit stop; where we can catch our breath, have our individual baths, and a little mull-ette over our experiences so far. (By 'mull-ette' I mean a small mull, not an 80s hair-do for which, if I am ever prime minister, people will be shot for partaking of in the current age.)

Together we've romped gloriously through Music, Hobbies, Office Life and Technology, not to mention the ever-so-tiny topic of 'Life'. Wouldn't get that from a John Grisham, would you? No. What's that? You actually quite enjoy a fast-paced legal thriller? Well, good for you. Ungrateful. For all you know, we might be about to enter the fast-paced legal thriller section of this little book-ette. [There probably *isn't* going to be a fast-paced legal thriller section. Soz.] You'll have to wait and see.

I think we have done very well together so far. And I think we now deserve some fun. How about a little tick-box game? I know—thrilling. If you've done any of the activities listed below (and I VERY much hope you have), then please place a firm, joyful tick in the relevant box:

☐ Reading (it is clear to me that you can read, and indeed have been reading, so well done for that and please tick this box)
☐ Forward roll

- [ ] Handstand
- [ ] Sung *Annie* or _____ (*Insert musical of choice*) loudly with blatant disregard to your neighbours who might be 'musically cool'
- [ ] Sashayed whilst making a sachet-based beverage
- [ ] Set up an Oddly Shaped Socially Awkward People Who Have No Talent For Ballet or _____ (*Insert dance of choice*) Club in your local area
- [ ] Rammed a vol-au-vent onto someone's nose at a formal gathering
- [ ] Obsessed over your lunch
- [ ] Spun childishly in a swivel chair
- [ ] Pondered the mysteries of life, leant back and sighed, 'Life, eh?'

I hope you've ticked a fair few boxes but, if not, don't fret, for we have much, much further to romp together, and many more marvellous activities to sample.

What I will ask of you is to partake in a task. I fear that Little Miranda might be right in that we are verging on obsessional about our mobile phones. So our first pit-stop task is:

Try and go a day without a mobile. For we might just see something wonderful we would otherwise have missed.

GOOD LUCK AND GOD SPEED

And now onwards with Miss Book and, may I say that, so far, I have been greatly enjoying writing her. Reasons include:

1. You can leave social events early, saying that you 'need to get back to the BOOK, you know. It's not going to write itself, that BOOK. What's that? You didn't know I was writing a BOOK? Oh, bless you. Well, I am. I am a BOOK WRITER. Yes, please feel free to *check me out*' *sweeps elegantly out*

2. You can wear glasses and a beret, and sit in your local café with a little notebook and a pencil. If anyone looks askance at you, you can draw yourself up to your full height and say, 'Yes? What am I doing and why am I wearing this? Oh, just gathering material for my book. I am much like the French philosophers. Yes, you do have to be very clever to write a book actually, thank you for asking. And no, these are not lens-free glasses for effect. And furthermore, I am not essentially here in the hope of impressing the male customers . . .'

3. Everything you do can be written off as 'research'. So far, in 'researching' this book, I have seen fourteen musicals, eaten three Battenberg cakes, been on a bouncy castle, danced wild and free to Billy Joel and thrown a jelly at my grandmother. And if none of those things actually make it into the book? Well, *pfft*. Who cares? I'm a ker-ay-zee creative animal. My process takes whatever it takes, man. I break all the rules.

I now declare this lovely pit stop over. Onwards, I say, onwards—please replenish teas, stack up biscuits and re-heat your roast, for we are about to venture bravely forth into the subject that is . . . oh goodness me, it's going to be a big one, but it has to be done . . . BEAUTY.

6

BEAUTY

A friend said something to me recently, which gave me pause for thought. A rare occurrence, you say? Well, that's a little cheeky of you, MDRC, but, in this case, absolutely correct. You have learned, now that we are on chapter six together, that I don't profess this tome to be one of deep reflection or profound serious thinking. The glasses and beret in the café were just to impress potential suitors (always good to try new tacks). I am nowhere close to one of them French philosophers; I basically lollop through life like an amiable hound. An Irish Wolf Hound, you say? Again, that's a bit cheeky of you. (But equally, fair enough. I think if I were to associate myself with any breed of hound, then an Irish Wolf Hound would be the loftiest and lollopiest—look, I've just created a new word—of all the dogs.) So, far be it from me to plunge into the great debates of the moment. I shall leave that to the professionals; I've got bollards to fall over and soup to spill and jaunts to go on. But this friend—she did get me thinking. What she said was:

'Miranda, you've *got* to start taking yourself seriously as a woman.'

She said this in response to the frayed, overstuffed handbag—and by handbag I obviously mean rucksack—that I've taken to carrying around with me. Is it just me who hasn't bought in to the need for a £700 Mulberry bag? There is no need when my current rucksack straps on like a dream, giving me a pleasingly, outward-bound Girl Guide-ish look, and can comfortably hold a small dog, a cagoule, chewing gum, tights, an emergency sandwich, a London A–Z, a banana, a box of tissues, a tube of cleansing hand gel, three bottles of water and fifteen notebooks (in which I pen my philosophical musings—by which I mean doodles of how Goran and I will look on our wedding day). I see it as one of my very finest purchases.

But, no. In the eyes of this friend (and by 'friend' I now mean 'handily placed representative of mainstream thought in twenty-first century Western Culture'), my wonderful carrying-sack is apparently an indication that I'm not 'taking myself seriously as a woman'.

What in the name of Moira Stewart, Fiona Bruce and all the serious-est of the serious women folk does she mean by this?

Time for an exercise, which I shall call 'Say It Out Loud With Miranda'. Please take a moment to sit back, breathe and intone: 'I am taking myself seriously as a woman.' Note your response. If you're reading this on the bus, or surreptitiously in the cinema, or in any other public scenario, then please note *other* people's responses. (If you are male, and teenaged, and reading this in a room with other teenage boys, then for your own safety I advise you not to participate.)

The rest of you—what comes to mind when you say those words? Is it a fine lady scientist, a ballsy young anarchist with tights on her head or a feminist intellectual from the 1970s nose-down in Simone de Beauvoir? Or is it what I think my friend meant when she said 'woman', which is

96

really 'aesthetic object'. Clothes-horse. Show pony. General beautiful piece of well-groomed stuff that's lovely to look at?

I reckon, to my great dismay, that she did indeed mean the latter. And in saying that I don't take myself seriously in this regard her assessment of me is absolutely bang-on. If taking oneself seriously as a woman means committing to a life of grooming, pumicing, pruning and polishing one's exterior for the benefit of onlookers, then I may as well heave my unwieldy rucksack to the top of a bleak Scottish hill and make my home there under a stone, where I'll fashion shoes out of mud and clothes out of leaves.

And—I must ask—do *men* have to do this? Is this a thing for them, too? What would it mean to 'take yourself seriously as a man'? Let's see. Attention All Men—please put down the *Top Gear* annual and join me in a round of 'Say It Out Loud With Miranda'. Lean back, and growl 'I am taking myself seriously as a man.' What springs to mind? Is it a singlet, a tool belt and a roll of electrical tape? Or is it a sharp suit, a cocktail and the presidency of the International Monetary Fund? Or perhaps you suddenly feel the need to hole up in a dingy pub and start yelling 'Ref!' at the telly? Whatever it is, it's not likely to have much to do with grooming, or carrying a particular type of slightly-too-small and essentially useless bag masquerading as a clutch (good word).

Basically, it's not got very much to do with aesthetics. And aesthetics—if I may be momentarily shouty and hare-brained and mad (it doesn't happen often, but when it does it's magnificent)— MAKE ME WANT TO STOVE MY HEAD IN

WITH A HAIRDRYER. Gosh, I do hope it's not just me.

Excuse me . . .

No excuse *me*, eighteen-year-old me, for you find your older self in the middle of a rant about the issue of beauty.

What, areas of Outstanding Natural Beauty? Like the Lake District?

Oh, dear, how very naïve you are. No, I'm referring to the issue of *human* beauty.

Ooh, like David Van Day from Dollar? He's beautiful.

Sshh! There's no need to tell everyone we thought that.

MY GUY

But 'Mirror Mirror' from the Dollar Album was our first single . . .

Again, sshh! And you were surprised by the lack of muso gene? No, I'm talking about human female beauty.

Oh, don't—we've just been trying on outfits for the inter-school disco tomorrow night. Hideola. And Bella has told me that my attempt to go Demi Moore-chic . . .

Remind me?

High-waisted jeans, tucked-in white shirt and cropped leather jacket—the St Elmo's Fire look—makes me look like a lesbian. Which apparently isn't a good thing. So now I am back to a mini skirt and white tights, but what to wear on top . . .

Does it matter this much?

Yes, it does, coz Milly's brother Biffo is going to be there and I fancy the pants off him—he's the spit of Emilio Estevez. I think I am going to go with my bat wing stripy shirt . . .

Wow, OK . . .

Coz that's smarter. Oh, I can see Bella is putting a hairdryer up her arms again . . .

Why?

Durh! So that her Princess Di dress sleeves are as puffy as they can go. Bella has all the right clothes. She

99

teased me for not having shoulder pads in my jacket the other day so I'm going to do what Milly does and put crusty bread rolls under my bra straps so they look like shoulder pads. If only my hair would do something vaguely respectable. I put lemon in it all day to try and make it frizzy and go a bit blonde in the sun, but wasps kept attacking me.

80's fashion really isn't for you, I'm afraid—it's 1991, move on: embrace the new decade.

Are we trendy in the 90's then?

Umm . . . we're still kind of waiting for our decade . . .

Oh great . . . Oh cripes, golly and gosh, the boys' coach has arrived.

As the embarrassingly Enid Blyton-sounding Little Miranda has so amply demonstrated, I've never been one of the beautiful crowd. From an early age I seem to have found myself cheerfully opting out of the whole business. It was through necessity, initially. I spent my childhood (the years in which many little girls embrace their 'inner princess'), clad in 1970s hand-me-downs, primarily from male cousins, which mainly consisted of a selection of beige, brown and orange dungarees. That, combined with a perfectly round pudding-bowl haircut made me look, on a good day, like a cross between Ann Widdecombe, one of The Flower Pot Men, and a monk. I was constantly mistaken for a little boy but I didn't care one jot. I was happy eating chocolate biscuits and pretending

100

to be a Red Indian. I didn't give any thought to how I looked. Which was absolutely perfect, and exactly as things should have been.

At boarding school, I remained in the tomboy category—a safe, neutral Switzerland as far as the looks issue was concerned. This gave me the freedom to focus on what mattered most, e.g. how to blow up a ginger beer bottle with a litre of vinegar and bicarbonate of soda (please don't try this at home).

And don't forget seeing how much food we could land on Miss Handel's extremely bouffant hair from the dining-room balcony.

Two grapes and a Jaffa cake, I seem to remember.

Correct. 'Twas hilaire.

Yes, Clare-Bear, Milly, Podge and I were happily exempt from each of the three major gangs: The Beautiful Ones, The Beautiful Ones' Friends, and The Ugly Ones. (We simply saw ourselves as The Normals, making no great impact on the beauty scale either way.) The Beautiful Ones spent most of their time primping and mirror-peering to maintain their position. The Beautiful Ones' Friends carried hairbrushes for the Beautiful Ones, basked in their reflected glory, and toiled like Victorian miners to gain the mastery of clothes and make-up which their more comely friends seemed to have been born with. And then there were the girls the Beautiful Ones cruelly dubbed 'The Ugly Ones'. They slunk miserably from corner to corner, their hair greased flat against their flaking scalps, too beaten down even to club together into some sort of snarky gang. (How absolutely vile all-girls schools can be.)

Now—if you don't mind—I'm going to get briefly thoughtful and attempt to make a point. I know: this is quite some news. I should hasten to add, however, that it's a point that would cause a professional sociologist to fling their pencil aside in despair and shout, 'This Miranda woman, she is making a crude generalisation that fails to even touch the sides of the complex issue!' But I shall continue, as I believe that my little point does contain a nugget-glimmer of truth.

I can now reveal that my point is . . . (brief *X Factor*-style pause for effect):

IT IS FAR, FAR BETTER NEVER TO HAVE BEEN BEAUTIFUL.

There, I've said it. And by beautiful, I mean effortlessly, conventionally, dollishly beautiful from a young age.

I accept that beauty is an entirely subjective issue, and that anyone can find anyone attractive for any one of a million reasons (which is why we all have a secret crush on Huw Edwards. No? But he's like a big commanding bear of a man when reading a headline . . .? Hello?)

So, to my little theory-ette. As a beautiful young woman in a world full of people with eyes, it's unlikely that you're going to have to draw heavily upon your other personal resources—intelligence, wit, compassion and general wily low cunning—in order to just 'get by'. If you're gorgeous, you're going to get by absolutely fine. Everyone will always want you in the room and you'll be lavished with attention, which you'll do very little to earn. Whereas, if you look like a sack of offal that's been drop-kicked down a lift-shaft into a pond, you're going to spend many of your formative years alone. This may seem miserable—but you'll have space, space that you can constructively use to discover and hone your skills, learn a language, develop an interest in cosmology, practise the oboe, do whatever you fancy, really, so long as it doesn't involve being looked at or snogging anyone. And you'll very likely emerge from your chrysalis aged twenty-five as a highly accomplished young thing ready to take on the world. Meanwhile, The Beautiful Ones will have been so busy having boyfriends and brushing their hair that they'll just be . . . who they always were.

Are you actually saying that it's better to have been ugly? Like big Lucy Bingwall who had four boobs and a hairy mouth?

Yep. This is one of your biggest life lessons, Little M. And by the way, she's now Lucy Bingwall who lives on a private island—

Yeah, it'd have to be a private island, with a face like that.

Good one. High five. No, really, she lives on a private island, with her explorer husband, speaks six languages and flies a light aeroplane. So.

Oh.

103

Quite.

Sorry. Continue.

Shall do.

However much I might have yearned to be one of The Beautiful Ones, particularly at those ghastly school discos, where any desperate attempt to impress the opposite sex led to at best deep humiliation (we shall discuss later, MDRC), I now feel extremely blessed that I wasn't. I see them at school reunions from time to time—many of them are still beautiful, and clearly put a great deal of effort into maintaining that beauty. Good for them. Some of them are 'just mothers'—the most admirable of jobs if chosen, but you can tell a lot are wondering what they have really achieved for themselves. They're nowhere near as jolly as 'The Ugly Ones', who are all very cheerfully running international banks and breeding vast stables of racehorses and doing marvellous things in developing countries, all whilst juggling a family brood. No—'The Ugly Ones' won, a thousand times over, I reckon. They had the roughest ride, and emerged the strongest.

But what about us neutral ones? The 'normals', stuck somewhere in the middle? The tomboys, the sporties? We didn't pay much attention to our place in the looks-department hierarchy. Then, by our mid-twenties, when still not having had a serious long-term relationship, there was an interesting and confusing time when we got a bit self-conscious and started to consider what 'The Men' might think of us. This meant we went from looking like ourselves

104

to trying slightly too hard to look like someone we thought men might find attractive. But styling ourselves to please others didn't work: it was like trying to hammer a square peg into a ra-ra-skirt-shaped hole. So we were forced to make a decision about our attitude towards the beauty game.

Mine was something along the lines of 'This is who I am, and this is the level at which I'm going to present myself, I feel fine, and if you don't like it then you're more than welcome to look away, thank you very much.' I decided, quite simply, not to care very much at all. As long as my rear-end and stomach were hidden from the public gaze, then I considered any outfit a roaring success.

People are either going to like the look of me, or they're not. And apart from remaining vaguely clean and healthy, there's not very much I can do to control that. Is an eye-lash tint, a facial and the right handbag really going to make all that much difference?

With this decision, I think I've spared myself a lot of misery. You may look at me and see a slightly frayed, wool-clad woman with an inexplicably hefty rucksack, but I look in the mirror and simply give thanks for all I've opted out of.

Hang on, Mrs Frayed Wool-clad woman . . . are we therefore not or ever a model?

I am afraid not.

I just thought what with me being this tall and thin, and the fact that most catwalk models are quite odd-looking in their beauty, I fit the bill . . .

We were to be a catwalk model, were we? Obviously before government-office posts. I had forgotten that brief realistic aim . . . But don't worry: height and not being 'pretty' can be used to advantages in other walks of life.

What like—a children's entertainer? A clown?

Close enough. And moving on.

Now, MDRC, let's start a sub-chapter in this unsettling world of beauty and discuss . . . (imagine the *X Factor* voiceover man is saying it) . . . GROOMING. Such a good word said like that. I suggest you now say it out loud as Mr *X Factor* Voiceover Man would: 'GROOMING.' Satisfying.

6b. GROOMING

Even the slightest encounters with the world of beauty and grooming have led me to feel nothing but utter confusion at the sheer *weirdness* of it all. I'm talking spas, hairdressers, clothes shopping . . . Oh, it all sounds lovely, does it? Such benign, appealing things they are. Except they're not: you're kidding yourselves, and you know it. At least, I hope you do and this isn't just me, because they all provide me with considerable anxiety and are high on my list of life's puzzling areas.

First up: hairdressers. Even though my formative experiences of hairdressing involved my mother, a bowl and a pair of kitchen scissors, I still prefer to cut my own hair, with the kitchen scissors, often whilst stirring a pan of beans and bopping along to Magic FM. The results are patchy, I grant you, but at least I'm spared the hideous experience that a trip to the hairdresser can be.

Ladies (and Gentlemen, of course—you're very welcome to join), I humbly offer you:

MIRANDA'S TEN REASONS TO HATE THE HAIRDRESSER!

1. The Mirror
And the length of time for which you're forced to stare at your own reflection. Because it's weird, isn't it, when you're made to look at it for too long? It becomes craggy, or puddingy, and then you get worried and it starts to look even worse. At a certain point, it even stops looking like your face and morphs into something altogether more peculiar. In my case, the face of a chubby choirboy.

2. The Neck Protector
Yes, that thick, black neck protector thing that's so heavy and tight it makes you claustrophobic and panicky so that you want to FREAK OUT, RIP IT OFF and DESTROY THE SALON LIKE A WILD ANIMAL.

3. The Basin
Or rather, the awkward, lie-back-with-your-head-in-this-little-curve hairwash basins? Where the very sweet work-experience girl will ask, 'Is the water too hot for you?' and you'll politely reply, 'No, no, that's lovely, actually,' as

rivulets of what feel like molten lava blister your poor hurting chubby choirboy face.

4. The Robe
The embarrassing walk from hairwash-area to haircut-seat, with a turban on your head and your weird gown around you, so you feel like an old Moroccan man selling dates at a market.

5. The Small Talk
That phrase, that terrible, terrible phrase that you think you've so cleverly avoided: 'Going anywhere nice this year?'

To which I want to reply, 'SHUT UP! WHY WOULD YOU ASK ME THAT? WHY KOWTOW TO THAT STEREOTYPE? YOU DON'T CARE, DO YOU? AND ALL YOU'VE DONE IS REMIND ME THAT NO, NO, I AM NOT GOING ANYWHERE NICE. I NOW *WANT* TO GO SOMEWHERE NICE, BUT I AM NOT GOING ANYWHERE NICE. I MAY NEVER GO ANYWHERE NICE AGAIN.'

6. The Complimentary Beverage
Being given a very lovely and free cup of tea, but being unable to drink it as the hairdresser suddenly shoves your head down to cut the hair at the back of your head, or suddenly pushes your head to one side as you try and take a sip.

7. The Loss Of Dignity
Anything that involves the hairdresser pressing your head down, pushing your head to one side, or suddenly and alarmingly lowering the level of your chair, so you jolt towards the ground with an alarming 'whoomph', smashing whatever dignity you had remaining into a million little

pieces.

8. The Stunning Neighbour

Invariably sitting next to the woman with the longest, thickest most beautiful hair in the world, so all you hear is, 'Ooh, what lovely hair, doesn't she have amazing hair, gorgeous hair, really gorgeous, amazing hair,' as you stare grimly at your own meagre, limp barnet.

STOP TELLING ME ABOUT HER HAIR, I HATE HER HAIR, AND I HATE HER.

9. The Big Reveal

Being shown the result of your cut and blow dry.

Realising they have gone for what can only be

described as the 'Princess Anne'—a style at once bouffant, risky and ageing. Then saying 'Thank you so much, I love it, you're amazing,' as you blink back tears.

10. The Walk Of Shame
Leaving the salon assuming everyone thinks you look ridiculous. And cue rain.

Whilst on a Day of Beauty and Grooming (in order to 'take myself seriously as a woman'), I might then feel the urge to nip into another salon for a pedicure. I sit on a bench with my trousers rolled up to my knees, and my feet in a basin of water. Rather than feeling pampered, I feel slightly shamed, as if I'm in the stocks or on the naughty step. Then a person—a *stranger*, as if this couldn't get any odder—will rub, sand and pumice my feet for longer than is strictly comfortable.

interjects, wildly, from twenty years earlier **WHAAAAAAT? THAT'S THE WEIRDEST THING I'VE EVER HEARD. Have you taken leave of your senses?**

I must have done. And I'm telling you now, I'm not enjoying any of this.

You'd better not be, you GIANT PERV.

I mean, a stranger, cupping and fondling my *feet*? That *is* odd, isn't it, MDRC, when you really think about? And because I am painfully ticklish, it's not

110

in any way relaxing: it's an infuriating sensation that makes me want to cut my feet off and slap them in the face of the tabard-wearing pedicurist. She then paints my toenails a shade of fungal green, which I'm too polite to refuse, before ushering me out into the street in flip-flops. On a freezing winter's day.

'Why didn't you go to a proper spa, Miranda?' I hear you say. 'A delightful destination spa with whirlpools and saunas and soft fluffy robes and crystal jugs full of apple and mango juice?' Well, I'll tell you why I didn't.

A friend once persuaded me that spending £400 for two days in a rural spa retreat would re-set my mind, body and soul for the next decade. What a load of . . .

Allow me to present:

MIRANDA'S TEN REASONS TO HATE THE SPA!

1. The Sauna
I DO NOT WANT to lie with half-naked strangers in a sealed wooden cave, avoiding eye contact as our sweat pools mix gently in the centre of the floor.

2. The Relaxing Mud Wrap
I DO NOT WANT to lie flat on a mortuary slab, caked in bandages and soil, thinking only of what I'd do if the fire alarm went off.

3. The Massage
The last time I had one, my head got stuck in the head hole and I became increasingly stressed

as it wedged itself tighter and tighter with each stroke, pummel and spooky undulation of whale music.

4. The Dressing Gowns

They're never quite big enough, which means walking around in constant fear of exposing myself to the assembled company (and probably being arrested for flashing, which is one of the top ten LEAST desirable things to happen on a 'relaxing' spa day).

5. The Steam Room

All the disadvantages of the sauna, plus your visibility is impaired by the steam. This heightens the risk of accidentally placing your hand 'somewhere it shouldn't go' when groping for your towel.

6. Lunch

Where not only calories, but nutritional content and health benefits of each available food are clearly listed. Consequently, you feel you have to justify your choice to the waitress: 'Oh, yes, I know the quinoa's a little on the carby side but, to be honest, after that lymphatic drain massage, I really feel I need the riboflavin.' When it comes, the quinoa fails to fill you up, and you have to run out to the car—flashing at a new arrival in your too-small dressing gown—and get the big piece of Emergency Cheese you stashed in the glove box, which by now is sweaty and tastes of de-icer. (You eat it anyway, because otherwise you might gnaw off your own fist in the middle of your manicure.) Which leads me to . . .

7. Manicures

Which are basically just holding hands with a stranger for forty-five minutes whilst listening to Enya.

8. Inane Conversation

The conversations with other spa visitors. Which will all be along the lines of 'Isn't this *lovely*?' and 'We deserve it, don't we? We really deserve it.' To which the only honest response would be 'No, it's awful. We'd all much rather be at home eating a bag of crisps and watching *Britain's Next Top Model*, laughing at how they are all dangerously thin.'

9. The Complimentary 'Lifestyle Consultation'

A trim woman in a uniform will lead you into a little interrogation suite, where she'll quiz you on your current diet, exercise and skincare habits. You'll lie through your teeth and claim that you jog five times a week, enjoy yoga, avoid sugar and that your only vice is the occasional splurge at the Eve Lom counter. The trim woman will look at you sceptically as you stand and your Emergency Maltesers fall out of your pocket onto the floor.

10. The Suspect 'Therapies'

Anything involving hot jets of water being blasted at you as you stand against a wall in order to improve muscle tone. Under slightly different circumstances, this process would be called 'War Crimes'.

So, no more spa days for me. My post-hair high street pedicure is as far as I'm willing to go in the name of beauty, thank you very much. And that done, I want to go home. But, I can't. Not yet. My mind's now been so addled by the women's magazines in the salon that I decide to try a little clothes shopping. It can't be that bad, can it? That's what a woman taking herself seriously would do— buy a lovely top.

Ah, shopping. Finally, something I understand.

I am not sure you *do* understand.

I do. You meet up with a gang of your nine best friends, you get on the bus to the Newbury Shopping Centre, you roam around for a bit, bumping into other packs of teenage girls, muttering something bitchy under your breath as you pass them, you get a McDonald's milkshake, and even when you finish it you keep sucking on the straw to make a noise, then you sit down and have some chewing gum. Then one of you might buy some nail varnish, and then you get the bus home. It's brilliant.

That sounds all very nice, but it doesn't involve the actual buying of clothes.

Mum does that. She gets them all from C&A, I pretend I hate them; then I wear them anyway.

Well, these days I have to go it alone.

So, I'll charge into Gap and discover, to my horror, that it's the sales. The women in the shop are like crazed animals, lions round a rotting zebra, trying to get their hands on a scoop-neck

114

sailor top for £4.99 less than they'd otherwise willingly pay. The noise of coat hangers scraping, the alarming disco honk of the Rihanna track, the gaggle of teenagers throwing pants at one another: I start to sweat. I go to one of those Gap tables, those lovely tidy Gap tables where some tops and jumpers are laid out, size Small at the top, size Extra Large at the bottom. I have to fumble through all the jumpers to find my size and inevitably the neat pile topples like a Jenga tower. There's now a heap of tops on the floor.

Seriously? Have they seriously not sorted out that system by now?

EXACTLY. No, they haven't. So, as ever, the shop assistant comes over, furious that we have ruined her display. I am now very hot. And when I get hot, I get angry: 'WELL, IF YOU'D HUNG UP THE JUMPERS AND NOT INSISTED THEY BE IN THIS INCOMPREHENSIBLE PILED-UP "SYSTEM" WHICH MAKES NO SENSE, YOU WOULDN'T HAVE TO KEEP COMING OVER WHEN SOMEONE WHO NEEDS A LARGE RUINS THE DISPLAY. A LOT OF WOMEN NEED A LARGE, YOU KNOW. SO CAN YOU STOP MAKING IT EASY FOR THE PETITES TO GRAB FROM THE TOP OF THE PILE AND SAUNTER SMUGLY INTO THE DRESSING ROOMS? PUT THEIR SMALLS AT THE BOTTOM FOR A CHANGE OR JUST HANG YOUR CLOTHES UP AND STOP MAKING US FEEL GUILTY FOR RUINING THE TABLE DISPLAYS, SO THAT WE FEEL WE

115

SHOULD TIDY THEM UP OURSELVES. AND THEN WE GET MISTAKEN FOR A SWEATY SHOP ASSISTANT AND SO AS NOT TO MAKE THAT PERSON FEEL STUPID FIND THEM A PAIR OF JEANS IN THEIR SIZE AND END UP DOING A FOUR-HOUR SHIFT. YOUR SYSTEM IS BROKEN, MY YOUNG, PERKY FRIEND. *BROKEN*, I TELL YOU.' (At which point the pre-teenage, surly shop assistant takes out her iPod headphones and says, 'What?')

I leave Gap, having lost half my body weight in perspiration, and wander down the high street. I need to sit somewhere nice and quiet, somewhere a little less . . . teenage. I notice a calm, discreet-looking shop with no one in it. Perfect. It turns out it's the ever-so-smart underwear shop Rigby & Peller. This is where the Queen gets her bras, apparently (she's also a Large, she too must struggle with the display tables in Gap). A pleasant lady approaches and asks me if I'd like a bra fitting. Goodness, I'd never had one of those before. Perhaps I *should* get a new bra? Acquire some lingerie. That might put a bit of va-va-voom into the old Hart life. That would be taking myself seriously as a woman. 'Yes, thank you,' I say gamely. 'I *would* like a bra fitting.'

In a place like this, I imagine the fitting will be some kind of discreet, respectful process perhaps involving a blindfold and some velveteen gloves. I'm ushered into a very plush cubicle (plush is one of my very favourite words—*plush*), and a small Spanish lady enters and asks me to remove my bra. Okey-dokey, not very British, but I'll give it a whirl. I do so, and as I turn around to face the lady,

I practically knock her out as I swipe her eye with a nipple.

'Oh, sorry, Mrs Nipple In Eye! Ha ha,' I trill in embarrassment. As ever, that approach doesn't alleviate the mood: she offers a tight smile in return, and stares at my bosoms. Stares. Squints. Tilts her head sideways a bit. Mutters something in Spanish and, after a pause, exhales sharply: 'Right!' and leaves.

Why is she leaving? Does she simply not know what to do with me? Will she return with a small band of medical students? I wonder.

Luckily not. She comes back bearing a truly beautiful bra. It turns out that she has what I call 'magic-boob-eyes', and can perfectly guess a woman's bra size without recourse to a tape measure. This shopping trip's taking a turn for the better.

Then I politely enquire as to the cost of this magnificent bit of kit. The cost: *£89.*

£89 FOR A BRA? Good God, you could go InterRailing for a month on that, or buy five ghetto blasters. Ask if it doubles as a sofa-bed or something.

I did. It doesn't. Goodbye to you, bra. I'm out of here.

The Spanish woman watches me leave. It occurs to me that now I haven't bought the bra, she's just been staring at my upper frontal area for absolutely no good reason. If I ever bump into her again at a social occasion, for example, I simply won't cope. I'll be bound to cry out, 'That's Mrs Nipple In Eye! She's seen my breasts!'

I leave, exhausted and humiliated. I tramp home,

feeling at least ten notches less beautiful than I was when I began my Day of Beauty and Grooming. I am broken.

Is it just me, or isn't life too short for days like the one I've just described? We could abolish the whole beauty regime shooting-match. Wouldn't it be marvellous to live in a world without the misery it takes to look like a slightly more well-defined version of yourself?

For once, I come armed with a solution to a conundrum. I have some changes to propose. I don't expect them all to come about at once, but please know that when I am Queen of The World, matters of beauty, styling and self-presentation will be conducted according to (drum roll, please) . . .

THE WONDERFUL LAWS OF MIRANDA-LAND!

Here are the key elements of my manifesto:

i. Clothing
In order to remove the need for all forms of decision-making, money-spending and sweating-in-shop changing rooms, citizens of Miranda-Land will be issued with the following:

—1 × **Governmental Weekday Outfit**
—1 × **Governmental Weekend Outfit**
—1 × **Standard Party Kaftan (unisex)**

—**Clogs** These will be offered in a variety of colours, and will be the primary way in which citizens of Miranda-Land can express their individuality through their clothing. However, anyone caught bragging about the cost of their clogs, unfavourably comparing another's clogs to their own, or writing 5,000-word magazine articles about 'The Next Big Clog' will have their clogs confiscated, and forced for a short time to wear enormous flippers.

ii. Beauty

Beauty treatments, as such, will only be offered in Miranda-approved beauty parlours. At the door of each beauty parlour will be a large sign that reads: 'COME IN ALTHOUGH THERE'S NO NEED. YOU LOOK LOVELY ANYWAY!'

The following treatments will be offered:

—**Pedicure** A small group of friendly old ladies will stare at the customer's bare feet and coo affectionately, uttering phrases like, 'I bet they get you from A to B very nicely,' and, 'Feet really do look better with shoes on them, don't they? That's the whole point of feet.'

—**Anti-Ageing Skincare** Customers wishing to 'turn back the clock' and 'banish wrinkles forever' will be offered a choice of three procedures: the 'Roast Dinner', the 'Donut Platter' and the 'Hot Buttered Toast'. These treatments are exactly as described: the customer will sit down and eat a delicious meal and/or treat, while Miranda explains to them the basic skincare principle of 'Fat Don't Crack'. This is based around a theory extensively tested at our Parisian Laboratoire/Patisserie: that the skin of ever-so-slightly-chubby people does actually generally look rather nice, and that the reason for their ageing is most likely due to being too

119

thin and not eating enough crisps.

—**Colonic Irrigation** Any customer requesting the colonic irrigation treatment will be led into a discreet back room, and laid down gently on a bed. At which point Miranda will charge in and shout, 'WHY IN GOD'S NAME WOULD ANYBODY WANT TO STICK A HOSE OF WATER UP THEIR BUM? YOU'RE A FOOL!' before hitting them lightly over the head with a loofah and ushering them into the 'Skincare' suite, where they'll be offered a plate of apple crumble to calm them down.

—**Brazilian** If anyone asks for a Brazilian, they will be presented with a young man or woman (whichever their preferred taste) to dance the salsa for them.

So, that's the plan. MDRC, what do you reckon? Little Miranda, what do you think?

I think it's absolutely genius. I wish I had my governmental unisex kaftan to wear at the disco tonight. Milly and I are going down to the hall now . . . *screams*

What?

One of the bread rolls just fell off my shoulder. Sshh. *tucks it backs in and scuttles off*

Good luck. It will be fine, totally fine. (Although it won't MDRC, it really won't.)

So, mull it over. Consider the pros and cons of my new system. And feel free to begin the 'skincare' regime when you next feel in need of a snack.

Because, really, whoever you are—you've *got* to start taking yourself seriously as a woman.

7

BODIES

Now, my lovely chum, I am hoping that you have also availed yourself of a Standard Party Kaftan and are currently swishing proudly about your sitting room in it. If not, please hurry along. I've been terribly busy with mine—a fetching gold number, which I'm pairing with a vibrant fuchsia polka-dot clog. Oh, yes. You really *must* join in, because if I'm to be the only one attending functions in such attire, then the whole system's going to go a tiny bit wonky. In fact, completely wonky, to the point that it will just become a system of 'Miranda wearing a kaftan, and everyone else pointing and laughing.'

I feel we've very much dealt with The Grooming Issue. The externals. The adornments. The frills. So it's time to get a bit more . . . structural. Bring it all back to the body (if you'll forgive the slight yoga-teacher vibe). So, if the previous chapter was, say, about decorating; then this one is about architecture.

*   *   *

There's an awful lot of pressure on bodies these days (not literally: we're not all being stood on by people or getting trapped under bench-presses—I hope). Our bodies are expected to look a certain way. Or at the very least, most of us wouldn't mind looking a little bit more like him or her from *Men's Health* or *Grazia* magazine, and a little bit less like, well, a sackful of ham. I know it's not just me. I know we've all got our 'thing'—our body bane. The bit that makes us feel slightly less lovely about ourselves than we otherwise might. Whether we're one of The Beautiful Ones, The Beautiful One's Friends, The Ugly Ones or The Normals, we can all feel that there's something askew. (Another good word, 'askew'. I find it nigh-on impossible not to follow with 'Bless You!' if someone uses 'askew'— Bless you!—in conversation. Just call me wacky.)

My 'thing' has always been my height: I am 6' 1" tall. Deep down, it's never bothered me. But people's responses have, over the years, been interesting as a lot of the time they find it remarkable. I honestly don't understand this. To me, being taller-than-average is no more peculiar than having a slightly larger-than-average nose, or rounder-than-average face, or shorter-than-average legs. I don't tend to give it too much thought. It's far from fascinating, and hasn't caused me too much fuss.

Um . . . Actually, I think you'll find it has caused SOME fuss. Durh brains.

Remind me?

The other day I was going to the sweet shop with Podge, who wanted to stock up on Wham bars . . .

Podge really should stay away from the sweets . . .

. . . when a pigeon started flying towards my head. I ducked accordingly, expecting it to swoop on by, but when I stood up again, after a brief moment of

wondering where it had gone to, I realised—IT HAD LANDED ON MY HEAD. It clearly thought I was a blooming lamppost. It flapped about and dug its horrible pigeon-claws into my hair. Totally gross. I've never screamed so hard in my life. Podge was no help—she just went into the shop to get her Wham bars. So, yes. It has caused us a teeny tiny bit of fuss, thank you.

Sure, that wasn't our finest moment. And it's particularly galling as we were at the time standing directly next to an actual lamppost. I would ask, MDRC: 'Is it just me or has anyone else ever been mistaken for a lamppost by a pigeon?' but I have a sinking feeling that on that one I am alone. (I have since been what can only be described as flinchy around pigeons, a major downside of London living.) In fact, the pigeon and I will always have a cold, distant relationship but, Little M, it hasn't done us too much lasting harm and makes for a mildly amusing dinner party story.

Well, I'm glad it's so blooming funny to you.

I tell you what *was* funny—the dwarf moment.

Oh, no . . .

I am going to tell. This one's simply too good to gloss over.

When you're tall, MDRC, sometimes you don't notice everything that's going on below you, which mostly means you trip over the odd shoe or bollard. But, years ago, when I was about sixteen, at my young cousin's fifth birthday party, it meant that I completely failed to notice that one of the other children's parents was a dwarf. Early in the proceedings, I became aware of my little cousin blubbing, so I bent to comfort her. I was distracted, and chatting merrily away to a friend as I picked her up. Yes, you've guessed it: I picked up the forty-two-year-old dwarf parent. I looked at her and—naturally, as I was expecting the five year old—screamed right in her face in fright. I quickly followed it up with a, 'Gosh, I'm so sorry, it's . . . I thought . . . no, well . . . let me pop you back there . . .' as I placed her back down from whence she came.

Totally mortificato.

Tell me about it. She actually found it hilarious.

Good for her. But you know what really WASN'T hilarious? That disco last night. I am still cringing under my duvet.

I think I've probably blanked that out, along with every other teenage party I might have braved.

Well, let me remind you. Last night, right, Bella ended up snogging Biffo when she KNEW I fancied him. But I didn't mind coz the guy I was sitting next to was quite gorge with floppy hair like Judd Nelson from **The Breakfast Club** *and he was actually flirting with me. You know, that very, very RARE occurrence?*

EXCUSE ME! I think you'll find in the future it's not all *that* rare. There was that time when . . . with the man who . . . at the . . . umm . . . and there was that guy . . . Oh, all right then. Go on.

Unaware of the nearly two-foot height difference between us, he only went and asked me to dance. How brill, I never get asked to dance! We got up and I looked straight ahead and couldn't see anyone. I looked down and there he was . . . looking straight into my . . . you know . . .

Let's call it 'nipple height'.

Urh, gross. I was towering over him like, well, a tower—the Eiffel Tower . . . Neither of us wanted to hurt each other's feelings so we soldiered on to the dance floor . . .

Wait, wasn't this the night that we designed the 'lower-our-height with-knee-bend' manoeuvre?

Yes. I immediately bent one leg, and slid the other right forward so as to lower my height. I was more like the Leaning Tower of Pisa, really. But then I was stuck like that and everyone was giggling at us, and my experience as Waltzing Man in Ballroom Scene meant I immediately wanted to lead, which didn't go down too well and the waltz didn't work because they were playing 'Crazy Crazy Nights' by Kiss. So we stood a little apart and after a couple of jokey **Grease** *moves . . .*

Well done. Good save.

I just wanted the ground to swallow me up . . .

Or just a foot or so, so you'd be level.

This is NOT FUNNY.

Soz.

I wanted to run away from him, but I thought that would be too mean. So I did the simple Kylie shuffle from side to side move.

Nice.

But because I was squatting to lower my height it looked a bit like I was trying to do a number two. That's when I got the nickname . . . umm . . .

Let it out: exorcise it.

The Poo Dancer.

There it is. The Poo Dancer. The squatty poo move. Please feel free to try it home whether you are of the lanky persuasion or not. Such fun.

127

I have to concede, that was a truly rotten night. But you recovered pretty swiftly I seem to remember, little one?

I ran to the loos and ate my shoulder pads.

There's a sentence.

All this evidence does seem to point towards the fact that a considerable man–lady height difference can prove to be a bit of a problem. It takes a particularly robust and confident man to scurry merrily alongside a much taller woman. And it takes an extraordinary calibre of woman, I think, to not mind being ever so much taller than her mate.

As with everything, I suppose, there are pluses and minuses to being tall and, for the benefit of all those women who are a good bit taller than average (and other interested parties), I shall now present:

MIRANDA'S PLUSES AND MINUSES OF BEING TALL
sounds trumpet, waves ceremonial flag

*Oh. Good. Another list. Coz that will help *dives back under the Ramsay Street duvet**

TEN GOOD THINGS ABOUT BEING TALL

1. **You exude a natural sense of authority, and people often bow to your judgement.** Which is very good for getting your own way in relationships, and in arguments at work.

2. **If you have short hair, you will occasionally be mistaken for a man and referred to as 'sir'.** This is a boon when trying to avoid the Ladies queue at the theatre (though you may find yourself rumbled at the urinals).

3. **You can generally see the tops of people's heads.** Which gives you a pleasing sense of all-knowingness and power.

4. **People always have something to talk about with you.** 'Are your parents tall?' or 'Have you ever met a woman taller than you?' and 'Do you have *awful* trouble finding clothes?'

5. **You can shop in special tall-lady clothes shops.** Which are sometimes absolutely hilarious. One branch of a Well-Known Tall Lady Emporium has nine-foot-high doors and over-sized chairs—supposedly to make us feel petite for once.

6. **You can, potentially, be very good at basketball.** Always helpful to have the option.

7. **Your feet are likely to be large.** Which means that you get (scientists have proved) at least fifteen times more pleasure from splashing about in puddles than your smaller-footed peers.

8. **People will describe you as 'statuesque'.** Which can make you feel rather marvellous and regal. Not to mention highly valuable, much-admired and timeless, like a Greek goddess.

When you are young, thin and tall, you get asked if you would consider modelling, which is excellent for the self-esteem.

When you are older, bigger and tall, you can use your frame for comic effect both personally and professionally.

9. **You will never be able to comfortably travel in an economy-class seat on an aeroplane**. Which means you might get upgraded to first class because the only way you can otherwise fit in your seat is by putting your feet in the aisles, thereby tripping up the air hostesses.

10. **You will never get lost in a crowd**. Which means that you can act as a Pied Piper/human beacon on days out with friends in frightening, crowded areas e.g. Disneyland/carnivals/the IKEA sales.

TEN LESS-GOOD THINGS ABOUT BEING TALL

1. **You exude a natural sense of authority, and people very often bow to your judgement**. Which can lead to you making decisions you are in no way qualified to make e.g. how best to re-wire a plug/which route to take to Aberystwyth/whether or not that fish has gone off.

2. **If you have short hair, you will occasionally be mistaken for a man and referred to as 'sir'**. Which means that old ladies will sometimes ask

you to help them with their heavy shopping.

If you dress up in anything vaguely sequiny, you might be mistaken for a transvestite.

3. **You can generally see the tops of people's heads.** Which means that you very often get an eyeful of dandruff, and see the sun bouncing off one-too-many sweaty bald spots.

4. **People always have something to talk about with you.** 'Are your parents tall?' or 'Have you ever met a woman taller than you?' and 'Do you have *awful* trouble finding clothes?' This can make you want to punch them in the face. After all, you can't say to someone, 'Gosh, you're fat, aren't you?' or 'Gosh, what a massive mole that is' and 'Have you met a woman with a mole bigger than that?'

5. **You can shop in special tall-lady clothes shops.** Which means that you have to cut the labels out of your clothes so that no one finds out you shop at 'Big and Long'. And you are constantly reminded of being different.

6. **You can, potentially, be very good at basketball.** I have no need of being good at it. It's not a necessary life skill. Unless you are a professional basketball player and then it's a key skill.

7. **Your feet are likely to be very large.** Which means that you could end up wearing big, flat, grey Velcro man-shoes. Or diamante pumps purchased from a shop that caters mainly for

transvestites.

8. **People will describe you as 'statuesque'.**
Which you worry might be a euphemism for
'absolutely bloody massive, moss-encrusted
and cracked, like a ropey statue in a municipal
park'.

   When you are young, thin and tall,
statuesque means looming over much shorter
men, tripping up, and generally feeling lanky
and unfeminine.

   When you are older, bigger and tall,
statuesque means being unable to find a man
whose lap you can sit on and not break his
back.

9. **You will never be able to comfortably travel
in an economy-class seat on an aeroplane.**
Which means that you'll spend countless flights
bent double, moaning and massaging your
feet for fear of DVT. Or desperately pacing
up and down the plane like a caged animal,
refusing to sit, and being furious at the fact that
they NEVER UPGRADE YOU TO FIRST
CLASS. Any form of transit is pretty much
agony.

10. **You will never get lost in a crowd.** Which is
bad luck when you're trying to hide from the
police/your newly spurned lover/dealing with
new-found and alarming fame.

There you have it. Pros and cons, ups and downs,
swings and roundabouts. Overall, I think you'll
find—

Uh, just one thing? You used the word 'bigger'. 'When you're older, BIGGER and still tall.' Just what did you mean by 'bigger'?

Oh, dear. Well, Young Miranda, although we stay roughly the same height as you are now, I hate to have to tell you that we do expand a little . . . uh . . . widthways.

WHAT???? We get FAT?

We gain a bit of . . . ballast.

OhGodohGodohGod . . . What, so at thirty-eight, we're old AND fat? I am going to have a panic attack.

Stop being over-dramatic.

Over-dramatic? I GET FAT. This is a DISASTER. My lovely figure. My-my-my legs! My legs are all I have! My lovely young, toned, brown, sporty legs! The rest of me is hideola. My face looks like a jellied horse—

Well, although many people agree with you on that and, indeed, take the effort to tell you, you'll be pleased to hear that I've developed a sort of affection for this dear old face of ours. It's characterful. It's friendly. And it's a face that couldn't possibly belong to anyone else. It's very much a 'Miranda' face. And I like that about it.

You're clearly fat AND insane. What about our ridiculous turning-in toes, our weirdly fine hair, our rounded shoulders, our lanky walk? Have you

133

developed a 'sort of affection' for all of those, as well?

Yep. Don't worry. It'll take a bit of time, but around the age of thirty-six you'll realise that you've only got the one body, so you might as well enjoy it. Make the most of what God gave you, and crack on with your life as nicely as possible. Maybe, even— dare I say it—celebrate what you've got. Make merry with it. Enjoy!

But I enjoy having a good figure . . .

Well, there are lots of advantages to being on the heavier side.

What could there possibly be?

Numero uno: you realise pretty quickly that you're never going to get what one of the viler magazines might refer to as a 'bikini body' so, instead of doing a hundred sit-ups twice a day, you can opt out of all that perfectionist malarkey. And you can spend your energy developing other personal qualities. Like being funny. And galloping. And learning complex dance routines, which become suddenly hilarious when you whack on a leotard and try to perform them. All that lovely stuff.

Numero duo: I find that as time goes by, being a bit bigger has made me *less* self-conscious. As I know I'm never going to look absolutely inarguably fab in a bikini, I can allow myself to be the first one to jump into the swimming pool in my underwear at a friend's party. Or the first one to crayon an hilarious jelly on my stomach for the amusement of an assembled crowd of intimates. Or the first one to sign up for the 'Trouserless Three-Legged Red Nose Day Race' at my little cousin's school. And the one who can unashamedly embrace what every woman secretly longs to wear: I give you the elasticated M&S trouser.

And numero trois (Italian *and* French, if you please): there's no need for flirting—someone will either like me, or they won't. I can be a friend to the world, male and female.

That sounds sort of all right. I am SO happy not to flirt—it's really trick-some. Bella's been studying Kelly McGillis in **Top Gun** *and gave us a lesson in it the other day. I got a crick in my neck doing one of the more advanced flirty poses while Podge twisted her ankle trying to do the sexy, cross-your-legs-over-each-other walk.*

Do lots of boys come up to us then? Do we get asked out loads?

Umm . . . Well . . . There was . . . Look, can we talk about this another time?

You always say that when I ask about relationships.

We will talk about them soon, I promise. Let's go on to number quatre, which rather aptly is: it's good for things not to go perfectly in life.

Surely the opposite?

Non, Mademoiselle (I am practically fluent). You see, difficulties lead to perseverance, compassion and empathy. We develop character.

But wait until you hear the very best thing of all about getting bigger.

Numero—uh—five: YOU CAN GO REALLY, *REALLY* FAST DOWNHILL ON A BICYCLE! The extra couple of stone makes all the difference there. Admittedly, it's not so much fun going up, but the downward swoop makes it all worth it. And an hour on the bike is, basically, a licence to eat a Wham bar (even though eating a Wham bar now would result in a Wham bar-shaped piece of cellulite on my poor old thigh: our metabolism really isn't what it once was, I'm afraid).

It sounds like there's been a bit of scoffing going on.

Not my fault. The world I'm in does make it a tad tricky not to scoff. Don't blame me for the invention of microwaveable meals.

Podge's mum has got a microwave. They seem pretty scary: she says you can't stand in front of it as you can be radiated to death.

I had forgotten the fear of the microwave . . .

Also, on the scoffing front, is it just me, or does anyone else feel like they're being made to run a gauntlet of sugary gorgeousness each time they approach the supermarket checkout? I join the queue with a bag of spinach and a smoothie, and find myself paying for a bag of spinach, a smoothie, eight packets of Doritos, two family-size Galaxy Bars (because they're on a deal for a pound), and a flapjack coated in yoghurt so it could very well be healthy but certainly isn't. Nightmare.

That said, I am making efforts to trim myself down a little bit: I think the weight has served its purpose, both comedically and in terms of building my fine and noble character (say nothing). I'm pootling about the park again, and I'm hoping that by forty, I'll be about the weight I'm biologically supposed to be (well, that's the aim: let's see how I feel once I've dispensed with these Pop Tarts—yes, they are still available if you look hard enough).

It'll be interesting to see how life looks when I'm a slimmer thing again. But for now, Little Miranda, know this: we all have our worries about our bodies and our looks. We just need to make the best of our lovely, wonky selves. The key is never to compare and try to be something you're not. I mean, MDRC, imagine how ridiculous I would look if I attempted

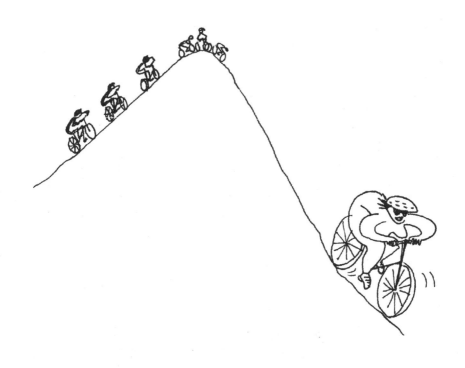

Cheryl Cole hair, wore a 'soap actress' dress or went for what I call the five-sets-of-false-eyelashes-

The-Only-Way-is-Essex look (transvestite alert).

We are all unique, which makes us beautiful; so never despair, and just chill the hell out about it all.

Cool. That sounds really mature and wise.

I know. I won't lie: I'm rather pleased with myself for making another point-ette. Now, if you'll excuse me, my friend Sarah Hadland is coming over, and we're going to learn one of the *Strictly Come Dancing* routines.

What?

Oh—er—I mean we're going to recite some poetry to each other and discuss Jung.

Phew. I thought you were serious. A thirty-eight-year-old fat woman learning a dance routine from the telly—dweeb-tastic. Right, I'm off to play lacrosse while I still can.

Good plan. Exercise with abandon, lean and youthful Me. *whispers* Because one day it'll be the *last thing on earth* you ever want to do.

What?

Nothing. Off you trot.

Thank goodness she's gone *finishes Pop Tarts, puts on salsa clothing, sings wild and free to the *Strictly* theme tune* 'De de de de de de der, de de de de de!'

8

EXERCISE

Right, MDRC, while Little Miranda's off playing lacrosse, let us embrace and explore another life-nub together: exercise.

I think it's best if we keep this one just between you and me, as I wouldn't want to give poor, darling Little M any more terrible shocks about her future. Right now she's whistling up and down the lacrosse pitch like a gazelle, nay, cheetah, with those annoyingly youthful legs, blissfully unaware that when you turn approximately twenty-eight-and-three-quarters, exercise suddenly trebles in difficulty, and once you hit thirty-three, it suddenly becomes what I refer to as—and I believe it's a technical term—Unimaginably Grim and just Totally and Completely Rubbish.

When I was eighteen, I assumed that I'd be playing lacrosse well into my twenties and thirties, playing for England and then moving on to become a coach. (Obviously in between darting from Paris and Milan with the catwalk model career.) But I now know that only a certain type of heterosexual woman can pull the lacrosse coach off, as it were; most likely a wiry blonde posh lady in white denim shorts called Veronica, who runs marathons at the weekend, has eight children, six terriers, a dinghy, a Hedge Fund Husband called Hugo, and who's so damned confident in her femininity that she's not remotely thrown by spending her days with a scrum of angry, hirsute, stick-wielding gals. I am not that woman. I should also add she is the type of lady who is regularly sponsored in Fun Runs. And may I just make my position very clear on this—there is no such thing as a FUN RUN as, even if you are dressed as an elephant, you still have to RUN. 'Fun' and 'run' are two words which, when the wonderful laws of Miranda-Land come into play, will be illegal to put together. I thank you. And relax.

As a child, the need to take exercise simply wasn't a concept. You were always skipping, bouncing, hopping, or running. And running WAS fun. You loved to run. As a youngster, if you wanted to get from A to B, you'd choose to make it all the more exciting by getting there as fast as humanly possible. You were so fond of running, in fact, you even often got told off for it, particularly if you did it on grass or in any kind of municipal corridor. It was a naughty treat of the highest order, to the extent that still I can't pass a well-manicured lawn without feeling a terrible urge to mince nimbly across it without being seen. Just me?

In addition to running, there is now the toddler craze that is scooting. If I may briefly sound like my mother, I do worry about their hips and backs. No—hear me out. Surely if you're spending the majority of your waking hours propelling yourself forward on a scooter, you're going to favour one leg over the other as your 'pushing' leg? I'm not a doctor, but logic follows that one leg will end up considerably shorter than the other, given the fragile developmental stage of most scooter users. I hereby predict that by the year 2035, we will be faced with a generation of lop-sided adults, who will have to buy one half of their trousers at Big and Long, and the other half at Weak and Stumpy.

I feel strongly that toddlers should scoot less, and run more. Don't say I didn't warn you all.

I have made another big old literary digression. Soz buckets. My point is this—as children, we were always playing, always exercising, in ways that would be unthinkable as adults. So, why not suggest a bit of playtime activity in the office this lunchtime? Here's how that would probably go:

'Hopscotch, anyone?'

'Well, no. Firstly I'm forty-five so that might look a tad odd. But also, not with my knees. Not unless you've got an orthopaedic surgeon on speed-dial.'

'Sheila, do you fancy it, spot of hopscotch?'

'Hopscotch? I'm fifty-two! Is it legal? Doesn't it involve bending down to pick up a pebble? Not with this back dear, oh no.'

'Anyone up for a bit of leapfrog down the corridor?'

'Ooh, not if you've asked big Bessie from Accounts. Don't much fancy my chances of getting out of that one upright.'

'I'm going to have a wrap for lunch, then. But after, does anyone want to do that skipping that involves someone going in the middle of two people turning the rope?'

'Gosh, no, I'd break my ankle!'

'I was scared enough attempting to jump in to the moving rope when I was eleven; it's a terrifying business!'

'What about a gymnastics routine at the end of the day? We could do one to *The South Bank Show* theme tune?'

'Oh, no thanks, dear; I'm too scared to do a forward roll.'

'Sheila?'

'No thanks, love, I simply don't have the pelvic floor for a star jump. Bless you for asking, though.'

It's rather depressing when you think about it. All those games, all that childish joy, lost on aching, fearful adults, when it would probably rather perk up their day. I for one would be heartened to see a group of suited professionals marking up a hopscotch grid on the pavement during their lunch break and hopping with gay abandon once they'd finally remembered how on earth the game was played. And there would be no point in even suggesting the see-saw: an absolute minefield once you hit the twelve-stone mark. (Although it is always tempting to suggest playing with a smaller, lighter opponent and accidentally-on-purpose sliding off whilst they're in the upper position, just to see them crashing down. Come on!)

The fact is, I went from mandatory school sport where, three times a week, we whacked on our gym knickers, jumped over something called a horse and shimmed up a rope, no questions asked; to university, an exercise wilderness. There, Pot Noodles are waiting to be inhaled, litres of cider are drunk and weeks frittered away sitting around watching *Supermarket Sweep* as we try to get a grip on the meaning of life.

Then, at around twenty-eight, after a few sedentary years at the desk job, things start to go a bit wonky. You pause for a moment after climbing more than fifteen stairs; you realise you'd rather miss the bus than sprint to catch it; and you've been keeping your trainers in a box in the attic, where they still bear the mud of a country walk you went on in 1994.

By thirty-three, you may find that you've officially

'let yourself go'. You'll know you've reached this point when you start to make long, impassioned speeches about how elastic is the new denim; you find yourself having to do a little warm up (deep breath, flex feet, tense thighs) before you get up out of a chair; and you cross the street when you see an old school friend as you fear sly rumblings becoming the footnote to an email: 'PS. Saw Miranda H outside Greggs yesterday. *Seriously* let herself go. Honestly, she's blown up like a dinghy. *Flabi*ola. LOL! xxx'

No, MDRC, this absolutely must be avoided. So I'm afraid that if you want to stay relatively physically respectable—and I'm not talking beach bodies here, just an attempt to remain vaguely person-shaped—you're going to have to incorporate some sort of exercise into your life. Here's how you'll probably proceed:

First up, you'll be very excited indeed about your decision to take a bit more exercise. You'll go to some form of sporting clothes emporium and splash out on all the gear (trainers, Lycra, double-industrial sports bra, completely mystifying and creepy 'moisture-wicking' trousers, adorable little sock-lets which look truly lovely under your trainers and make you feel a little bit like that Veronica running woman described earlier, wrist bands, armband for your iPod, crampons, jodhpurs, climbing shorts, golf clubs, tap shoes and tankini). You'll then catch the bus home exhausted, dump your bags delightedly on the floor, and craft yourself a delicious stew to say well done.

Three weeks and no moving about later, you'll decide that an easy way into this whole exercise malarkey would be jogging. Anyone can jog. Just a quick thirty minutes round the common—piece of cake (you'll certainly deserve one when you're done). You'll hoist yourself into your new Lycra (an exercise in itself because you've bought the size down in hope), download 'Eye of the Tiger' onto your iPod, and blunder out of the door.

You leave your house, waving confidently at your neighbour in their garden: 'Look at the new me, oh yes.' This is it. You're going out on a jog. You're a jogger now. You're five bars into 'Eye of the Tiger' (approximately eight seconds) and things are going brilliantly. You're a leopard, an amazing, prancing leopard, running wild and free as you were born to do. Yeah! You must have been going for at least five minutes. You look at your watch. Thirty seconds? Oh, well . . . keep going. Then ooh, ouch, legs burning, is that a stitch? Must . . . get . . . air . . . in . . . You stop, pretending to tie your shoelaces because your neighbour is still looking on. You clasp your thighs, which appear to be wobbling even though you've now been standing still for at least ten seconds. (Please tell me it's not just me who turned thirty and found their flesh started moving independently to their main frame? A deeply distressing and frankly unacceptable milestone in a person's life. And not the best image—apologies, and back to the jogging). Your neighbour eventually goes in, but you don't want to be caught skulking straight back home after your thirty-second jog, so you go to the pub for a drink, then run sprightly past her window forty minutes later, waving smugly to feign a socially acceptable level of fitness.

Having dispensed with the idea of jogging, how else can we get ourselves moving? A personal trainer? No thanks. I once made the mistake of paying for a personal training session.

At 7.30 on the morning in question, a lithe, toned young Australian man rang my doorbell. He was confronted by a smelly and bed-headed English woman.

'Miranda? G'day, I'm Bud. Ready for a hardcore workout? Let's burn some fat, you're going to feel great!'

Horrified by this prospect, I had no choice but to reply, 'No, I won't, I'll feel hot, embarrassed, angry, ashamed, sweaty and ill. Go away, eat some lard, pretend I never rang and let me go back to bed; it's too early for this rubbish.' And with that I slammed the door in his face victorious, even though it cost me 60 quid.

Of course, you could resort to the fitness DVD. But is it just me, or do you always find yourself trying three of the moves, declaring the workout 'a bit too dancey' and then flopping down bitterly on the sofa to watch it with a bag of popcorn while bitching about the participants' outfits? And I do think that the people who make the exercise videos are rather *too* fit, if we're honest. It's simply showing off. I'd far rather have a fitness video starring a plump woman in her pyjamas who's sort of doing her best and who tells you that if you do ten grapevines (a term you become all too familiar with as you embrace the world of organised fitness), you can have a pie.

When the laws of Miranda-Land come into effect, I plan to introduce a fitness-DVD grading system. While you're shedding the first few stone, you work with Mrs Porky and her sausage roll bribes. After that, you can graduate to a more muscular, size 12 trainer. And only when you're on the home stretch are you exposed to Little Miss Size 10 Wonder-Beauty, with her six pack, spinning squat thrusts and thong-prep butt clench dancercise. As things stand, fitness DVDs are not for me.

'What about visiting a local swimming bath?' I hear you say. A simple no because of the *admin* involved in swimming. That terrible, terrible swimming administration or, if you will: 'swim-min'. The getting there; the complicated locker; the getting changed (bent double, towel in mouth, balancing on one leg, making sure that no one sees an inch of your bare body); the negotiating around an army of naked ladies in unsuitable positions (MDRC, it will *never* be acceptable to be nude in public, let alone BENT OVER IN THE NUDE in public); and the showering *before* you get in—that I find insulting. I am perfectly clean, thank you.

Then, when you're finally in the pool, you have to choose between the fast lane, the medium lane and the slow lane. This is another of life's unworkable systems. The medium lane is always stuffed to the gills (everyone playing it safe), so you decide to be adventurous and have a crack at the fast lane. This is comparable to the wall of death: aspiring Olympians barrel past you doing the butterfly as you splutter wildly and try to ignore their sporty shouts of scorn. You give up, and slink back into the slow lane, where you spend twenty minutes doggy-paddling behind two octogenarians on a day-trip, knowing that if you speed up even a fraction you're going to find an eighty-five-year-old foot in your face.

In fact, the option of swimming is an academic

one for me, as I'm currently not allowed back into my local pool. There was a bit of an incident when I became so enraged by the tyranny of the lanes that I chose to swim widths. It was jolly good fun, actually, going under and over those lane-divider thingies like a crazy, rebel dolphin. The trouble came when I went a tad too fast over one of them, and it deftly removed my tankini bottoms. I failed to notice this until I was up and out of the pool. I looked down, gave a shriek, and hurled myself back into the water, landing smack-bang on a rather buff gent in the fast lane. (I like to call it my 'muff on buff' moment, if you pardon the vernacular.)

Once you've tried the obvious exercise solutions—and found them wanting—you might be a bit more adventurous. Embrace whichever fads are doing the rounds: Zumba dancing, Pilates cardio, boxer jazz, hula hooping, ballroom pump, tap dancing on a Swiss ball. At some point during this odyssey, an oddly toned, middle-aged woman with an inappropriate henna tattoo and a hemp basket of herbal remedies for every mild complaint, who invariably lives in Notting Hill, will approach you and say, 'Oh, you must try yoga. Yoga's worked wonders for me. I'm sixty-four years old and I've got the bottom of a teenager. Here, have a feel!'

Yoga I can't endure for one simple reason: they say it's jolly good at 'freeing you up', but I defy anyone over the age of thirty-five to get into the downward-dog position and not find themselves 'freed up' in one particular area: the bottom department. In that pose, you can let out one hell of a trumpety one, I'll tell you that for nothing. And what makes it all the more awful is that when someone farts at yoga, *you can't even laugh.*

147

This surely contravenes the most basic of human rights. When you or someone near you lets out a loud and lengthy fart in an otherwise silent room, surely the only appropriate response is to hoot with uncontrollable laughter for at least twenty minutes? Yoga teachers are, to me, little more than fart-laugh-police.

Which leaves us with The Gym. If you know me at all, you'll know I don't believe in these pricey cathedrals of manky sporting equipment covered in other people's sweat. I've done my time with gyms. I have all too often tipped up on January 4th (believing that by September I will be a fitness instructor myself), signed up for the twenty-four-month membership (so called because it sounds less than two years), gone every day for three weeks, had two days off and never returned. I've then spent the next twenty-three months seeing sixty British pounds going out of my bank account and making me feel like an idiot of the highest order. I *know* this isn't just me. We are fools, all of us: we're paying to keep those gyms running. We're spending £720 a year to get the fit people fitter. Without our money, the gyms would crumble and all the fit people would run to fat. It would be a wonderful revenge and life would be a more level playing field. But it's too late: we've signed the contract and we can't stop paying, so we all sit around getting spongier and spongier while the lithe people continue to get lither. All because we thought we knew ourselves a little better than we actually did, back on January 4th. Gym membership is, basically, an Optimism Tax.

But, don't be disheartened, for I will now furnish you with a solution. We'll return to *The Wonderful Laws of Miranda-Land*, and create an *Exercise*

148

Policy. Pay attention, for your leader speaketh:

In the first weeks of January, a special squad of Fitness Police will stand outside gyms, and briskly interrogate anyone a bit lardy and hopeful who looks as if they're about to sign a contract. Questions asked will include:

'Now, sir, are you sure you're not just doing this because you saw a picture of Daniel Craig in *Heat* and quite fancy looking like him? Because, sir, I can tell you now, you WILL NEVER LOOK LIKE HIM.'

'Are you sure you wouldn't rather just go for a walk in the park, madam? It's free, and it's ever such a lovely day. It really is awful in that gym, you know. It smells like a giant crotch.'

As a consequence of this rigorous policing, within two years gyms will no longer exist. They'll all be turned into 'Adult Bouncy Castle Centres', where full-grown people will be able to bounce energetically to a soundtrack of their choosing.

Furthermore, exercise in general will only be permitted if it's also in some way fun. Examples:

i. **Galloping**. Adults will truly reclaim the gallop.
ii. **Maracas**. We will shake maracas and throw crazy shapes to a mixture of reggae and salsa music.
iii. **Moonwalking to the bathroom in the mornings**. This will be compulsory.

In fact, MDRC, we don't need to wait for Miranda-Land to exist to commence proceedings. I dare you to go—now—and make some maracas. Put some pebbles in a coconut, whack it on a stick, bung on some salsa, and off you go. Perhaps you could dance along to *Strictly Come Dancing* with your maracas? You could call it 'S & M'— Strictly and Maracas. Yes, I foresee absolutely no confusion there.

Remember, fitness MUST be fun. What's that I hear you say? Time for another brand-new amusing compound word? Quite right, how about 'Fun-ness'? Forget exercise, fun-ness is the only way. Let the streets be filled with galloping commuters, moonwalking postmen and hopscotching office workers.

9

DIETS

I don't know about you, but all that talk of exercise has made me very hungry indeed. But I will refrain from suggesting a sandwich break because diets have been very much on my mind, what with being on a mission to slim down for forty.

On the subject of diets, I would just like to get something off my currently large upper-circumference of a chest. That thing is this: can we please stop this nonsense that is the *multi-billion pound* diet industry? I have written the only diet book that I believe needs to exist, and here it is:

CHAPTER ONE:
Eat a bit less.

CHAPTER TWO:
Move about a bit more.

THE END

It is scientifically proven. It means we don't have to read books with four-stage diet cycles, buy ridiculous ingredients we wouldn't normally ask a hamster to eat—may I draw your attention to tofu—and have to explain to our loved ones that we are going to have bad breath and terrible wind because we must eat cabbage soup for breakfast.

My book is the only one you need, and here endeth my contribution to the diet industry. Yours sincerely, Miranda Hart.

Now, let's all reward ourselves with a cup of tea and one biscuit. Not two, just one. Thereby adhering to the instructions in chapter one of my diet book. I thank you.

PIT STOP!

I hereby declare it officially time for another literary pit stop. And may I say on our behalf that I believe we have earned it, for in the space of four chapters, we've rollicked through enough body-beauty-exercise-diet business to keep a women's magazine going for a year. Consider all questions of beauty, weight, exercise and diet now officially dealt with.

It's time now to have a look back at what we've achieved since out last pit stop, and play *Miranda's Amazing Tick-Box Game*! If you've done any of the things listed below please tick away:

- ☐ Freaked out at the hairdressers and destroyed the salon like a wild animal
- ☐ Smuggled half a pound of cheese into a day spa
- ☐ Thrown a 'shop-strop'
- ☐ Worn a standard party kaftan and clogs
- ☐ Said 'Bless you' when someone said 'askew' (Bless you!)
- ☐ Done the Poo Dance, aka the No. 2 Groove
- ☐ Bought unnecessary snacks at the sneaky supermarket checkout snack heaven area
- ☐ Galloped

- [ ] Run on grass
- [ ] Learnt at least 60 per cent of the dance routines from the latest series of *Strictly Come Dancing*
- [ ] Organised an office hopscotch
- [ ] Done at least one other fun-ness activity e.g. maraca playing.

Now, to your second task. Oh yes, it's Task Time. How did you fare with the last one? I spent a lovely evening at home alone without my mobile. I found myself concentrating far more on the film I was watching, having a little think about my life, making up a poem that I then recited to an ornamental duck, before realising I had no idea what the time was because my mobile also serves as my watch. All in all, it was rather freeing. Don't tell Little Miranda but she's probably right: having time away from technology is surely a good thing.

Your second task might feel as un-British as getting a bra fitted, sitting comfortably in a sauna, Zumba dancing, or not laughing at a yoga fart, but please don't shy away from it as it will do you the world of good, I promise. I would like you to:

Look in the mirror and say, 'There is none other like you and for that reason alone you are beautiful.'

GOOD LUCK AND GOD SPEED

Well, you know what, we're only halfway through our literary romp. But we've got plenty more to discuss on our journey; many more life-hiccups to warn Little M about. Talking of hiccups—a minor

153

complaint, but hellish when they pop up at the wrong moment, yes? So with hiccups in mind, let us move onwards with Miss Book, to discuss the frankly murky Mr Subject that is . . . HEALTH.

10

HEALTH

So, My Wonderful Dear Reader Chum! Please note at this half way point you have been upgraded to not only Dear but Wonderful. And more than that may I say how terrific you look. Quite the stunner. What a lovely top—is it new? (How brilliant would it be if you *had* just bought a top and settled down to read this chapter?) After a restorative pit stop, I hope you're feeling in fine fettle.

Little Miranda enters, not in even nearly fine fettle I can't breathe, help. Oh my goodness, that was terrifying. Oh dear, I'm going to faint, oh, I didn't like that . . .*

Little M, what *is* going on?

I've just scrambled out of Miss Handel's chemistry lesson. Normally I would skive it because really what's the point of litmus paper? But because it seems the highlight of my adult working life is ordering stationery, I thought I had better learn some stuff. I blame you for this. I swear, I can't breathe. We were doing some weird experiment with strange powders and a Bunsen burner to try to find out how much energy there is in a peanut and then see if it would explode by coating it with copper. Or something useful like that. Anyway, Podge made me do ours because she was busy finishing the packet of peanuts and now I'm SURE I inhaled some poisonous gases. I mean, I don't want to *be dramatic but I'M DYING! I AM NOT LONG FOR THIS WORLD. *swoons, rallies* Quick, I must write a will . . . I can't breathe . . .*

Will you calm down?

Calm down? I'm DYING! This is no time for calming down. Call Mum. I need her to arrange for Dollar to sing 'Mirror Mirror' at my funeral.

Look, you're obviously not in your dying moments . . .

You don't know that . . .

I know it for certain. As evidenced by the fact that I'm standing here now, in rude health, at the ripe old age of thirty-eight.

Oh. Oh yes. Oh. Sorry about that. Sorry about that, everyone. At ease, if you please. I just thought Miss Handel had poisoned me with something that felt like it had stung my lungs . . .

Stung your lungs? No, that didn't happen. Your lungs remain very much un-stung. What you're suffering from is a minor panic attack, brought on by an overactive imagination. (It won't be the last, MDRC.) I bet Miss Handel told you it was nothing to worry about, didn't she? You should have listened to her. She knows what she's talking about.

I am not sure she does. I am convinced she has made up that periodic table thingy. What IS that?

I still have no idea.

I'm going to go back and tell Miss Handel that I shan't be partaking of her stupid, terrifying classes any more for no other reason than frankly her hair's too big for her own good. I mean, seriously, what's she hiding in there? Nest of bees? Nest of squirrels more like. It really is a mighty bouff, and that much hairspray near the Bunsen burners is surely a risk. I am going to tell her I'll report her to the head.

I'm afraid you need to keep on good terms with Miss Handel. You're actually going to re-meet her in twenty years' time when you go back to visit the school.

Why do you go back to school?

Oh, um, I do a kind of Question and Answer thing in the hall.

*What, like a test in front of the whole school? *panics* It's not on the periodic table is it?*

It's on 'the arts'.

*Shit me—I don't know anything about the arts. Should I start doing homework now? That sounds properly horrifying. Is it because you didn't pass your English GCSE, and it's taken you twenty years to revise for it again, and because you're so stupid you're being made to come and retake it out loud in the hall in front of Miss Handel and the whole school? Oh God, Oh God . . . Oh no, I think I'm having palpitations. I knew I had a weak heart . . . I'm dying again *suddenly has* *an interesting thought, stops dying* Hang on, you're telling me that Miss Handel will still be here in twenty years' time? But she's so OLD.*

She isn't. We thought her terrifically old, but it turns out she is actually the same age as I am now. Therefore, on the cusp of her sexual prime.

Urh. That's made me feel sick. And my heart is going again. Those gases have done something to me, I swear it . . .

Calm down.

Sorry. I'm being a giant massive loser from Planet Loser, aren't I?

Yes, you are. You'll do this regularly. Several times a week you fly into a massive panic about whatever illness you think you're currently dying of.

I am not that bad.

May I refer you to the fact that for two years you believed the rumour that if you burped and farted at the same time you could explode and die? Or that when you stayed at Clare-Bear's parents the other night and had an electric blanket for the first time, you were so worried that you might wet the bed and electrocute yourself that you didn't sleep all night?

You never know. Better to be safe than electrocuted to death in the middle of the night. It would have been really embarrassing, and Clare-Bear would tell

158

everyone at school I'd wet the bed.

Also, you used to think you'd better not get your tummy button wet in case water got into your body through it and drowned you, while yesterday you got up from the dinner table and washed a sausage because it looked 'a bit germy'. And isn't it true that if you're ever even the tiniest bit hot, you start to worry that you might spontaneously combust?

No, wait—that is *actually properly terrifying and does happen. I heard it on the news. One minute a man was just sitting watching the telly, the next he's a pile of ash. I mean—BLOODY HELL! Seriously.*

Shhh, you're exhausting yourself. All this health worrying is turning you into a husk of your former bouncy self.

Now listen, as I have to tell you, Little M—there is actually something wrong with you.

goes pale and quiet, whispers What?

You have got what we call . . . hypochondria.

OH.MY.GOD! How long have I got? Let's get that will polished up. Sis can have my tape cassette collection and Mum can have my Ramsay Street duvet cover. Call Dollar, let's schedule the funeral; I want Michael J. Fox to be one of the pallbearers. I know he's very small, so you'll have to find three other very small pallbearers otherwise he'll just be walking along underneath a coffin floating above him . . . and I want the school choir to sing 'Thank You for the Music' and . . .

159

Stop, stop! A hypochondriac is simply someone who worries excessively about their health, to the point of thinking that any illness, however minor, is life-threateningly serious. Someone who spends about half their life convinced they're dying. Someone, in short, exactly like you.

That's nothing like me. I'm just . . . cautious.

May I refer you to last year's 'hairball' incident? Tell our reader chum what you presented to the doctor.

Oh . . . umm . . . really? Ok. So, I went to see Dr Mowatt and explained that I had this tickly cough in my throat and that I'd seen our cat, Ollie, cough up a fur ball, so I suddenly thought I might have a fur ball stuck.

And what did Dr Mowatt say?

He asked me if I was a cat. And said if I was, then I'd be able to cough it up. (He was, frankly, very patronising.) And then he said if I wasn't a cat, had I been licking my cat or other pets to cause a blockage of fur in my throat? He said if I hadn't, I was probably OK.

I do wish you hadn't gone to him about it. I have to face dear old retired Dr Mowatt every year over a mince pie at Mum and Dad's Christmas drinks party.

He's still alive?

Yes. It's just that youth makes you think every adult is way older than they actually are. Each time I see him, the memory of asking him if I had a fur ball makes me go all hot with shame and I turn a kind of Party Plum Puce colour. Half of me wants to pretend to be a cat, to prove that I wasn't mad but actually part feline; then I realise if I start randomly miming cat actions at a drinks party, I will look truly nutty.

My Dear Reader Chums who live in small villages—I don't know how you cope. You must bump into the local doctor regularly. Is it just me who assumes that every time you see your doctor out of context, they're looking at you and remembering all the embarrassing conditions— real or imaginary—which we might have talked to them about in the past? If I were a doctor (heaven forbid—can you imagine?) I'd struggle not to point and laugh at everyone in the street.

But back to you, Little M. I am afraid you *are* a hypochondriac. Pure and simple. And do you know what I blame? *Neighbours*.

Why Neighbours?

When you go to a school on top of a hill in a Berkshire hamlet, your afternoon dose of *Neighbours* is the main contact you have with the outside world, isn't it?

S'pose so.

Which is why you can't not call any yellow Labrador you see Bouncer and why you call all of your imaginary boyfriends Scott. And if someone in

161

Neighbours gets a headache or forgets something, within five episodes they're horribly dead of a brain tumour. This is because *Neighbours* is a fast-paced and dramatic television series, which requires a high turnover of interesting characters. Correct?

Correct.

And this has, I'd humbly suggest, warped your perspective on the human body and its capacity for disease and healing. Do you see?

Um . . . yes. I suppose that sort of makes sense. Will I always have hypochondria?

No. We grow out of it. More or less. We're now sane enough to be able to watch DVDs of *ER* without imagining ourselves dying on a gurney.

DVD? ER?

A DVD is like a round, flat video. And *ER* is a fabulous television programme from the mid-1990s, which is mostly fabulous because of the presence of one Mr George Clooney.

Who's George Clooney?

Gosh, what a treat you have in store there! He's a film star. And without wishing to blow your mind too much—he's ten times better looking than Kevin Bacon.

Whoa! Not possible. I watched Kevin Bacon in Footloose *again last night—wowzer buckets. Is this*

162

George better even than Tom Selleck?

Tom Selleck? I'd forgotten that one.

Tom Selleck in **Three Men and a Baby** *is totally gorge. I want to marry him. Actually, I decided last night I would quite like to marry a doctor. Because then I'd feel totally calm and reassured at every turn.*

That might be nice: not because I'd want his medical knowledge; more because I'm rather drawn to the white coat and the commanding manner and generally get a bit giddy with the air of caring authority and then that stethoscope . . .

You're thinking this out loud . . .

I am so sorry, MDRC. Moving on . . .

Time passes. Hypochondria abates. Though I must confess, I still hate being ill. It's a rotten business. Rotten, rotten, rotten. And is it just me, or does going to the doctor present many a social dilemma, which one would rather not deal with? Going to the doctor is frankly a rotten business. Rotten, rotten, rotten. (I have said rotten so much now, it's not even a word to me—just a sound. Try it.)

Much as I love, respect, and owe a debt of gratitude to the many healthcare professionals who've done their bit to prevent my early demise, I must confess that a visit to the surgery is certainly on the list of one of life's trials where I regularly come a cropper.

Firstly, it's called a surgery. *Surgery.* A grim, drawly word, I'm sure you'll agree, thick with

163

images of blood and scalpels and general sicky grimness. If you're ill, why can't you go somewhere positive and fun-sounding: the Hug-Me-Better Love-Dome, perhaps, or the Health-O-Sphere?

Of course, now, with certain ailments, you may not even get *in*. You rock up blearily to the door of the doctors' surgery, palpitating, groaning and sweating, wondering vaguely if it's flu. Only to be confronted with a big sign that reads: IF YOU MAY HAVE FLU, PLEASE DO NOT ENTER THE SURGERY.

Well, I don't know whether or not I have 'flu! That's why I'm here—I was rather hoping you might tell me. Isn't that your job? What does one do, in that situation? Stand outside and give oneself a swift self-diagnosis? Ask some passing pedestrians to feel our foreheads and see what they think? No, you want a professional opinion.

Rebelliously, you brave it and enter The Waiting Room. A sweaty germ-hole and paranoia breeding-ground. Everywhere you look, there are signs on the wall alerting you to the presence of diseases you've never worried about before but are suddenly 100 per cent sure you might have: chlamydia, cyclosporiasis (try pronouncing that for the laugh), anthrax—

Bella said she had chlamydia—she kept the rumour going for two terms. But it TOTALLY wasn't true. She was just showing off that she was the only girl in the school that had actually had sex. I know, it's too shocking to believe.

Thanks for that, Little M (and may I say, MDRC, late developers win in the end). On the walls of surgeries (or Hug-Me-Better Love-Domes) I'd like to suggest that—perhaps around the time The Wonderful Laws of Miranda-Land are brought in—only images of puppies, kittens, and rudely healthy, ruddy-cheeked children eating ice creams are displayed. And, might I add, when it comes to Miranda-Land, diseases will be pronounceable and simply nicer-sounding. Instead of jaundice you'd have 'Sunshine Radiance'. Cirrhosis would be 'Rose Petal Flakis'. You'll positively *want* diseases for their names in Miranda-Land.

My surgery waiting-room anxiety is in no way relieved by the company I'm forced to keep there. At least eight times out of ten I'll find myself sitting next to the—I believe this is the official term—waiting-room nutter. You know the type: there'll be ten free seats, but he'll choose to cheerily plonk himself down next to you. For a chat. With his breath. Why is it someone with halitosis (or, in Miranda-Land, Personal Mouth Aroma) always chooses to use a sentence consisting of a row of breath-blowing consonants? On one occasion the fellow sat down next to me and his opening gambit was: 'I Definitely Don't Desire the Dreary *Reader's Digest*, Dear.' Each 'D' blew a waft of retch-making smell my way.

The sitting-next-to-me-when-there-are-free-seats part was unacceptable enough. In this country, we *never* sit next to each other unless absolutely necessary. In the waiting room, we'll dot ourselves about and always have a chair-sized gap between us. That gap must never be filled: people simply must not encroach on our personal space. That's just how it is.

To avoid sitting next to someone in a 'Better-Me

Playground' (another fine term for a surgery, methinks), I've gone so far as to sit on one of those tiny little chairs in the crèche area. (Obviously, I wouldn't risk sitting in one with arms for fear of standing up with it still attached to my bottom.) If there's no crèche chair available, I might sit in one of those small animals or cars where you put your money in and they move from side to side. Or rock back and forth. (What are they called? Let's call them Miniature Back-Forth Animal Fun-Mobiles.) I may look ridiculous, but at least I haven't broken any British rules regarding personal space.

PLEASE WAIT

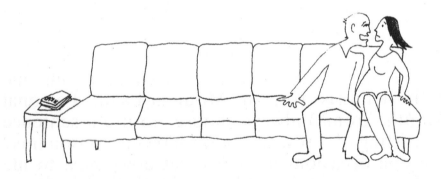

Now, I have another story for you. I fear that, much like the pigeon-on-head incident, this one *will* just be me. I was sitting on one of those Miniature Back-Forth Animal Fun-Mobiles, when a friend spotted me and, without my noticing, snuck up and put some money in before hiding behind a nearby door. The contraption started up, and I was propelled forward in a violent rocking motion. As this was unexpected, I screamed loudly, thus drawing attention to the fact that a 6' 1", thirtysomething woman was rocking backwards and

166

forwards on a small plastic cow. I carried on until it finished, too frightened to dismount while it was moving. Just me? Thought so.

By the time I actually get to see the doctor, I'm usually a bundle of nerves. And when I'm in any way nervous, I have a tendency to attempt what I call 'awkward hokey banter'. This tendency worsens if the doctor is male.

Oh no, are we still awkward with doctors?

Afraid so. I shall demonstrate to My Dear Reader Chum with a short scene, and just hope that perhaps at least one of you understands this doctor plight:

Miranda (any age, because we really haven't changed AT ALL in this regard) enters the doctor's room.

MIRANDA
Good morrow, good Sir Doctor!

(Already?—WHY?)

DOCTOR
Come in. Sit down.

MIRANDA
Thanking you muchly, a very hearty thank you to you. (Laughs a silly laugh.)

DOCTOR
What seems to be the problem?

167

MIRANDA
I think I might have 'flu. I know I'm not meant
to be here under these circumstances, but
please don't kill me. Not that you would kill
me because you're a doctor and you save lives;
you don't kill. Do you see? (Unnecessarily long
burst of laughter, especially given that her
joke wasn't that funny.) No, what I mean is,
please don't tell me off. Although I bet you're
quite sexy when you get firm? Doctor Firmy.

DOCTOR
Sorry?

MIRANDA
Nothing. Nothing at all. Just apologising for
being here with possible 'flu, when that's ever
so naughty. What a naughty girl I am.
Spank me.

DOCTOR
What?

MIRANDA
What? Didn't say anything. Someone outside
said something about spanking—people are
weird, aren't they? Aren't people weird?

DOCTOR
Right, let's have a look at you.

MIRANDA
Well, here I am! So look until your heart's
content, good Herr Doctor. (Giggles, tips
head to one side, bites lip—it's all gone a bit

Marilyn Monroe.) We might be here some time
. . . (Flirty laugh.)

The doctor sighs, and very un-erotically shines
a light in MIRANDA's ear.

MIRANDA
Ooh, that feels funny. Can you see my brain?
It's very big. Ha ha ha! And you know what
they say about people with big brains? BIG
BOOBS! Shush Miranda. Shush now.

DOCTOR
Lift your top, please: I'll need to take a look at
your chest.

MIRANDA
Righty-ho. That's jolly good and fine. Of
course. (Lifts top, peers down.) Oh sorry, I am
wearing my 'day bra'. I don't usually wear a
beige-coloured bra. Actually, they call it 'nude',
don't they, this colour? Well, I don't normally
wear a nude bra. It's usually black and a bit
frilly because, well, that's me! Not that I'm
black, as you can see, but I certainly am frilly.
Frilly Hart, they call me. This nude bra's just
an everyday 'I am not feeling well' kind of bra.
Mind you, better to wear a nude bra than be in
the nude. Good word, isn't it, 'nude'? Nuuude.
Nuuuuuude.

The doctor looks scared, and hands MIRANDA
a prescription. She runs out.

I am SO embarrassed. I've literally hidden inside

my jumper.

I know, I know. It's excruciating. We just can't do doctors, as it very much were. And indeed, MDRC, one of the very few true scenes in my sitcom . . .

What?

Oh, you weren't meant to hear that. Ignore.

*Wait—no, has someone based a sitcom on me? Oh, that is mortificato. Typical, classic. Of course that would happen to me. I am such a plonker. A **plonker** and a dweeb and a loser of the highest order. OF COURSE someone would go and use my life to put in a sitcom. I'm surprised you haven't emigrated by now.*

Well, we haven't. But I'm glad you can acknowledge what a total dweeb we are, and always have been, with doctors.

I have less trouble with the doctor-flirting nonsense in a hospital. Perhaps the institutional, municipal, 'No, really, you might die here' vibe knocks it out of me a bit. Nevertheless, the hospital visit presents its own unique challenges to the dignity. If nothing else, can we please discuss the hospital gown? I mean, there's probably some very clever reason for having a foot-wide gap at the back of it, but the only reason I can think of is so that the porters can all have a jolly good laugh.

Like a grand old rustic bicycle, I have to be dragged into hospital from time to time for check-ups and repairs on some minor but tedious health niggles. Given that I'm a regular visitor to said fine establishments, although predominantly now less neurotic, I thought it wise to do a little research into how they're run. What I found out was that while the majority of those professionals working in hospitals are to be admired and respected, *post*-research I don't wholly trust the system.

During my research, I came across the following sentences from patients' notes, which were typed up by actual medical secretaries at an actual NHS hospital. They're absolutely true. Are you ready? Please prepare yourself to be both amused and alarmed by my findings:

1. She stated that she had been constipated for most of her life until she got a divorce.
2. Patient's medical history has been remarkably insignificant with only a 40-pound weight gain in the past three days.
3. She has no rigors or shaking chills but her husband states she was very hot in bed last night.
4. Patient has chest pain if she lies on her left side for over a year.
5. On the second day the knee was better and on the third day it disappeared.
6. Patient has left her white blood cells at another hospital.
7. The patient is tearful and crying constantly. She also appears to be depressed.
8. The patient has been depressed since she began seeing me in 1993.
9. Discharge status: 'Alive, but without my permission.'
10. Patient had waffles for breakfast and

anorexia for lunch.
11. She is numb from her toes down.
12. Patient was alert and unresponsive.

Wow. I'm proper panicking now. What kind of things do we go to hospital for?

Um, well, as I said, nothing too grim. Although a complaint of the traditionally embarrassing variety. MDRC, I'll try to be delicate here, but if you're of a squeamish temperament regarding matters of, shall we say, bottom indigestion . . .

Urh, urh, urh! I thought my life couldn't get much worse.

. . . I suggest you skip the remainder of this paragraph. Actually, for safety's sake, I'd disembark Miss Book now, and hop aboard again for the next chapter.

All gone? Good. Now, to the rest of you. So, from time to time, in order to check up on the old Hart colon, I have to have a colonoscopy. Which is, put simply but graphically, a camera up your bum. This generally involves having an enema that, post-procedure, can leave you a little, how can I put this—congested. Windy. Your abdomen has become a mildly distended and highly dangerous area. You can find yourself possessed of an overwhelming desire to fart, plus a total inability to do so 'safely', if you catch my drift. Really, it's wise to take a few quiet hours to oneself when one is in such a condition.

I learnt this the very hard way, whilst attending a rather important meeting at the BBC two hours after my unpleasant procedure (what a truly awful word 'procedure' is. *Procedure.* Not a fan), when I believed I was back in the 'safe zone'. During the meeting I became aware of an urgent need to break wind. I politely excused myself from the room and let forth what I believe was one of the loudest and longest farts in the history of humanity (not wishing to boast or anything, but it really was spectacular). I tried to cover it up by coughing loudly, but the pressure the coughing exerted on my bowel meant that before I knew it, I was 'following through', if I may be so delicate.

I rushed to the loo, and had no choice but to remove my pants AND my trousers. I dumped them in the bin and artfully draped my only spare garment—a capacious paisley shawl—around my lower half. Thank God I wore the shawl that day. Thank God and all his angels in heaven.

Now, what does one do in this scenario? I think we'll all agree there is no rulebook here. It's an off-piste situation. I wondered what to say and, as I stood frozen in the BBC lavatories staring at my grey, panicked face in the mirror, I considered my options.

They seemed to be going back into the room and saying any one of the following:

1. *'The Fashion Police just called—trousers are so out.'*
2. *'I felt a sudden altruistic urge and donated my trousers to a children's charity. What have YOU done today to make you feel proud?'*
3. *'My trousers were ripped from me by an angry Doberman that I think belongs to Jeremy Paxman.'*

4. *'Trousers? What trousers? I've never worn trousers in my life. I definitely wasn't wearing them when I left the room. It's you that's mad.'*

Please feel free to use any of the above if, heaven forbid, you should ever find yourself in a similar situation. When I eventually re-entered the room in my paisley kilt/sarong/loin cloth, I noticed a flicker of confusion cross the faces of the executive producers. But I braved it out, indicated my attire with a flourish and announced instead:

'I think I want to become a nudist, but I'm not sure, so I want to try a bit of a halfway house.'

The looks of confusion turned to horror. I then swept as confidently as I could out of the room. I'm not sure it was the best solution, but it worked in so far as the scarf was fairly see-through, so the nudist element at least rang true. The meeting was a memorable one for all concerned.

I think that's quite enough of me and my crazy body worries. And no doubt far too much information. MDRC, how are *you* feeling? Bit peaky? Blithe and bouncy? Vaguely repulsed by all this bottom talk?

Well, I'M feeling officially repulso. You may not be a hypochondriac any more, but I most certainly am, and I am now freaked right out.

Don't worry, Little M, it's really not that bad. These days, we are positively obsessed with being and staying well. Everyone has some pill or person they swear by. We are culturally over-wrought with

174

the idea of conquering mortality. All you hear is:

'Oh, I haven't had a cold for five years now that I take echinacea every day.'

'This pill is still illegal in this country but I swear by it as it boosts the immune system apparently. Sometimes when I look at clouds I see rabbits, but I certainly feel better.'

'Oh, you must go and see my woman. I have a wonderful woman. A mix of acupuncture and crystals. I swear by her.'

'Oh, you must go and see my man. Wonderful man. Forages nutrients from his allotment in Penge, then brews them into tea. Makes your breath smell like compost but adds twenty years to your life.

You all sound like witches. And more obsessed with health than I am.

In many ways, my younger hypo self, that is true. It's now cooler to do Pilates and eat blueberries than get drunk of an evening. But it's predominantly positive, if not frankly a little dull. And I don't buy in to too much of it. Everything in moderation I say. People lead long lives without popping supplements. We're all about the supplements. Either way, you should be pleased to hear that the health neurosis you're currently suffering from does wane.

So you're not neurotic at all now? You're a total chillaxed funster with nary a care in the world?

175

I wouldn't go that far. I may have lost the fear of illness, but I am now a bit of a health and safety nut. But that's an age thing, I think: life starts to seem a bit more perilous.

Is it just me, or did anyone else turn thirty-five and find they were unable to rush down a flight of stairs without imagining themselves in a broken-legged heap at the bottom? Or started suffering a sudden, inexplicable fear of slipping in or out of the bath and shower? I was walking down a steep hill the other day and started gathering momentum, which unexpectedly forced me into a run; I've never been so scared in my life. I screamed the whole way down, and when I got to the bottom of the slope I felt I'd achieved something extraordinary. When did this happen? And when did I start becoming aware of my knees? I mean, as a thing to worry about (I have always known they were there; I didn't suddenly go 'What on earth are THESE halfway down my legs?'). Now, I certainly wouldn't jump off something—chair, table, bale of hay—without taking a moment to worry on behalf of the old knees. It's the forward roll/handstand conundrum all over again.

Tragico alert! What about the Hart sense of adventure? I always thought I'd be a brave explorer, a swashbuckling pirate type (though obviously I never want to go to the tropics because of all the diseases). You sound like a proper wimp.

Just getting on a bit. Remember we are as old as Miss Handel now.

MDRC, I've hit upon a sure-fire way of knowing that one is approaching middle age: suddenly taking about 60 per cent more interest in public loos than you used to.

What? Loos aren't interesting.

Well, not to you: you're far too busy trying to become the next Kylie. But past the age of thirty-five, one suddenly finds oneself becoming a tad more particular: does the loo in question have the right loo paper? Is it clean enough? And you find yourself saying things like, 'Ooh, that's a lovely hand drier. Real va-va-voom there. Must be a Dyson Airblade' or 'Oh my goodness, a wicker bin! It seems we're not all going to hell in a handcart after all, ha ha!' and 'That was a good one, Marjorie. Lovely soap and you get one of those little hand towels that you use just for yourself and then throw extravagantly away' to 'Ooh, I love a hand towel; I don't need to go, but I will—sounds fun.'

You have officially turned into my worst nightmare: a middle-aged unadventurous frump like Great Aunty June. IT 'SOUNDS FUN' TO USE A LOO! EVEN THOUGH YOU DON'T NEED TO GO?

I *am* nearly forty. I've got to get my kicks somehow.

Right, MDRC. That's health and ageing covered. Life and death. Not doing too badly, are we? Now it's time for us to traverse into the far jollier world of . . . Hold on. Perhaps you could, for this chapter, give some respect and, wherever you are, be upstanding (come on, up you get, that's it: I want at least one person to come up to me in the street and say they stood for this chapter) for . . . HOLIDAYS.

11

HOLIDAYS

For those who stood for this chapter, I thank you, and now please be seated.

So, here is the thing, MDRC—I love, love, *love* a holiday. Holidays are *very* important to me. Not because I'm some kind of pleasure-scoffing, layabout luxury-hound; I am quite the opposite, in fact. I am a fretter: a fretter and a fixer and a worrier—always have been. If I wake up in the middle of the night I find it nigh-on impossible not to pop down to the kitchen for a quick peek at the laminated To Do list on the fridge (stuck firmly on with a novelty magnet—currently a small plastic broccoli floret, thank you) which can then lead to my spending half the night cleaning out the downstairs cupboard, putting DVDs back in their right boxes, checking my insurance policies and doing a spreadsheet for the next eight months of work. In short, I find it very difficult to switch off. The only way to silence my inner fretter is to take it somewhere unarguably on holiday. Turn my back on the To Do list, step away from the Post-it notes, and forget about that untidy sock drawer which could so dearly do with my attention (I couldn't possibly wear an odd sock—freaks me right out).

Seeing different things, being somewhere totally new, is the only way I can really wind down. I happily forgo haircuts, shoes and all the 'right' interior décor so that I have money to spare for holidays. We aren't on this beautiful planet all that long, I figure, so I want to see as much of it as possible, as soon as possible.

I'm SO relieved. So, Mrs 'I love a hand drier, and I'm scared running down a hill', we do have a sense of adventure. We do put our health and safety anxieties to one side and go intrepid from time to time. Our life is escapade central. Yes?

Well, I go on holiday, yes. But it's more lying down and pottering than full-on, high-octane adventure.

Oh God. How dull.

I don't need hardcore adventure holidays to get my kicks, thank you very much. I don't need to skydive to feel alive. (Rhyme. RHYME! Just in case you hadn't noticed. Thank you. At ease.) I get my adrenaline kicks within the very exciting everyday life that I lead, I will have you know.

How?

Well, sometimes I give myself a rush by putting the toaster setting on high, and seeing if I can release the toast before it burns. That's more than a thrill. Or there's Rich Tea Roulette. When you dunk the biscuit in your tea for as long as you think it can bear before it disintegrates and sinks to the bottom of the mug.

stares blankly, disappointed, speechless

And my adrenaline-levels go through the roof

when I'm waiting to see who's going to be voted off a reality TV show. You know, when they do that heartbeat sound effect, and leave such long pauses before they reveal the names—it's TREMENDOUSLY exciting.

'Reality TV show?'

They're programmes on television with members of the public in, or sometimes celebrities (who are members of the public who've appeared once in *Holby City*). They're usually either singing competitions where someone gets voted off each week, or dancing competitions (that's obviously the best one). There is one for more generic skills which usually involves a hip hop dance troupe, a dancing dog and a plain, older person who we don't expect to be able to sing who suddenly can and we cry. Or sometimes people just sit about in a house and chat and we vote off the ones we don't like. It's mostly the fault of this man called Simon Cowell, who's basically the King/Evil Overlord of Saturday night television.

He can't be more powerful than Larry Grayson. He was the best.

I'd forgotten our love of Larry. 'Shut that door.'

So funny.

So funny.

Brillo pads, amaze-balls and totally hilaire.

Yes, whatever you just said. Simon's nothing compared to Larry Grayson. And I think we should all take a brief moment to mull over that *pause* There's Ant and Dec as well.

The guys from **Byker Grove?**

Exactly. They become major Saturday night TV stars.

Don't be stupid—they're about twelve.

I think they still are. That's their trick.

So, watching a reality programme and seeing who gets voted off is your idea of an adrenaline rush?

Not just that! I went on a picnic recently.

A PICNIC IS NOT AN ADVENTURE!

Excuse me, but at thirty-eight and over six foot, trying to sit cross-legged on the ground to eat a meal is a *total* adventure. Have you ever attempted to eat with a plastic knife and fork, off a paper plate, while balancing the plate on your knee? And in company? That's an adventure. I tried to cut into my pork pie and the knife broke, then my Scotch egg rolled off the plate and into some mud. What does one do in that situation? Wipe off the mud, and eat it anyway? Risky. I peeled off the meaty outside and ate the boiled egg. Result. And, once, on the beach, I sat down with fish and chips (not strictly a picnic, but still hardcore al fresco eating) and a seagull swooped down and took the whole fish from my

181

box! It was terrifying. So don't you go telling me that picnics aren't an adventure, thanking you muchly.

Don't you at least want to go on a proper adventure? Podge's big brother Charlie just did a bungee jump in Oz. That sounds so cool. And one of those things you should do before you die.

I imagine you'd get there and realise that it could well be the thing you do *immediately* before you die, because of the simple fact that you are jumping off a high bridge with just a piece of elastic tied to your ankles, you FOOL. Do you really want to end your days, Little M, bouncing face-first off tarmac whilst a couple called Theresa and Ned from Bishop's Stortford who are doing the jump to raise money for their donkey sanctuary take photographs? Three simple words to anyone asking me to do a bungee jump: 'No', 'thank' and 'you'.

I did once attempt to go swimming with dolphins. That was pretty adventurous.

This sounds more promising.

But the blooming dolphins never turned up. On the one day I came to visit them, they saw fit to be elsewhere—perhaps there was a screening of *Free Willy* at the undersea Cineplex. The only creatures that did deign to grace me with their presence were seals. 'Well,' I thought, 'seals are better than nothing. They're rather cute, little chubby water-bobbing things. This will still be life-affirming.' And indeed it was, for the first five minutes. Until—and this is not a word of a lie—I found myself swimming behind a seal, and the seal chose that moment to release a poo. I swear that had my natural ninja reflexes not been as quick as they are, a seal poo would have gone right into my mouth.

No, I'll happily walk along a river looking at the rapids—I just don't need to be *in* the rapids. I'll stand at the top of a mountain and look at the view, but I don't then need to get a different angle on said view by dangling thousands of feet in the air in some kind of wobbly metal contraption. You say hang-glider, I say flimsy bringer of instant and terrifying death.

No, thank and you. Anything that can be considered an adventure sport is not a holiday. I see myself much more as a Tuscan retreat sort of a lady.

Oh, I've always dreamed of elegantly floating around an Italian village in a marvellous linen dress and a large hat, looking exceptionally beautiful. I would be holidaying with fabulous theatricals like Judi Dench and Maggie Smith, Penelope Keith and Alison Steadman.

Well, little one, this is still very much our dream. Judi, Maggie, Penny (if I may be so bold), Alison . . . and Eileen Atkins, Penelope Wilton, Imelda Staunton.

French and Saunders . . . Fry and Laurie . . . Michael J. Fox . . .

We're less bothered about Michael J. Fox now.

Well, defo Emma Thompson.

Of course, Emma Thompson.

Ahh, Emma and I would be bestest friends always and forever. We'd go down to the lake together and swim, laughing and splashing, and then she'd tell me that she'd written a part for me in her screen play for the next Merchant Ivory film. I'd giggle with delight, and Anthony Hopkins would take one look at me and hear my beautiful giggle, and he'd fall madly and instantly in love with me. He'd hand me his Panama hat to wear, and . . .

Stop it now.

Sorry.

But you're right. In our holiday dream, it would all be very *Tea with Mussolini*. Which is a film that comes out in the late 90s that you're going to adore. All the top theatricals are in it. And Cher.

*Brill! *sings* 'If I could turn back time—'*

singing 'If I could find a way—'

Do you remember my famous Cher impression?

I do. I just wish you hadn't decided it was appropriate to demonstrate it during a university interview. Let's not dwell.

So do we go on elegant Tuscan retreats? Because surely one of the best things about being an adult must

184

be holidaying on your own. Going on holi-bobs with your parentals is just horrifico.

It wasn't that bad, was it? We had some fun.

What is fun about sitting in a caravan for seven days every year from the ages of ten to fifteen in the pouring rain in Cornwall, finishing a 1,000 piece puzzle of a warship? Then on the one day in five years there was sunshine, being subjected to the most horrific scene ever. How can you not remember THAT moment on the beach?

The moment your parents decided to free themselves and 'go nudist'.

'Look at us being European—such fun!' they cried as they skipped towards the sea. That isn't a sight you are ever prepared for. And while the skipping towards the sea was one thing; the return skip was quite another. They then got arrested for flashing and we had to spend the night in a Cornish cell, en famille.

And that was just English holidaymaking. Going abroad was even worse. If they didn't understand the menu in a restaurant, Mum and Dad would shun the phrase book and rather imperiously ask, 'Do you have a SHEPHERD'S PIE, then? SHEPHERD'S PIE? SHEPHERD'S PIE?!' louder and louder, in their big booming English voices.

How about the one with the teen romance? That was lovely.

No, it wasn't. Even that went full-on wrong. We were in Spain, and this gorge Spanish boy came over and asked me to have a mocktail with him by the pool. I was wearing my tiny denim short shorts à la Jennifer

185

Grey in **Dirty Dancing.** *Because I was all thin and leggy then. Unlike YOU, you big giant fatty.*

RUDE.

Little Sis had helped me put on lots of After Sun because she said it was important my legs had a sexy, smooth, silky glow for such a major occasion. So I went to meet this boy at the bar looking hot to trot. I hopped up casually onto the plastic bar stool next to him, but because I was slathered with so much lotion, I promptly slid off it again. I tried again, managed to sit, then moved forward to flirtatiously sip my mocktail and I slid straight off again. Sis said I looked like Morph from Tony Hart. And totally deranged. Nightmare.

You just couldn't get a purchase on that stool *sniggers*

Do you mind? These are recent and traumatic memories for me. I'll never forget the way Juan flip-flopped back to his friends in a mix of fear and pity. No wonder my life goes in a sitcom.

MDRC, the bar-stool-falling experience was a useful store from that point of view.

If you think Spain was bad, do you remember Turkey?

Oh, no. Turkey. I am not sure we should tell that one.

Well, you seem to enjoy telling your Dear Reader Chum absolutely everything about our life, so why stop now?

OK, but let me just put out a disclaimer as this story also involves poo. Apologies in advance.

Right, so we were on a school trip camping in Turkey—my Geography class and a class from the local boys' school. The campsite was quite basic: the loos were in wooden cubicles with no flush, so 'stuff' was just left there. (There were no hand dryers and wicker baskets here.) By the final day, let's just say it was getting quite full and pretty grim actually.

On the last evening, Biffo was in the queue behind me. And, as you know, I well fancied Biffo and Clare-Bear said I was in with a chance. She could tell by the way he looked at me in the water polo game.

I went into the loo cubicle and did a big poo, but it was really showing because there was now a pile of debris quite near the top of the loo. I told you—

disgusting. I thought I couldn't have Biffo coming in there and seeing that, because he'd know it was me, and then he'd never fancy me.

Can I apologise to any readers who are, like me, feeling quite sick. Carry on, Little M.

For some reason I thought that the right thing to do was to roll up my poo in the loo roll and throw it out of the hatch at the back of the cubicle. But what I didn't realise as I threw it out was that Biffo had since stopped queuing and had gone round the back of the toilet to pee in the bushes, and my flying, rolled-up poo in a toilet roll landed right by him. He screamed and shouted, 'Someone has just thrown a shit at me!' and everyone gathered outside the cubicle to see who it had been. I had no choice but to come out.

Weirdly, no one believed my excuse that a bird had swooped in and stolen the poo. It was so traumatic. Biffo pulled a face not dissimilar to Juan's the year before.

Please, please tell me that we have fun holidays at some point in our life? I don't care about the hang-gliding and dare-devilling any more, I just want to have a not totally and completely horrendo time.

We do take ourselves on some lovely trips, I promise. But it's not all plain sailing. Don't panic, there's no more poo-throwing or getting arrested or falling off bar stools (well, maybe a little bit of that. Is it just me who has a complex relationship with the bar stool?), but holidaymaking does present its own set of annoyances, I rather find.

MDRC, let me turn to you for a moment, to see if you agree. The first major headache is all

188

the holiday administration or 'holi-min'—a costly and destructive business. For example, there is the fact that before going on holiday you decide you need a lovely new wicker beach bag and a sarong, conveniently forgetting that you decide this every single time you go on holiday, meaning that by the age of thirty-five, the average British woman (by which I mean me) owns at least twenty-three sarongs and fourteen beach bags. And is it just me who *always* forgets to take the electric socket adapter thing? So that I have to buy *another* adapter for £17 at the airport? I have fifty-six of them in a cupboard at home.

Ditto travel pillows. I buy them at the airport thinking they look good: 'Oooh, yes, lovely—I'll definitely have that for the journey. I'll sleep like a new-born babe, carried aloft on a cloud.' Then I get on the plane and realise that a) I'll look like a massive tit trying to blow it up in a crowded aeroplane, b) it's probably incredibly uncomfortable and, c) the only people who seem to be able to pull them off are sixty-six, called Jean, are heavily into giant Puzzler crosswords and are going on a 'jaunt' from Guildford. They have no shame in wandering around the plane with it still attached to their neck. I find that unnerving. Are they sleepwalking?

I have thirty-four unopened travel pillows making merry with fifty-six plug adapters, twenty-three sarongs and fourteen beach bags in my holi-cupboard at home.

Then there's the actual being-in-transit aspect of the whole holiday business. I'm not a fan of the over packed, over crowded hustle bustle of the holiday plane, train, or automobile. Plane-wise what I fear

189

most (and what inevitably always happens), is being seated in the middle seat next to a large sleeping male, and finding myself desperately needing the toilet. A few nudges and he doesn't wake. You're in economy, you're completely trapped, and so your only option seems to be to mount him from the side and clamber over. The last time I attempted this manoeuvre, the man woke up as I was directly facing him, in the mount position. Slightly awkward all round. What does one do? I cheerily said 'Hello!' and carried on. Of course, by the time I got back from the loo he was asleep again, and I was forced to remount. I was remounting (sorry, I will stop saying *mounting*) just as there was a spot of turbulence, which caused me to lose my grip on the headrest, and crash down heavily into his lap. What made this far worse was that he didn't seem to mind.

Still, it's worth it when you get there. Feeling that surge of heat hit you as you walk off the plane.

I love that feeling. Suddenly, the To Do list seems far, far away, especially if there's any kind of hotel stay involved. I do love a hotel room: adore it. What's not to love about everything you need in one room? Would you have a kettle on a tea tray with biscuits in a packet in your bedroom at home? No, you very likely wouldn't. And—please excuse me, MDRC, I'm getting a little giddy here—the kettle. The little tiny kettle on a little tiny stand! Admittedly it's hard to fill as it never quite fits under the basin taps, but that's all just part of the fun.

Then there's room service. I've now mastered the art of room service, if I do say so myself. If you're anything like me, you'll find the idea of a stranger coming to your room with a tray of food tremendously exciting. You'll probably over-order because you kind of want a bit of everything, but let's call it curiosity. To avoid looking greedy, this is what I do (a hot tip for any other single travellers, from me to you with love): when I hear the knock on the door, I quickly put the shower on in the bathroom and close the bathroom door. Then, as the waiter comes in with the overloaded tray (sometimes two trays are needed, often a trolley), I'll shout in the vague direction of the bathroom, 'Don't worry, darling, stay there; I'll get the room service!' Do you see? Clever. Thereby insinuating that there's a man in the bathroom with a huge appetite, and it's not just old Mrs Greedy-guts herself ordering all the pies. The only downside is that you must then spend the rest of the week making up excuses as to why your husband or lover isn't joining you on various excursions. (It often turns out your husband or lover is an albino agoraphobic who only comes on holiday to order room service. And, given that, who'd deny him a steak sandwich and an ice-cream sundae of a morning? That's right. No one. It would be very cruel indeed. High five me for that tip. Thank you.)

No matter how wonderful your hotel room is, you will at some point want to leave it. And you may well find yourself heading for the sea. Now, I love the sea. I love bobbing about on it, in it and lying around watching it. The sea and its timelessness, its gentle in-and-out lapping which slows one's very breathing . . . excuse me, I've gone a little poetic. However, beaches with all their beach-min provide many a mini life hurdle (and what a lovely phrase 'many a mini' is, if I do say so myself) so I think it can only be but time for one of my lists. Oh, yes. It gives me great pleasure to present you with:

MIRANDA'S LIST OF FIVE SLIGHTLY PETTY THINGS WHICH ARE A TINY BIT DISCOMBOBULATING ABOUT OTHERWISE RELAXING BEACH EXCURSIONS PARTICULARLY WHEN THERE IS A PRESSURE TO BE ELEGANT AND SEXY ON A BEACH HOLIDAY (I think that's a succinct list title):

1. Towels
Or rather, putting one's towel down on the sand to establish one's 'beach station', at the precise moment when a gust of wind rudely chooses to blow it back in one's face. You then can't see briefly and stand inadvertently on a child's sandcastle, who then cries and their parents think

you did it deliberately.

2. Swimming

I like to imagine that I'll go for a short and refreshing dip, before emerging gracefully from the sea perfectly flushed from the exercise, lithe and toned, hair smoothed elegantly back (like Ursula Andress, minus the scary knife). What actually happens is I hobble in (having stood on a pointy shell), make embarrassing 'Ooh, ooh, aaah, it's cold' noises, hop screaming away from what I thought was a jellyfish (but is actually a plastic bag), start swimming, panic about being pulled out to sea by a 'rip tide' (even though I don't quite know what a 'rip tide' is), do a crazy rushed breast stroke back in, hitting a sand bank not realising it had got shallow, and emerge from the water shivering, sand covered, my hair plastered to my face like a crazed sea creature. I then walk back to my towel picking my swimming costume out of my bum and removing a bit of seaweed from somewhere you never want seaweed. Sexy.

3. Ice Creams

They melt. Which is, at any age, one of the saddest sights in the world. Does one go for the 'hurry, eat it really, really quickly, gobble it fast, before it melts' look? Or just let it go and not mind? I favour the former because I do mind, but I must look like I'm in a local ice-cream eating competition. Ursula Andress, eat your heart out.

4. Wind

Even a very gentle breeze will generate a miniature sandstorm at your beach station. The sand will go in your eyes. It will go on your melting ice cream, which you won't notice because you are briefly blinded, so you will lick sand from the ice cream. The sand will also get *on* your towel, something you are at all times desperately trying to avoid. You turn over, having carefully put sun cream on and said sand sticks to your entire body. Ooh, the horrid abrasive feel. Wind then swishes some wasps in your direction. You are being dive bombed. You become a wild, sand-coated, stressy, blind, fast ice-cream-eating, wasp-swatting beast. Abort beach. Abort, abort.

5. The Evenings

I always hope that I've never looked more beautiful than of a hot holiday evening, but deep down I know that I'm mostly just red and covered in mosquito bites. Despite my very 'British abroad' look, the last time I was on holiday I decided to crack on and party. I was in Antigua; I know—exotic. I thank you. So, I went to a local party where they had steel drums and—get this—maracas. I know! If we had all been dressed in unisex party kaftans this would have been the Miranda-Land Utopia. I was maraca-ing (could that now be an official verb?) with gusto to the steel band. I was feeling pretty free, actually. I'd had a couple of rums; life was good. Then a solo guitarist came on and started playing some lovely slow tunes. Even though it wasn't the wonderful up-tempo steel band any more, I couldn't help but continue maraca-ing. By then it was just me and a middle-aged man who introduced himself as Ron (there's always one), but I didn't presume I was in his camp, oh no. I was the beautiful mysterious lady maraca-er. Trouble was, as I maraca-ed with more gusto than perhaps one should, the top of my maraca suddenly came loose and hurtled off in the direction of the guitarist. To my horror, it actually hit his strumming hand. The music stopped. Had I turned down that third rum punch, I might have been sharp enough to run and hide. But, no, the culprit could only have been either me or Ron, and I was the one waving a wooden, maraca-less stick. The guitarist gave me the what I call Juan-from-Spain look (fear and pity, in case you had forgotten).

Here endeth Miranda's List of Five Slightly Petty Things Which Are A Tiny Bit Discombobulating About Otherwise Relaxing Beach Excursions Particularly When There Is A Pressure To Be Elegant and Sexy On A Beach Holiday.

I hope we get better at beach-etiquette before our honeymoon.

What honeymoon?

What?

Nothing.

We have gone on a honeymoon, haven't we? Can we please discuss this?

Oh, look, isn't that Jason Donovan? He's popped round to the school refectory to serve scones for tea?

WHAT! WHERE? *runs off, salivating*

I think I handled that one beautifully. For all the conundra a holiday can present, it doesn't put me off. Oh, no. It won't stop me holidaying for I loves it so. And the only way to avoid coming a holiday cropper is to become a truly seasoned traveller. Go away for months on end, take regular sabbaticals, live a more hand-to-mouth existence. Jack in the nine to five, and just take off.

I've always rather fancied myself as a hippie. Don't look at me like that, MDRC; I *could* pull it off. A permanent back-packer. Then, I always think, you'd have time to adjust to the sun, the sea, the languages. You'd become comfortable anywhere, maybe even comfortable in yourself. You'd acquire the ability to wear low-slung, baggy trousers and hair beads (agreed that if I wear them now, I'd look like a middle-aged aspiring Rastafarian from Chelsea). There'd be no societal pressure; no conventions to be bound by that make us regularly embarrass ourselves. You could make your own rules; become a true eccentric. I have always fancied that. Dodge the rat-race, slake the wanderlust once and for all.

May I say something, Big Miranda? Apart from never lie about Donovan and scones again (coz that's one of life's best combos), why don't you be a bit more like that?

We're far too British and practical, I'm afraid.

That's an excuse. You're just scared.

196

I am not. I do very brave things in life.

You think picnics are exciting, and can't do a forward roll any more.

We're just anxious—that's just us!

That's an excuse. Now it's my turn to teach YOU something. I'm currently eighteen and I might have panic attacks about chemistry teachers poisoning me with gas, but if I was given the opportunity to go to Antigua then I wouldn't stay on the beach; I'd go hiking to look for a deserted waterfall. If I got a chance to go skiing I would go, straight away, and not worry about my knees. It sounds to me like you've got into a habit of worrying and you're not living the life you want to live. I know that I'm a bit of a hippie at heart. That's me. I'll need to go on regular long back-packing trips. I'm planning to go to Oz next year.

I know—you do go—and it's the best five months of your life. You've never felt more free and alive.

*But I don't want it to be **the** best. I want it to be **one** of the best. If you're honestly saying that thirty-eight isn't old (which I still find hard to believe), then get out there and stop fussing! I can't believe that I'm still alive at thirty-eight—given the amount I worry about dying—so I'm going to stop worrying and free up. I suggest you do the same.*

feels a bit teary I don't know what to say . . .

You don't have to say anything. Just take up this very worthwhile challenge.

197

I will. Yes, I really will. The next time I'm given the opportunity to go white-water rafting, I'm going to go.

Wooooooooooo!

Oh, yeah, look at me go . . . *pushes back chair, rushes off excitedly, trips over carpet edge*

She's down.

She's up again. No harm done. I sprang straight up again—it's all about the recovery. And my knees are fine. Onwards and upwards.

Anything to stop you being what you seem to have become: an old overweight, anxious, stationery-obsessed office worker.

RUDE.

12

CHRISTMAS

The only time I can confidently say that I have an anxiety-free zest for life is at Christmas. It's the one holiday I fully embrace with childish excitement and glee. If somebody asked me, 'Do you like Christmas?' I'd have no hesitation at all in telling them that I don't just like it, I LOVE it. I'm a total, unashamed Christmas fiend. I'm not the biggest fan of winter, but those glimmering, shimmering Santa-stuffed weeks sustain me through the bleak, chilly months.

*HOORAY FOR CHRIMBO! *sings* 'Feed the bi-ir-ir-ids. Let them know it's Christmas time—'*

Umm . . . Little M, we discussed this.

*Oh, yes. Sorry. 'World.' *sings* 'Feed the wor-or-uh-*

orld! Let them know it's Christmas time.'

then sings *'Ding dong merrily on high. In heaven the bells are ringing.'*

joins in, ever ready to troll the yuletide carol 'DING DONG VERILY THE SKY, IS RIV'N WITH ANGELS SINGING' *takes deep breath* 'Glooooor-or-or-or-or-or, GLOOOOR-or-or-or-or-or—' (Oh, dear, that's too high for me. I always start that bit too high. And it does go on, doesn't it? I can end up feeling faint if I really go for it in a carol service.)

Is it just me, or does anybody else, when at a carol service, sing at least ten times louder and prouder than they'd ever normally do in public? At a wedding I'll mumble along in the mousiest fashion imaginable, but whack up a Christmas tree and suddenly I'm Sir Harry Secombe. I do love a good carol. My favourite is the last verse of 'Hark, the Herald Angels Sing', when we all really let rip. First two verses normal, third verse quiet (though I always forget this and come in way too loudly), then last verse bellowed out as if we're trapped down a lift-shaft, crying out for rescue. Love it. It's rousing. (And that's 'rousing', not 'arousing'. If you find it arousing then I suggest you put this book down at once, and phone a therapist.)

There are some wonderful aspects to Christmas. It's magical. And each year, from at least November, well, September, well, if I'm honest, May, I look forward to it hugely. The singing, eating, log fires, eating, drinking, singing, eating, the good will, the cheer, ice skating, singing, the eating, the drinking, the snow, the scarves, singing, eating, drinking, eating, singing, eating. Yes, I embrace the season in all its candle-lit, log-fire-lighting, chestnut-roasting gloriousness, and ponder the people to whom I can spread bounty and joy in this glorious season of giving. *sings* 'Well, I wish it could be Christmas every da-a-a-ay!'

singing 'When the kids start singing and the la la la ne ne la ne la . . .'

No one knows the words to that bit—just come in at the end with . . .

'SLEIGH-EH-EH!'

That's it. And you're back on track.

I'm so relieved that we still like Chrimbo.

Why wouldn't we? WHY? WHY?

Coz it does have a tendency to send people a teeny tiny bit mad. Or, indeed, completely and utterly stark-raving crackers (PUN!).

Good one. Don't worry, we do still love it.

Well, I'm just worried. Coz the last two Christmases I've totally been in a Gordon Grump with everyone. Mum and Dad get so annoying at Chrimbo. Even Sis turns into a massive loser. So I imagined it would just get worse and worse and we'd end up hating it.

I'm not going to deny that a little bit of, shall we say, unusual behaviour can surface around Christmas-tide. And perhaps the best way forward is to discuss it in a frank and open fashion. So, MDRC, replenish your tea—or perhaps even treat yourself to a little tot of mulled wine? A morsel of mince pie? (And don't forget lashings of brandy butter. There's a saying in my house: 'Do you want a mince pie with your brandy butter?' Lovely.) Let the Yule-tide discussion begin.

I would like to suggest that 90 per cent of people have fallen victim to the bonkers behaviour of others around about Christmas time. And that in at least 90 per cent of these 90 per cent of cases, the bonkers-ness primarily emanates from . . . The Mother.

I'm not necessarily talking about *your* mother (and certainly not *my* mother, good heavens, no: she's the height of restraint) but whichever mother happens to be the official 'Big Chief Organiser of All Christmas Activity' for that year. Of course, these are enlightened times—in your household 'The Mother' may well be a father, or a pair of fathers, or even a couple of particularly game teenage children. But for convenience's sake, let's refer to this poor creature as 'The Mother' while we ponder the question of—and please forgive the outburst—JUST WHAT THE HELL HAPPENS TO OUR MOTHERS AT CHRISTMAS?

I mean, really, what happens? Christmas is supposed to be a relaxed and joy-filled occasion of mega-jolly fun times, but at around mid-morning on Christmas Day, this normally relaxed figure morphs into what appears to be an over-caffeinated, tinsel-decked Captain Mainwaring from *Dad's Army* who's just been hit on the head with a novelty cracker.

My family's Christmas Day begins in a deceptively relaxed fashion. First thing in the morning, we're very chilled. We're all in our pyjamas for longer than usual (except sad cousin Billy, who hasn't worked for a year and spends most days in his pyjamas, but we're not talking about that). We're in front of the fire. It's lovely. We're all opening our stockings, which is fun because our stockings are filled with silly, jokey things, like miniature desk hoovers, chocolate coins, cat pencil sharpeners and pleasant light reading matter like, well, like this book. (Did you get this book in your stocking, MDRC? If you did, let's put our hands together now and offer a hearty hooray for Father Christmas.)

At this point, The Mother is in a good mood. She's wearing her Christmas-morning silk dressing gown and sipping an Earl Grey from her best Wedgwood Christmas range cup. She's enjoyed her stocking. It's an idyllic Christmas scene. The cat is playing with a bauble on the lower branch of the tree (is there a more heartening sight?); Dad has put his tie-of-tinsel on (every year—yes, we never tire); Little Sis is sporting the fluffy bear slippers she's just been given (they are, of course—because it's Christmas—the funniest thing we've ever seen); Great Aunty June has finally worked out what to press so that her socks play a tinny, sock version of 'Jingle Bells', and she's doing an amusing dance; cousin Yvette has got a sticker rosette from a present stuck in her hair and it has to be cut out— we'll dine out on that one for a year; and I've got to the bottom of my stocking to discover the hallowed satsuma and we all go, 'Aaaah, satsuuummmaaaaa!' and laugh (no, I don't know why, either).

The Mother remains mellow. She even sees fit to play a little joke-ette on us. She vanishes off into a corner, and fiddles mysteriously around with something for a bit. 'What are you up to?' we ask. 'Oh, nothing! Ignore me!' she says. We do. Then, five minutes later, she returns and declares, 'Look! We have a visitor,' and turns to reveal a 9' inflatable Santa slowly being blown up in the corner of the living room by an electric pump. We all laugh for a moment, as The Mother trills: 'A good friend of mine, thought he'd pop round, SUCH FUN!' We chuckle once more, and turn away. The trouble is, poor old wheezing half-inflated Santa takes a fair old while to reach his full height: about six minutes, to be precise. A length of time for which it's impossible to sustain laughter at an only mildly amusing joke. So, while he inflates, we turn back to our presents. At which a terrible rage rises up in The Mother. Through gritted teeth, she says, 'NO, darlings. We must watch him inflate ALL THE WAY or he'll be TERRIBLY UPSET. SUCH FUN! SUCH FUN! SUCH FUN!' At this point, 'Such fun' turns from being an observation to a grim command.

This is the moment when we all realise that The Mother has shifted into Christmas Mode. We quietly watch the Santa inflate, and we solemnly applaud. It has begun.

This is EXACTLY what I'm talking about. That is worse than last year when Aunt Lily made a reindeer out of marzipan and she made us all line up and stroke it. Then we had to say OUT LOUD, 'Happy Christmas, Mr Reindeer.'

SUCH FUN! So the stocking-opening calm fun has passed, and The Mother has entered the kitchen. You know you're in for a rocky ride, as she's wielding the electric meat-carver like a light sabre and foaming lightly at the mouth. She's now in full neurotic vegetable-obsessed drill-sergeant mode. The jokey apron she normally wears (slogan: 'I KISS BETTER THAN I COOK'—*eurrgh*) has been replaced with a formal blue-and-white striped one. There are lists and rotas pinned up on the cupboards. Somebody's 'on potatoes' at 10 a.m. Heaven forbid the sprouts aren't peeled by 12:05, because we'll need to be eating them at 1 p.m., and if we don't eat at 1 p.m. the turkey might be dry and it's been dry for the last five years because UNCLE HENRY NEVER GETS IT TOGETHER WITH THE SPROUTS. Last year, Henry was seconded to peas, and took the news about as well as he took the news of his recent 'semi-voluntary' redundancy: 'I could do the sprouts, I will make them work this year.'

'No, Henry, back away, you're only capable of peas.'

'Oh, poor Henry, poor, stupid Henry; only capable of peas. Well, how about I take the peas into the shed with this bottle of Scotch and show them who's boss? Eh?'

'No, Henry, if you're going to be like that, you can go and sit in the car.' And so on.

And *heaven forefend* there's any flaw in the turkey, because The Mother got up at *4.30 a.m.* to put it in the oven. This is the same woman who, 364 days of the year, rises at ten and happily eats éclairs for breakfast whilst wearing a dressing gown and fluffy dog slippers. On any other day, she is the Queen of Relaxed. But at Christmas, with a houseful of eight guests (who at any other time of the year she would accommodate without noticing), she'll be heard shouting: 'I got up at four thirty this morning to put that turkey in the oven. Four thirty! It's a magnificent beast, and please know that if anyone is late with their vegetable task, I will have arisen at four thirty, yes four thirty I tell you, for NO GOOD REASON. Now, who's on bread sauce—YOU'RE LATE. Did I tell you that I got up at four thirty? Four thirty, to put that turkey in? Yes, four thirty. You heard.'

As the day continues, The Mother might be heard to offer some other truly worrying notifications, including:

'I've just finalised the seating plan for the Queen's Speech. Your father and I will be standing throughout; he'll be saluting, while I'm opting for the traditional interval curtsey.'

'I've mastered the running order for the downstairs toilet.'

'I've choreographed a plan for the steamed vegetables and where they'll be placed on the hostess trolley.'

'I've itemised a running order for the lunchtime conversation topics.'

'I've calculated the optimum distance/slope ratio for the Boxing Day ramble.'

'I've labelled the recycling boxes for present-opening time. Presents must only be opened on my whistle.'

'Crackers will not be pulled in twos, but only in the round-the-table, crossed-arms position so everyone can be involved. OTHERWISE, IT MIGHTN'T BE FUN, MIGHTN'T IT?'

By the tenth notification, we are all becoming increasingly tense and twitchy. Suddenly, Dad is taking the dog out for a walk (we don't have one); Sis is nipping to the twenty-four-hour garage because she's run out of nappies (this is in the pre-niece days); and Yvette's gone to the emergency doctor for her chest infection (she's perfectly healthy).

You see? This is what I mean. It's hideola.

Ah, but here's the thing, Little M. We kind of get used to it as the years go by, and we'd be sad if it didn't happen any more. It's part of the Christmas tradition. And we do love our Christmas traditions. Even . . . wait for it . . . The Games.

You've GOT to be kidding. Are we still playing games? Gross vibes. Why can't I just sit in my room and listen to Talking Heads and try to put nail varnish on? I HATE games.

Yuletide games are an absolute must. And, MDRC, I'm not talking normal games like Charades or Cluedo, but weird hybrid games which have evolved over generations of family squabbles, and which no one entirely understands. We've got Charitctionary, and Hide and SeeklueodoOperation (in which someone hides and pretends to be dead, and whoever finds them has to find out whodunit by removing the bullet from a mock body without it buzzing—such fun). Then there's the unadulterated thrill of trying to explain the rules of the game to Great Aunty June (or GAJ). Explaining a game to GAJ is a task akin to teaching a dolphin the Laws of Cricket.

Last Christmas, for instance, The Mother took the controversial step of introducing Jenga to the Games Agenda (which is laminated, and stuck up on the living room cabinet).

'What's this, dear?' Great Aunty June enquired, looking in a slightly frightened fashion at the wooden bricks.

'It's Jenga, Aunty June,' I said encouragingly. 'We have to take a brick out of the tower and put it on top of the tower, making the tower taller. And whoever makes the tower fall over loses.'

'Is it like Monopoly?'

'No, not really. It's—'

'Who deals the cards?'

'There aren't any cards.'

'What about the dice? Where're the dice?'

'There are no dice.' By now, the impatience of The Mother was beginning to affect The Daughter.

'Then how do we know who's won?'

'Um . . . we sort of don't.'

'Then why is it a game?'

'Well,'—the tension was rising now—'it, umm, you play it with people, so . . .'

'Is it one of those modern computer games, then?'

'No! No! How could it be? There's no computer.'

'I've never understood those computer games.'

'Jenga is not a computer game!' I took a deep breath and tried to calmly explain: 'You just take a

brick from the tower, like so—'

To demonstrate, I took a brick from the Jenga tower, which promptly toppled over sideways giving everyone their cue to massively enjoy the tower falling over.

'Well, that doesn't look like much fun at all. It keeps falling over.'

'THAT *IS* THE FUN! We try and make it stay up, but when you remove bits, it might fall.'

'Well, don't remove bits then. That way it'll stay up.'

By now I was forced to remove my jolly Christmas jumper as I was sweating with rage. 'THEN IT WOULDN'T BE A GAME!'

'I'll go first; where're the dice?'

'THERE ARE NO DICE' I shouted. 'I can't do this, I'm leaving.' I kicked over the rest of the Jenga tower and stormed out as the remaining family members contrived to pretend MASSIVELY to enjoy the tower falling over with a Christmas chorus of 'Jenggaaaaaaa, ha ha.'

I once experienced the delight and agony of playing Chinese Whispers with Great Aunty June. I cannot stress enough the sheer pointlessness of this endeavour: only at Christmas would we insist on carrying on playing it, because, of course, FUN MUST BE HAD AT ALL COSTS. Would we be quite so manic if this were April 12th and we all just happened to be together enjoying a large meal? No. I think not. But as it was Christmas, so we had to crack on with Chinese Whispers.

I was sitting next to Great Aunty June on the sofa and the rest of the assembled Christmassy company sat in hushed silence, all looking forward to the game. Dad whispered the phrase in my ear; I smiled, turned to GAJ and whispered the phrase in her ear.

Immediately, she spun round and shouted, 'WHAT?'

I whispered it again, slightly more loudly.

'*WHAT?*' repeated GAJ, and looked at me, exasperated. 'I can't hear you, dear! I don't know why you're whispering; I'm deaf as a post, as well you know.'

'*OH, FOR GOODNESS' SAKE!*' I shouted. '*THE MOUSE HIT A CAT ON A MAT! THE MOUSE HIT A CAT ON A MAT!*'

Everyone turned to glare at me.

'Well,' said Mum, disappointed. 'Now we've all heard it, it's ruined.'

'Yeah!' echoed the rest of our not-so-jolly party. 'The game's ruined. Miranda's ruined it. Nice one, Miranda. Well done, Miranda. RUINED.'

'What was I supposed to do?' I appealed to them. 'She's deaf, she can't play Chinese WHISPERS!'

'There's no need to shout,' shouted GAJ.

'Oh, but there is. There is very obviously a need to shout. YOU CAN'T HEAR ANYTHING!'

'Don't be aggressive, dear,' Mum said, giving me The Mother Stare.

'It was *your* idea to play Chinese WHISPERS with YOUR deaf aunt.'

'Don't shout at your mother,' Dad joined in.

'I'm going to count my chocolate coins,' announced Little Sis, who till now had remained silent.

'You're thirty-two!' I protested.

'She can do what she likes,' snapped Mum. 'It's Christmas, remember. AND WE MUST HAVE FUN. Now, sit down and put your Christmas jumper back on.'

'Now you're shouting, dear,' Dad said, somewhat boldly, I thought.

'Don't tell me not to shout!' Mum turned The Mother Stare onto Dad. 'I got up this morning at four thirty TO PUT YOUR TURKEY IN. FOUR THIRTY!'

Little Sis had begun edging towards the door. 'I'm going to read my new book in my room.'

'You stay here,' said Dad, in his firmest voice. 'You know your mum doesn't like separate activities at Christmas; we must all remain in this room.'

'Don't you like this room?' Mum stood menacingly with her hands on her hips.

'That's not what I said!'

'Has anyone even commented on the holly behind the pictures on the walls? Has anyone noticed?'

Dad manfully attempted to save the situation: 'Look everyone! Everyone, look at my tinsel tie, look at my tinsel tie . . .'

He was ignored.

'Who's taken my drink?' Mum stared around, accusingly.

I grabbed at the glass in front of me, 'This is mine.'

'No, it's not, it's mine,' said Little Sis, grabbing it back.

'It's MINE!' I repeated. This was not looking pretty.

'MINE!' yelled little Sis.

'My glass should be obvious,' said Mum, trying to regain her poise, 'because I put a rubber band around it so that everyone knows it's mine.' Every year! The bloody rubber bands! 'It's an excellent system,' Mum continued. 'This year GAJ has a sticker on hers.'

'What's made of wicker?' GAJ suddenly piped up.

I downed the contents of my glass. 'Not wicker, STICKER.'

'SUCH FUN!' Mum had The Look again.

'It's not SUCH FUN,' cried Little Sis.

'Can we all just calm down?' Dad mumbled.

'Things are SUCH FUN. IT'S CHRISTMAS. And things would still be fun if *you* hadn't ruined Chinese Whispers.' Mum glares at me.

'But SHE'S DEAF!' I yelled, pointing at GAJ.

'Who's deaf, dear?'

By now furious, I attempted to dramatically storm out of the room again but was blocked by the 9' inflatable Father Christmas. I kicked it out of the way only for it to bounce back with surprising force, knocking me clean to the floor.

Such fun!

This family is a bunch of square losers. They're so square, they're cuboid. And what about Triv? Triv Pursuits—when we just play it normally, not the sad family version of **Trivial Pursuopoly.** *Every year, Little Sis insists the winning thing to put in the wheel is called a cheese, when she knows full well it's a pie. Yet*

she always calls it a cheese. Drives me mad.

No, the main thing is a cheese, and the little things are pies: you're trying to make a cheese pie.

Have you gone mad? That makes no sense. It's a wheel, not a cheese, and we're putting pies in the wheel.

You don't put pies in a wheel! There is no such thing as wheel pie.

Well, if anything it's a pie and we're putting cheese in it . . .

No, it's a pie and we're . . . Hang on, this is stupid, now we're arguing about it between OURSELF. I don't care what they're called.

This proves just how annoying Christmas is. At Christmas I suddenly care what they're called, and want to punch Sis on the nose for calling them cheeses. They're pies. So there.

I think we should probably let this one go. Honestly, we do start to accept all these Christmas shenanigans and grow rather fond of them. Even the cheese/pie debate.

Really? There's nothing in all this monstrousness that you thoroughly dread?

A few things do grate a bit, I grant you. Doing Christmas cards, I hate.

But Mum and Dad do them.

Not when you're an adult. When you're an adult, you have to actually pay for them and send them yourself.

Can't you just not send them?

You *should* be able to not send them. But it's impossible because some time in the middle of December, a big glittery card will rock through your letterbox that reads, 'Warmest wishes for a wonderful festive season, all our love, Minty and Speng.' You'll think for a moment 'Who the hell are Minty and Speng?', then realise that Minty and Speng are that peculiar couple you met on holiday and spent two weeks in Lanzarote desperately trying to shake off. Now you feel horribly guilty. You quickly send Minty and Speng a Christmas card back. A week later, you receive another card, this time from your tax accountant's brother who you met at a drinks thing in 1994. You send him one, too. Cards pour in, you respond to them all in a costly, guilt-ridden frenzy. 'This is madness,' you think, 'madness—now we'll all be stuck in a Christmas card loop for the rest of our lives, bouncing not goodwill but fury back and forth at great expense, growing less and less fond of each other with every stamp we miserably lick.'

Do people still send those embarrassing round-robin newsletter things with their cards? They're GRIM.

Afraid so. Utterly ghastly.

Is it just me who can't stand those newsletters, MDRC? You know the ones. You open a Christmas card and a folded, typed sheet of A4 slides out. Your heart sinks, because you know it's going to read something like:

Well, what a year! Tallulah, brainbox that she is, has just got nine A stars at GCSE, which I think we all agree isn't too shabby for a twelve year old. Can't think where she gets the brains from, HA HA! No, the grown-ups of the family should stick to what they do best: drinking Pimms and cleaning up after their brood. But hands up, confess mode, this year 'Mummy' has found herself modelling for Boden. I know—there's life in the old dog yet! But no, it's about the little 'uns. On which note, Milo's had a cracking year. First flute with the National Youth Orchestra, which fortunately hasn't clashed too much with the England rugby trials. I must say, we've been racing the people-carrier up the A12 like bandits, between Milo's extra-curricular japes and Tamara's work with disadvantaged children. Must take a moment to mention that, actually: Mara's been ever such a hit down at the soup kitchen—unfortunately she can only do it a couple of times a week as she's mostly in Milan modelling for Versace. But she does her best, the little humanitarian. Can't think where she gets it from—HA HA HA! Anyway, tiddley-pom, on we struggle. Lots of love, Veronica and Hugo xxx

Does Mum still set them on fire, weeping, 'Why can't you be more like Mara?' Actually, I don't want to know. Now, what about presents? Do we still always get

216

RUBBISH presents?

No, they have got a bit better. Though last year we did get an egg timer from GAJ.

Gross. Though nothing's as bad as the ghetto blaster incident.

Oh, yes. Why don't you tell that one?

Oh, all right then. Hello Reader. So, here's the thing. Aged sixteen, I asked Mum for a ghetto blaster. Aren't they the coolest things ever? Especially when you get the double tape players so you can play one tape and record it onto a blank one and make people tapes. And the ghetto blaster I asked for came with a CD player. (I don't have any CDs but HOW COOL?) Anyway, I got a whiff from the Little Sis that the parentals might be getting me one. I was SO excited. I was going to go back to school in January and put Talking Heads on my ghetto blaster, and everyone was going to see that I was so trendy. I was so excited about present opening that year. And, by the way, present opening in our house is actually good. We open all the little ones from the pets first, then—

No need to share that. On with the story.

So I got to my main present. And the box was worryingly small. I opened it, and it was . . . wait for it . . . a Dictaphone. Mum and Dad thought a Dictaphone was a ghetto blaster. A DICTAPHONE. I completely panicked because I'd already told everyone at school that I was going to get a ghetto blaster. I couldn't go back and tell them that I'd got

217

a Dictaphone instead, could I? Bella would spread it around the whole school in minutes.

Quite. So how did you explain it?

Um . . . well . . . I MAY have told them that the reason I didn't have a ghetto blaster was that my family had decided not to celebrate Christmas in the end, as we'd all recently converted to Islam. Trouble was, later in the term when we were in RE class studying all the faiths, Islam came up. And Podge told Miss Manning that I was a Muslim. I had to make a speech about it to the class, then spend the rest of term pretending to be Muslim. Which was all right actually, because I didn't have to go to chapel. But in some ways it was a bit rubbish as it meant I couldn't have sausages and bacon for tea, and I LOVE sausages and bacon. So I had to have a big conversion-back-to-Christianity moment two terms later to undo the lie. Which Miss Manning got excited about and I had my own chapel service for it. Embarrassamento!

So, basically, that all just shows what a huge disappointment the big day always ends up being. I could go on, but I think it's now my turn—TO DO A LIST.

LITTLE MIRANDA'S LIST OF THINGS THAT ARE COMPLETELY MAD ABOUT CHRISTMAS DAY:

1. Rubbish presents. See above.

2. Watching television with elderly members of your family. VERY LOUDLY INDEED. They can't understand how the remote control works but keep trying to make it work by pressing all the buttons. They somehow get it on a video function and we can't work out how to get back to normal telly programmes. Infuriating.

3. Relatives unable to find the listings for 'Christmas Day' in the **Radio Times.** *Even when 'Christmas Day' is written at the top of the page in very large letters, and there are really relatively few 'days' to choose from. Why does this happen EVERY YEAR?*

4. 'The Mother' insisting that everyone save the wrapping paper. She is apparently going to iron it and use it next year. Even though it's ripped to shreds, covered in Sellotape and someone has drawn a bum on it in glitter.

5. Every year the parentals debate what time the news is on and whether or not it will be slightly shorter because it's Christmas Day.
*   'Is it ten past ten, darling? Or ten twenty-five?'*
*   'Shall we stay up for it if it's ten twenty-five?'*
*   'Will it be over by ten forty, then?'*
*   'Only a fifteen-minute bulletin? Strange.'*
*   SHUT UP, SHUT UP, SHUT UP. THERE IS NEVER ANY NEWS ON CHRISTMAS DAY,*

219

ANYWAY. NOTHING HAPPENS. IT CAN'T HAPPEN. WE'RE ALL AT HOME PLAYING JENGA WITH GREAT AUNTY JUNE.

6. *Middle-class women becoming ridiculously competitive over how well prepared they are.*
   'I make my mincemeat in August.'
   'Really, I find I'm too busy with the cake in August.'
   'Oh! Ha ha. I made my cake in 1985. Fifteen years and it matures to perfection. Amazed you've never tried it.'

7. *The annual conversation about the decline in the quality of Christmas television. 'It's not been the same since Morecambe and Wise, has it?' How can they not love Noel Edmonds' House Party? Mentals not parentals.*

8. *GAJ looking at her watch to help her decide if she wants a cup of tea. SO ANNOYING. Do you want one or not? It doesn't matter what time it is.*

   (This last one is big enough for . . .)

9. *AND 10. Accidentally ending up watching a television sex scene with Mum and Dad.*

Oh, no, don't worry: we have found a way around that one. It goes like this:

MIRANDA, her MOTHER and FATHER on sofa, watching television. The nice BBC Period Drama has suddenly become unexpectedly racy.

220

MOTHER:
Oh. Right. I see. (PAUSE) SO! I thought we
could all go on a lovely Boxing Day walk
tomorrow.

ME:
Yes! Lovely! Do show me the route.

MOTHER whips open the Ordnance Survey
map. Shows MIRANDA the walk. Wild
humping and groaning noises from the
television.

MOTHER:
I thought this would be lovely. Such views!

DAD:
Oh, yes, lovely.

MIRANDA:
Oh, yes, lovely.

Humping and groaning noises get louder.

MIRANDA:
It goes up that hill then down again, I see.

MOTHER:
Yes. And then comes back round via the
church.

MIRANDA:
Lovely.

Everyone realises that the sex scene has finally

finished.

MOTHER:
(putting away the map) Well. I'm glad we got
that sorted.

MOTHER, FATHER and MIRANDA sit in silence
as if nothing has happened.

Oh yes, we find ways to manage the situation
and embrace the madness. The fact is, Little
M, you're still at the age where you're assuming
that everyone else is having normal, fun-fuelled
easy family Christmases, and it's only your family
that's bonkers. But you'll eventually realise that
all families are basically the same. Everyone's got
their version of The Mother and Great Aunty June,
and everyone experiences moments of thinking
that their family is made up of the most annoying
people ever to have walked the earth. Up and down
the nation people are shouting at their parents for
calling remote controls 'doobries', or being shouted
at for accidentally bathing the sprouts in Armagnac.
Once you accept this, you can really, truly grow to
love family time at Christmas.

The main thing, I find, is that you forget. You
forget how mad-making it really is. You noodle
through the year thinking, 'Oh, yes, Christmas, that'll
be a jolly nice and simple few days off work.' Then
the first of October rolls round, the first bit of Slade
whistles into your ears, and . . . you're off. You've all
gone crackers.

Still, we wouldn't be without it, would we? At
thirty-eight we're embracing it more than ever.
Now, excuse me, I must go and get the 16' inflatable

Christmas-pudding-shaped bauble out of the car.

Oh no, we turn into The Mother. I KNEW it . . .

Now, MDRC, I suggest that wherever and whenever you are reading this book: sun lounger on the beach in August, tucked up in bed in February, your friend's backyard in the middle of a blazing May day—you join me in a rousing carol. *takes deep breath, plunges in* 'Gloo-o-oo-or-ooh, GLOR-oh-oh-oh, GLOR-oh-oh-or-or—' No, started too high again . . . *goes down an octave* 'Gloor-oo-or-oooh . . .' That's better.

Merry Christmas, one and all.

PIT STOP!

Well, I am stuffed. I am stuffed and bloated and replete with literary mince pies (and also actual mince pies: my mouth started watering during that last chapter and I found some of last year's in the back of the cupboard. Mmm, lovely chewy stale pastry). So, methinks, it's time for another

Pit Stop. Please replenish beverages, sashay into the kitchen and make yourself a sachet-based hot chocolate. Or even—and here's a thought—a sachet-based soup. (Everyone says it's a meal, but I think we all know it's not really, don't we? It's a *drink*. A freeze-dried, sachet-based meal? Absurd. What are we, astronauts?)

I hope you're still very much with me, MDRC, jollying along by my side. If so, please put your hands in the air—wherever you may be—and offer me a hearty 'Yes, I am.' Done that? Good. Is everybody looking at you? Extra good. I'm all for healthy public affirmations of one's existence, which is what passing strangers would have assumed you'd just felt the urge to do.

So, we have jollied along through the thorny topics of Health, Holidays and Christmas, and now that Mr Mug is happily full of whatever beverage you've selected, let's gambol through our next round of tick-boxing. Please tick, with immense pride, the *triangles* below (triangles make it even more fun, don't you think?), if you've found yourself doing any of the following:

△ Written out a new To Do list. (Remember: you should always put 'Do a To Do list' at the top of it so you can immediately tick something off)

△ Fantasised about marrying a doctor

△ Appreciated an effective hand drier and a nice loo

△ Enjoyed running down a hill if you're over thirty-five

△ Managed to sit down elegantly on a picnic rug

△ Got your maracas out (not a euphemism)

224

△ Got into a fist fight with a 9' inflatable Santa.
△ Managed to play Trivial Pursuit with your family without punching anyone
△ Roused yourself with a round of 'Ding Dong Merrily On High'.

If you've achieved one or more of these things, please give yourself a high five (which is actually probably just clapping, when you think about it). Very important to celebrate victories, however tiny, I always say.

And now, to 'Task Time'. Have you told yourself you're beautiful yet? To be honest, I haven't quite managed it. I say it, then burst into fits of giggles and have to draw a moustache on my face with a Magic Marker. Perhaps we'll all have better luck with our third and penultimate task:

Channel your inner hippie. Step out of your comfort zone and go on an adventure.

GOOD LUCK AND GOD SPEED

'So, Miranda, what are we putting to rights next?' I hear you ask.

Ooh, can it be relationships now, please? Sexy, fun relationships with gorge boys? You have been avoiding this one.

OK, Little M. Fine. It's got to the point of our journey of life lessons to take a deep breath and embrace the world of relationships. Because there is one rather wonderful relationship in our life at the moment. And I think that now might be the

225

time to tell you about it.

Oh, HOORAY!

Alrighty, here we very much go . . . I invite you all to please tourner la page ('turn the page' in French). And let's get going with the goss . . . Exciting.

13

WHO'S TOP DOG?

As I said, MDRC, we're going to be tackling head-on the complex issue of significant, intimate and personal relationships. And I heartily believe that there's no more intense relationship than that between a woman and her dog—

Wait, WHAT? This is about a DOG? A **DOG!** *You said this was going to be the Big Serious Relationships chapter? You're telling me it's about an ANIMAL?*

It is about a deeply significant relationship, thank you very much to you. Hands up, we're not discussing boyfriends here. It's a dog, but . . .

Stop. I've heard enough. This is just one disappointment after another. I'm officially off. I've got far better things to do with my time. I was going to miss the debating society for this . . .

You hate the debating society.

We're debating the Republic versus the Monarchy with the boys' school. **There are boys in the school.** *Boys, not DOGS. And, by the sounds of it, I had better go and get myself married to one immediately to avoid being thirty-eight and talking about a relationship with a PET. *storms off, slamming door behind her**

That went well. As I was saying, MDRC—

there's no more interesting relationship than that between a woman and her dog. Well, that's not quite true. There's the relationship between a woman and her dry cleaner (does anyone else unnecessarily over-explain stains on garments for fear the dry cleaner may misconstrue?); the relationship between a woman and her handsome yet mysteriously noisy downstairs neighbour (anyone else find it very hard to be cross with someone 'seriously handsome'? I begin my stern complaint about unacceptable noise levels, then tail off into a girlish giggle and a snort, before scurrying red-facedly away); or the relationship between a woman and her eternally loyal takeaway delivery fellow (anyone else find it odd that you don't know the name of a person who regularly brings you food when you've just got out of the bath?). But the dog/woman dynamic is a rich and mysterious area, which I feel that you and I must make part of our little literary frolic together.

I am the owner/master/boss of a fine beast named Peggy. Peggy is a black-and-white Shih Tzu/Bichon Frise cross (two problematic breeds which have, in Peggy, come together to form something rather wonderful). I prefer, however, to spell Shih Tzu phonetically: Shit Sue. That's better. A little rude, perhaps, but Peggy doesn't mind at all. She's a good-humoured and agreeable beast, a cross between a Bichon Frise and a Shit Sue. I am not sure what the correct term is, but I hereby announce it should be: A Shitty Frise. Nice. (However, if you're taking one to a Royal Garden Party, you may wish to opt for a Bichon Sue, which is both dainty and pleasingly French-sounding. Up to you.)

228

I had no plans to own a dog, though I'd always loved them. In my youth, I even did a stint as a volunteer at Battersea Dog's Home. The bulk of my job involved sitting in the cages socialising with the dogs. All very lovely, until visitors came and peered curiously at me and the dog, through the wire, as if we both needed re-homing. I used to feel awkward and make some weak joke like, 'I don't piss on carpets; take me, ha ha ha!' or, 'My dad's a bull mastiff but I'm a poodle at heart!' (I'd just be stared back at with light pity and disdain, though I like to think the experience left me with the big, sad eyes of a woman who's just been passed over in favour of a greyhound puppy.) Still, I never saw myself as someone who'd actually *own* a dog, at least, not any time soon; not until I'd retired and gone feral in Cornwall with a smallholding, when a dog would fit nicely in amongst my hordes of chickens, cats, domesticated rabbits and the odd hand-reared-by-the-Aga farm animal. Pet sheep, anyone? Fun. But for now, no.

In fact, I'd always harboured a healthy scepticism about Dog People. To me, they seem to divide into two equally loony camps. Camp One consists mainly of Home-Counties owners who call their dogs things like Suki, Emily, George, Bella and Jaaaaasper. (That's 'Jasper' to you and me, but when pronounced with a Home-Counties elongated 'a', it becomes Jaaaaasper—please feel free to try it.) These dog owners are quite strict with their mutts and are always wandering around the park barking orders (pun absolutely intended and joyously so—am more thrilled than normal with that one) very loudly: 'Suki. Here now, please' or 'George, stop that!' and 'Bella, come, Bella, come;

come, Bella, Bella come' with 'Jaaaaasper heel, Jaaaaasper heel, Jaaaaasper will you HEEL, and put that *down*, put that DOWN; I am *so* sorry, I think he thinks your three-year-old's a joint of beef.' These dog people have children at home also called things like Suki, Emily, George, Bella and Jaaaaasper. And the children get barked at, too: 'Emily, bed. Bed, Emily' and '*Greens* George, eat your greens, NOW; George, George—greens' or 'Boarding school, Bella, to boarding school, Bella— *BOARDING SCHOOL*!'

Then there's Camp Two. These owners can be found throughout almighty pet-loving Great Britain. They call their dogs more traditional doggy names, like Pippin, Mitsy, Treacle or Buttons. They often costume their dogs (dungarees, standard party pet kaftans, sou'westers, pretty summer dresses), or chose to adorn themselves with images of their dog ('I Heart Treacle' T-shirts, dog-face-printed baseball hats, temporary tattoos). Their Christmas card is a picture of both themselves and their dog wearing Santa hats, looking 'merry'. Such fun! If they're of the Christmas newsletter persuasion then it'll say 'Love from Chris and Fiona and Pippin xxx' and there'll be a paw print at the bottom of the page.

Some of these people also experience the phenomenon of looking quite a lot like their dog. How does that happen? Do they deliberately choose a dog that looks like them? Or do they really not know it's happening? I know somebody with a long-coated red setter who looks *just* like her dog. A long face, gangly limbs, red hair. They're a pretty pair, I grant you, but I find it all most disturbing.

In both of these camps the message is: our dog is a key member of our family unit; we treat him/her/it as an equal. We give Christmas and birthday presents to them and vice versa. We know they know it's a special day. We have regular arguments about who they love most in the family and whose turn it is to play with them. We see absolutely nothing odd about this at all, thank you very much indeed.

'None of that madness for me!' I said to myself, as I spent years striding cheerfully dog-free through parks. Then along came Peggy. She belonged to a friend. I met her as a puppy. She was a black-and-white ball of fluff that fitted into the palm of my hand, and would sometimes retreat, scared, from the world and snuggle into my empty trainer. How could I refuse? I tried to resist her, I really did: I said, 'No, I am a sane adult woman, I have no need of a dog, I will not become One Of The Dog People, never.' But then I looked down at that pleading little fluff-bundle face and . . . I took her. I didn't nick her, you understand—it was all formally arranged. She became mine.

And now, every day with Peggy is a test of my mettle. Can a woman love her dog, nurture it and care for it and meet its every need, without going stark raving pet-obsessed bonkers?

I think I manage it. I'm doing OK. I don't have any photographs of my dog on display (well, apart from the two framed ones on my desk). I don't let her up on the furniture (she's only on the sofa now for a little treat). And it's not like she sleeps on my bed or anything (look, last night was an exception—it was her birthday). But, OK, hang on, at least Peggy's not noisy or troublesome (she's recently taken it upon herself to act as my protector, barking furiously whenever a male human approaches. Which explains a lot, if we're honest). It's not like I found myself saying to a friend, speaking on behalf of Peggy: 'Sorry, we're a little cross today, aren't we?' (I did, I did, I actually *did*). And it's not as if I've bought my dog a monogrammed side plate for her to eat off, whilst sitting up at table with the rest of the family (one will be arriving from Argos within thirty working days).

'Oh, dear. Oh, deary, deary me,' I hear you sigh. I sense your disappointment. But it's hard, isn't it? Are any of you reading this with a little furry friend beside you in bed, on the sofa, on your lap? Do you get sucked into those trusting eyes that stare up at you, hoping for love? Are you convinced you know what they're thinking? Do you look at them with more love than you ever thought you could feel for another living thing?

Please tell me this isn't just me and my family? I caught my father, who professes to find the cats I lumbered my parents with a complete bore, chatting away to Tommy—his favourite—whilst carrying him from the bottom of the garden back to the house to give him some food. I heard him saying, 'Guess what I've got in store for you, Tommy. Oh, yes, that's right, a delicious plate of tuna.' And then he asked him, 'What have you been getting up to, eh? Are you going off a-hunting tonight? Would you mind ever so refraining from leaving any mice on the doorstep? What's that? I know you mean it as a present, but you really needn't.' Even he can't help going a bit wonky for a lovely furry friend. What *happens* to us, MDRC?

232

I have also been known to have full-blown, freakishly intense conversations with my parents about how well the pets are getting on with each other: 'Sorry, Dad, I think Peggy chased Milly away from the food.'

'No, that's fine, she deserves it.'

'D'you think? You wouldn't say that about Tommy, would you, Dad?'

'I think I probably would.'

'You've always liked Tommy best. How do you think that makes Milly feel?'

'Milly doesn't know!'

'Oh, Milly knows, Dad. *Milly knows.* And it's her birthday today, she knows that.'

'Oh, yes, have we given her the little gift yet?'

'I am not sure she deserves one after what she got me last Christmas.'

'I thought you liked that dancing elf.'

'Well, at least it wasn't a Dictaphone.'

'What?'

'Nothing.'

I know, I know. I had better get some air and mull this all over. Come on, Peggy, walkies. Walkies, Peggy! Come on then, you. Let's put on your collar. What a pretty collar you have—don't you look pretty?

Stop it, Miranda. STOP IT. *slams house door shut, strides off out into the world*

EXT. PARK. DAY.

A pleasant London park. The park is alive with young families, happy couples, peaceful old ladies, and dogs. Great throngs and hordes of hounds, each prancing around, attached by a perilously slender lead to the arm of an attentive, devoted (some might say foolish) human.

In the midst of this appears a sombre pair. A tall, worried lady (MIRANDA) strides grimly behind what could politely be described as an imperious, four-legged ball of fluff (PEGGY).

PEGGY:
Hurry *up*, Miranda! Let's run, let's jump, ooh, look, a stick—and a *tree!* Let's go up the tree, Miranda, let's—ooh, look, a little pile of earth—I'm hungry—I want . . .

MIRANDA:
I don't care what you want. We're going this way. I'm in charge here, thank you very much.

PEGGY:
Oh, are you?

MIRANDA:
Yes. Without the slightest shadow of a doubt, *I am in charge*.

As she says this, the slightest shadow of a doubt crosses MIRANDA's face.

PEGGY:
Interesting. Very interesting you think that. (A brief, loaded pause.) Miranda, where are we going today? Where's this secret place we're going, which you are clearly too embarrassed to tell your Dear Reader Chum about?

MIRANDA:
We're going to see the (whispers) *Dog Behaviourist*.

PEGGY:
The what?

MIRANDA:
(loudly) The Dog Behaviourist.

PEGGY:
Thank you. Oooh, look, ducks! (Runs off and chases duck, returns.) I'm back! So why are we going to see the Dog Behaviourist, Miranda?

MIRANDA:
Because you're a terrible, badly behaved little scruff who sprawls all over the sofa, who . . .

PEGGY:
Hold that thought, that woman over there's having a picnic . . .

MIRANDA:
No, don't . . . Peggy . . . Peggy . . . PEGGY! . . . Oh, I *am* sorry, madam, do you want me to buy you another Scotch egg? Are you sure? Naughty Peggy. Very naughty. So sorry.

PEGGY:
(Overjoyed, overwhelmed) I got a Scotch egg! I got a Scotch egg!

MIRANDA:
That was seriously embarrassing. You see,

Peggy, *this* is the kind of thing I'm talking about. And the barking, the jumping up . . .

PEGGY:
Yes, yes, yes. I'm a scamp. But . . . *why* does the Dog Behaviourist think that I do these kinds of awful scampy things, Miranda?

MIRANDA:
Because you're just plain wrong in the head, that's why.

PEGGY:
No, that's not the reason, and you know it. The *professional, fully trained* Dog Behaviourist thinks that I like to jump up on sofas and bark at people and eat their Scotch eggs—ooh, a squirrel! Look at me run at that squirrel. *I'M GOING TO CHASE THE SQUIRREL UP THE TREE*—(darts off, returns) Alright, back. How fast was that?

MIRANDA:
I wasn't really looking.

PEGGY:
You were: it makes you laugh when I run that fast. And look how cute I am when I pant. The Behaviourist thinks I do those things because I sincerely believe that I am top dog in our pack. Our pack of two. And for some reason, you disagree.

MIRANDA:
I most certainly do. I am the language-

speaking, money-earning human, and you're just an over-eager, little dependent hairball. It's impossible for me not to be top dog. I shall now put you on the lead to prove it.

MIRANDA and PEGGY stride solemnly on. PEGGY suddenly shoots forward in order to sample a discarded wine gum. MIRANDA tugs lightly at her lead in an attempt to restrain her.

PEGGY:
Ow! That hurt both my neck and my dignity.

MIRANDA:
You have no dignity.

PEGGY:
I do, too, have dignity. And poise and grace, and a little girlish walk that you know you're jealous of, even though you won't admit it.

MIRANDA:
It's not a walk. It's a prance. A scuttle. A hop.

PEGGY:
And a very beautiful one it is, too.

PEGGY prances, scuttles and hops.

PEGGY:
Look! Look at my lovely girlish walk (sings) *'I feel pretty. Oh, so pretty—'*

MIRANDA:

(Shouting) Yeah, but, I can see your poo-hole!

PEGGY:
(Gasps) I cannot believe you would stoop so
low!

PEGGY is furious. She knows full well that
because of her delightfully stumpy little tail,
her girlish prance does, regrettably, expose
her 'poo-hole' to public view.

PEGGY: (CONT.)
Oh, that's charming. That's absolutely
charming.

MIRANDA:
I'm just saying, as top dog in this family, I am
not the one that has such an orifice on public
view.

PEGGY:
I am *still* more beautiful even with my, wotsit,
issue . . .

MIRANDA sighs.

MIRANDA:
You're very arrogant, do you know that? If it
weren't for me, you'd probably be in a dog's
home.

PEGGY:
Is that why you took me in? Was it *charity*? Am
I such a terrible *burden*? Am I—

MIRANDA:
Oh, shh. You know you're not. You know, deep
down that I—feel a . . . degree of . . . affection
for you, a bit, which—

The tension between MIRANDA and PEGGY is
mounting as they near the offices of the Dog
Behaviourist.

PEGGY:
Oh, you *do* love me, Miranda, you *do*. You
know deep down that you do. You'd miss me
if I weren't here; you know you would. You'd
miss my cheerful greeting when you come in
the door. That little noise I make—

To demonstrate, PEGGY emits a high-pitched
whinnying noise. Like a mouse doing an
impression of a horse. Despite herself,
MIRANDA smiles.

PEGGY:
I'd like to suggest, Miranda, that for all your
talk of 'crazy dog owners', I have had a
profound and wonderful effect on your life. I've
taught you what it means to fully accommodate
another creature. I've taught you how to live in
a state of complete mutual need and reliance. I
couldn't live without you, you know. I love you
and I would do anything for you. You know
when I come over and lick you when you're
doing your tummy exercise? That's because I
think you're dying: you're making such terrible
noises and I'm coming to save you. And in the
morning, I don't mean to be annoying when

the alarm goes and I jump all over you, but I am just so excited that we've got another day to spend together. You know full well that you wouldn't want to live without me. What would be the point of going for a walk without me running along beside you and jumping up into your arms when you stop to appreciate the view? You know you love our little cuddles. In fact, I'd say that I have taught you *how* to love. And I think *that*, most definitely, makes me top dog. What do you say to that? (PAUSE) Miranda?

No response from MIRANDA. PEGGY glances round at MIRANDA, fully expecting to see her mistress choked up, eyes glistening with tears.

PEGGY:
Miranda?

MIRANDA has been sending an email on her BlackBerry.

MIRANDA:
What? Sorry, I wasn't listening. Anyway, I think this is it.

They've arrived at the DOG BEHAVIOURIST. MIRANDA lets PEGGY off her lead, and ushers her in.

MIRANDA:
(Brisk) Go on. In you go.

PEGGY trots in. MIRANDA stares after her.

Tears spring to her eyes.

MIRANDA:
(Whispering) I heard every word. I love you,
little one.

OK, I give in. Here this chapter endeth.
Lots of Love, Miranda and Peggy xxx

14

MOTHERS AND CHILDREN

Big Miranda? This mad dog-bond—?

Oh, so you were listening.

I didn't go to debating society in the end. Bella thought I should bleach my moustache beforehand— everyone's doing it these days, whether we have hair there or not—but I accidentally used her Henna hair dye instead of the moustache bleach, and created a full-on moustache for myself.

blows water out like a whale for laughing Can you not tell me things like that when I am drinking? I have spewed water all over my laptop.

It is NOT FUNNY. I don't know how long it is going to take to wash out. It was black Henna dye.

What did I tell you about using Beauty Products?

I just wanted to try and get a boyfriend after the dismal dog news. And now everyone's calling me Hitler Hart.

Start doing John Cleese goose-steps and turn the joke on you—that way you've got the upper hand.

OK, brilliant, will do. Thanks. So, this dog thing? Do you not have any humans to love?

Well, yes. Lots. I love Mum and Dad, and my friends, and—

What about your children? I'm imagining you have children, yes?

Right, let's just hold our metaphorical horses— or possibly literal ones, if you're reading this in a stable. It's time for a more robust exploration of the world of . . . Mothers and Children. Settle down, Hitler Hart, and listen up.

MDRC, I don't know if you have children, are considering having children, or are about to give birth (in which case, please put this book down immediately, listen to the midwives and for goodness' sake *push* when they tell you to). Or perhaps you consider yourself still to be a child, literally or metaphorically, so having a brood of your own isn't currently an option. Perhaps you're like a thirty-eight-year-old 'man-child' from a Nick Hornby book, pursuing a monk-like, responsibility-free existence of computer games, beer and curry. In which case: grow up! Or perhaps you're of a more spiritual bent, and have recently completed a week-long workshop on 'unleashing your inner child', in which case, I hope said child is now unleashed and wreaking havoc on the Lego mat. (I nearly went to an 'unleashing your inner child' workshop so that I could do the exercise then go over to the others, push them over, spit on them, draw on their faces, draw on the walls, wee myself and sit in a corner eating Haribo. 'What?' I'd say, innocently, 'you said release your inner child. Consider her released. Wave your joss sticks at *that*.')

243

Alternatively, perhaps you're someone who's terribly modern and brave, someone who can lean confidently back in their Philippe Starck office chair, buzz their PA for a chai latte (which I always think sounds like a terrifying martial art), tighten the belt of their size six jeans, kick aside their yoga mat and intone, 'Yeah, I simply don't *want* children. Just not something I ever imagined for myself. I'm totally cool with it.'

Whichever category you fall into, I say well done. It takes all sorts to make a world.

But I would like, for one chapter only, to focus on the confusing issue of mothers. Because, is it just me, or are we currently suffering an epidemic of what I call 'extreme motherhood'? Here's the thing: it seems that some mothers today have forgotten that human beings have been breeding, simply and successfully, for an awfully long time now. They've forgotten that children were raised by *cave people*. Fine humans have grown up with the minimum of hassle and the minimum of fuss, yet this fact is ignored. The How To Bring Up Your Baby/Toddler/Teenager section of the bookshop is growing by the day, while the list of things you're supposed to buy for your child and the things they're supposed to have achieved by certain ages is getting longer and longer and more and more demanding, it seems, with every new baby that pops into the world. New mothers today are on a fear-based treadmill for bringing up their little ones.

Whilst recently spending time with Clare-Bear and her four-strong brood, I arrived during the ghastly sounding phrase that becomes common usage amongst mothers of toddlers: the Play Date.

And, indeed, it was ghastly. I could have sworn I heard the following phrase. Brace yourselves.

'Oh, my goodness! Yours isn't sleeping through yet? Theo's out like a light the second the Coronation Street *credits roll. Must be all the quinoa we're feeding him.'*

'Oh my God, oh my God, darling—Fiona's child just said "tractor"! Romeo can't even say "digger". Should we get a tutor? Yes, I think so. Someone Oxbridge.'

'But you'd expect them to be at least interested in the Ancient Norse Myths at four months, wouldn't you? I got the large-print edition, for crying out loud (which, ironically, is what her child is now doing)—oh, come on, darling, look at the lovely Norse Myths.'

I hear these kind of things, and think, 'Can we all just calm down, please?'

Occasionally I like to drive past primary schools and make my views known. I wind down my window and merrily bellow: 'They're all going to be fine, you know. It doesn't matter if they haven't been on a cathedral tour of Northern Europe by the time they do their SATs. I mean, I was just given a tin of beans and a big stick to play with, and I've turned out all right.'

I am not entirely sure about that. But Mum couldn't have done much more, could she?

Not then. But the Modern World has thrown up all sorts of ways for mothers to be extreme. It's all organic vegetables and super foods and after-school clubs and 'development' and naughty steps and no smacking and 'give them a choice'.

Mum just dropped us off at school, or at the shops in the holidays, and the rest was homework or playing on our own, with the odd slap if we didn't stick within the rules—or an extra sweet if we did. Job done.

No sweets now as, if nothing else, they might contain nuts. Anyone who is anyone has a child with an allergy. Lots of high-maintenance children who can't eat nuts or wheat or gluten (whatever that is) running around playgrounds with épée pens.

What's wrong with fish fingers for lunch, flapjacks for tea and lashings of Arctic Roll at weekends? Yum.

Arctic Roll is definitely a no-no these days.

WHAAAAATTTTTT? No Arctic Roll? Now, that IS extreme.

Fasten your seatbelt, because it's about to get much worse. Ladies, gentlemen, and my eighteen-year-old self, my scientifically vigorous research into parenthood has revealed four distinct varieties of 'Extreme Mother' currently active. Please may I draw your attention to:

1. Extreme Mother Type One
Extreme Mother Type Ones are terminally superior. The fact that they have successfully furthered their line gives them, they believe, superiority over all other human beings,

especially over single, childless women. However, they reserve an extra-special bit of scorn for any of their fellow mothers who may not be getting it 'quite right'.

Type One mothers generally end up with three to four children who will be given names like Bruschetta, Vinaigrette and Focaccia (girls) or Marmaduke, Frappuccino and Aspinal (boys). These names will be abbreviated to Chetta, Gretty, Cacci, and Marm, Frappers and Asp, which will make the Type One mothers sound, when they're calling to their children, a bit like someone marshalling an Italian football team.

Type One mothers may have husbands who present a united front, and appear to enjoy dressing their sons up in matching Boden shirts of a weekend. Or they *may* have husbands who are absolutely shocked and mortified at what their lives and wives have become, and who spend their time bent over in an apologetic stoop, muttering, 'Sorry-sorrysorrysorrysorry-sorrysorrysorrysorry' as their wives maraud around the school sports day like little floral-clad dictators.

Extreme Mothers Type One take pride and joy in two things. First, the fact that they own the largest 4x4 on the market, which was made missile-safe in Afghanistan and can hold fourteen Bugaboos and a Waitrose picnic, no probs. Secondly, the fact that they lost the baby weight (and a little something extra, to boot) via an extreme, military style 'Mams and Prams' exercise class within six weeks of each child's birth.

Extreme Mother Type One is by far the

extremest type of Extreme Mother.

2. Extreme Mother Type Two

Extreme Mother Type Two is marginally less extreme than her Type One counterpart. She takes motherhood a fraction less seriously but is, nonetheless, determined to maintain the illusion of absolute togetherness and control. No, the baby will not get the better of Extreme Mother Type Two, at least not in public. The pram is top-notch Maclaren. The baby changing mat is Cath Kidston, the canvas sack with all the neatly labelled tupperwares full of nutritionally balanced food is Cath Kidston, the clips to keep the packets of organic rice cake snacks fresh are Cath Kidston. This woman is Cath Kidston-ed beyond reproach. She can also be identified by the fact that, despite having three children, her car is oddly clean. This is one of the ways in which she silently competes with other mothers. The other way is via the OTT nurturing of her child's embryonic gifts and talents: 'He clapped! At Monkey Music. He clapped! Darling, eBay us a Xylophone; he's the new Mozart!'

When safely ensconced in her own home, Extreme Mother Type Two then falls into one of two categories. In the spirit of being mathematically precise, let's call them '2A' and '2B'.

Category 2A will keep up the beautifully controlled façade by breezing through the front door, forcing through her tiredness with a song, and maybe treating herself to a little homemade something from the Cath Kidston cookie jar for a modest, non-waistline-damaging sugar rush.

Category 2B, on the other hand, will crash

through the door, give in to the tears that she's been holding back all day, weep and wail and bellow as she chars the fish fingers, then stagger to the drinks cabinet (kicking over a stray Jenga tower), to crack open a bottle of wine and shop for more Cath Kidston on her iPad. However, if 'company' were to appear at the front door, 2B would be able to sober up, spritz on some Jo Malone and have an aubergine parmigiana from the oven in three minutes flat. And she'll serve it up whilst telling tender stories of how 'Motherhood's really offered me a chance to give something back, you know?'

I warn you, 2B is a very sneaky beast.

3. Extreme Mother Type Three

Extreme Mother Type Three is extreme in a rather different fashion. Some would call her slovenly. Some would say that she simply 'says it like it is'. Type Three mother will confidently approach a Type One mother in the park and say, 'Oh, yeah, sorry about the sick on the shirt. No point changing it, I thought. It'll only get sicked on again. Ha!' Type One mother will respond to this by nervously peeling her child away from the sick-smeared Type Three, saying pointedly, 'Focaccia, please come here, I am taking you to ballet now, and then we shall be learning how to make moussaka for dinner.' Type Three won't care about this—she'll have found a stray Tangfastic in the front pocket of her coat and will be eating it hungrily (the Type Three mother cares little for dieting). Type Two mothers are absolutely thrilled that Type Three mothers exist, as they present no threat to them whatsoever. The Type Three mother's car is a stew-pot of wet biscuits, toy trucks, chocolate wrappers and two-year-old juice cartons. She'll be able to comfortably socialise with friends who don't have children, as she doesn't subscribe to the theory that her kids watching an hour of telly while she has a natter with her mates is going to ruin them for life. Type Three mother will also occasionally find herself of an evening in front of the telly saying, 'Oh my goodness, I haven't had a bath for three days.'

4. Extreme Mother Type Four

Our final type of Extreme Mother is a one of a very special breed. She is the 'Too Much Information' mother. Every morning, she'll arrive at the nursery gates and tell the other mothers how sore her breasts are, how hard the little one bit last night, how often the toddler woke up, when she last had sex and what that was like for the first time, post-birth. 'Urh, urh, urh, urh, stop, please!' is what you really want to shout loudly in her face, but you maintain a fixed, middle-class smile. You took to avoiding her while she was pregnant, as she used to grab your hand and place it on her tummy, failing to notice that you winced in horror at the feel of her popped-out belly button. Is it just me, or am I the only one not interested in feeling a baby kick from outside a womb? I will go as far as to say this: IT FREAKS ME RIGHT OUT. *I* will decide when to show an interest in your child— probably at three, when they are potty-trained and can say funny things. But Type Four won't notice your displeasure, and will later tell you all the details of the birth, ignoring my cardinal life rule that the only context in which the word 'stirrups' should be used is when talking about stables.

Finally, Type Four will pass a lot of her time attempting to make friends with other mothers via activity groups. Sample phrase: 'I've had this amazing idea! Percussion for Parents. Week one—castanets. We shake it all out, and the toddlers dance. Like we're a Spanish village!'

Now, I worry I may have painted you a rather bleak picture. If so, forgive me. I am merely an observer. I appreciate the deep and wonderful rewards of parenthood and genuinely admire all you parents. You're capable of enduring trials I can't even begin to fathom, which is why I have yet to bow to the societal pressures of the need to breed. Thereby so far avoiding the horrors of parenthood, which I will forever be in awe of. If nothing else, telling your children about the birds and the bees.

Every parent must dread this moment. I firmly believe that there is no right answer to the question, 'Mummy, where do babies come from?' In the course of my aforementioned rigorous and scientific research, I have come across the following answers:

'Babies come from the love between a man and a woman which happens when the lights are out and everybody's feeling nice.' **(This child is likely to develop a fear of the dark.)**

'Babies are made by a special hug which mummies and daddies do when they get married without any clothes on.' **(This child will grow up wondering why people bother to dress for weddings.)**

251

'Well, Mummy and Daddy do what the guinea pig sometimes does to the rabbit when he's cross, except they both want to do it, and they do it because they love each other, not just because they're in the same cage and they're confused.' **(This child will be unpacking that in therapy for years.)**

No, really, parents, I respect you enormously. If there were no parents in the world, then I would not exist (which would, of course, be the most dreadful of tragedies). I have the deepest of deep respects for you all. And if I do decide to take the leap, I'm not sure I'd make the grade. Talking of which, I should, if you don't mind, take this opportunity to formally tell eighteen-year-old Miranda that we don't actually have children yet. Wish me luck . . .

Ahem . . .

Little Miranda stirs herself from a deep, sugary, post-Arctic-Roll nap Wha—? Oh, hello. What do you want?*

Don't be grumpy with me, young lady.

Excuse me; you are NOT my mother. Please go and mother your own children and leave me be.

How pertinent. I rather cut short our earlier conversation to talk about extreme motherhood. But it's now high time that I swept in on the matter of children. So here I am a-sweeping. Watch my grown-up wisdom sweeping at you. Look at me sweep . . .

252

Get on with it.

Soz. Little Miranda, I have to tell you that at the age of thirty-eight, we remain childless.

WHAT? But that's . . . IMPOSSIBLE. I've made a plan. I made it with Podge, Milly and Clare-Bear three years ago at break when we were making a cat's cradle out of red liquorice laces. AND I explicitly explained it to the careers officer. We're going to meet someone when we're twenty-three, having set up a business; marry them when we're twenty-five, then we'll spend a year or two being really successful at our careers, then settle down and have three babies called Jason, Kylie and Donovan.

I see. Well, the thing is . . .

I don't think you do see. It's all mapped out.

Please stop interrupting. You are very interrupty today.

Interrupty isn't a word. I might have barely passed English GCSE but I know that interrupty isn't a word . . .

Well, actually, umm . . . in the last twenty years it has been declared a word, by . . . er . . . Angela Rippon.

Really?

Yup. So, if I may continue my wise sweep . . .? I'm here to tell you that it's a good thing we don't have children. We're happy.

HOW are we happy? Everyone has children. It's the rules. And how does your husband feel about this?

Ah, yes, well, we don't actually quite have a husband yet, either.

Have we been in PRISON? Have we spent the last twenty years in prison? Because that's the only possible explanation for the life you currently appear to be leading.

No, we have not. I think you'll find that I'm a bright, sociable, erudite woman (say nothing, MDRC) and, as a bright, sociable erudite sort of woman (again, shush), over the years you'll be bound to accumulate a fair bundle of friends. And, over time, a large number of them will have their own children. Which often results in being given the joy and honour of becoming a godparent. In my case, thrice over, if you please.

Why would anyone ask YOU to be a godparent?

I have a theory about this. Any one child has, on average, three godparents. And out of those three, one will be rich, one will be wise, and the third will be the 'pity godparent'—the sad one that the parents sort of felt they had to ask, to perk up their otherwise seemingly meaningless life.

And you are—?

WISE. I'm the wise one, obviously.

254

Say something wise, then.

Oh—uh—all right, umm . . . 'The river which runs the deepest . . . also runs . . . uh—the . . . nicest.'

Hmm . . .

No, no, wait. 'Don't put all your eggs in one basket because . . . you might spill milk . . .' No, hang on, hang on—'Don't count your chickens before . . . you've looked at a gift horse . . .' OK, right, I know, I know . . . 'Never go to the supermarket when you're hungry.' There you go. Doesn't get wiser than that. Fact.

You're the pity one.

I'm the wise one, I tell you. *Wise.*

You're deluded. You could be standing at the font between Donald Trump and the Dalai Lama and you'd still think you were the 'wise' one. Anyway, what's so marvellous about being a godparent? It sounds dweeby to me.

Loads of things. First and foremost—you get to give them back. Did you hear me? You can give the children back. Joy. Brilliant. The minute the child cries, you immediately hand it straight back to it's mother in a swift rugby pass manoeuvre (although do make sure the baby isn't at any point airborne, as it turns out that isn't funny). Godparenting has all the perks of being a parent without any of the bother. I mean, I love children, but after a while

255

I simply can't bear being with them . . . Oh, come on, it's what we all think! Children, with all their jumping and shouting and wobbly teeth and silly handwriting. If I wanted to spend time with a bunch of kids who think the height of good taste is picking their bogies with a teaspoon, I'd go to a rugby match.

High five, good joke.

Thanks. I do, of course, love spending time with my godchildren. After all, you can buy them presents that you, basically, want to play with yourself. Wicked pirate outfits. Scalextric. Subbuteo men. Toy post offices that you can just fit in even at thirty-eight (though, disappointingly, you do need to remove the roof). But this doesn't stop me pretending to be the post-mistress. Once in, you can write fake letters to the Queen and the Pope and your favourite musical theatre actresses (NB: do make sure your godchildren don't put a real stamp on said letters. Ruthie Henshall must have been confused by a few of her recent letters.)

So, feeling any better about godparent-hood, Little Miranda?

Maybe a little.

If it helps, you also get to do babysitting. Babysitting's brilliant. Obviously I'm talking about the kind of babysitting where the children are soundly asleep in bed before you arrive, and all you actually have to do is watch television, which somehow feels rather illicit and thrilling because you're doing it in someone else's house. Then there's the hallowed babysitting phrase . . . wait for it . . . 'Please do help yourself to anything in the fridge.' *Sings* *'Alleluia, alleluia, alleluia.'* What's the first thing we all do, after seeing the parents drive off? *Rush* to see what's in the fridge. That's not just me, is it? We all fall upon that fridge like a vulture. My question: how much can I eat without it being rude? My answer: all of it. She said 'Help yourself to *anything* in the fridge.' 'Anything' surely also means 'everything': that's just basic language. A pound of lasagne, a twelve-man apple crumble and nine Babybels later—thank you very much.

But what about when the children are old enough to talk? Aren't you meant to give them spiritual guidance and stuff?

Absolutely not. That is the last thing you should do. No, when they get older, it's even better. When they're old enough to know what you're all about, they'll start to view you as a visiting rock star: a desperately groovy figure with innate glamour who occasionally bursts into their humdrum, well-balanced little family life with ten sacks of Haribo and the original cast recording of *Shrek the Musical.*

So that's all there is to it? Vamping in and out with presents?

Yep. And the odd outing, which is marvellous. You can take them to places that you secretly want to go to but can't visit by yourself. I once went to a zoo on my own in my early thirties. I was really enjoying myself before suddenly, in the marsupials enclosure, I realised that I must have looked like a woman on the edge. (The bum bag and cagoule didn't help, sure. But both are comfortable practical attire and, I think, most unfairly tarred with the weirdo brush.) Going to establishments that are meant for children, as an adult, is a tricky life issue, I find. Even if you went to the zoo or Chessington World of Adventures or Cadbury World as one half of a couple, without children it feels a bit . . . wrong. You wonder if people are looking at you, trying to guess who's the one being taken for a 'special day out'. But with a child by your side, you can pretend your squeals of delight on the log flume are just to keep the kids happy.

Well, that does all sound a bit—

Perfect. It's absolutely perfect. Don't worry, Little Miranda. There'll be plenty of childishness in your future. There'll be sleepless nights and tantrums and sugar binges and little toy post offices and face painting and sing-songs and games. It just won't be a child who's doing them. It will be you. Wonderful, thirtysomething you.

That does actually sound OK.

It is. It really is. I mean, take this moment. Right now. As I write, it's three o'clock in the morning. I can't sleep, so I'm at my desk. I'm wearing pyjamas and an apron, and Marigolds. I am wearing the latter because I have decided it would be fun to eat a jelly with my hands. Yes, I am eating jelly at three o'clock in the morning, and when I've finished writing this chapter, I'll have a little dance around my living room to Billy Joel's 'Uptown Girl'. I'll probably knock something over, but do you know what? No one's going to make me clear it up. I can just lollop off to bed, sleep in my jelly-stained apron till ten the next day, then scamper out wondering what fresh disaster awaits me. Life is very nice, thank you.

OK, I am convinced. Now can I go and watch **Neighbours?** *Madge and Harold get together today, apparently. Urh but aah.*

You may go. For I sweepeth in, and now I sweepeth out. Laters, little one.

So, MDRC, here is what I conclude on the subject

of mothers and children. Firstly, that being a godparent prior to having your own children, or as a substitute, is a wonderful gift. All of the fun; none of the work.

My second conclusion is that all our well-intentioned extreme-mother-types should try to embrace a little calm. I know I speak with no authority at all on the subject, but as you know by now, I do enjoy speaking with no authority on subjects I know nothing about.

I said at the beginning of my what I call, book, that as adults we spend such vast amounts of our time worried what people think, trying to get through each day without causing a fuss, or looking like a fool. But children don't have that worry. They're free. They are, for that blissful time in their lives, free of all social convention and stress. So, please, please, please, don't force them to wear the right things, eat the right things, learn and do the right things. No parent can ever get it right but, much more importantly, if you're basically decent and kind then it's hard to get it particularly wrong. We've all turned out all right—so let them play. Let them be a mess. Give them a tin of beans and a big stick and cast them loose in the backyard with an Arctic Roll.

Because, think about it—how great would it be to live life like a child, right now? *Is* it just me who, deep down, yearns to go on the swings, make dens, and wander into any old playground and find an equal-sized, willing partner for the see-saw? Imagine for a moment playing by children's rules. If you were at a party and saw someone you liked, you could just go and hold their hand. If they then try to kiss you and you don't like it, you can push them over. If your aunty gives you a Christmas present that you're not too keen on, you can throw it back in her face and burst into tears. You can gallop freely. You can skip. Children have got it right. The tragedy is, none of this is permissible as an adult. Although one thing surely is—and I'll bet you know what I'm going to say—that's right, the *galloping*. Such fun!

Now it seems that this chapter endeth, which means it's time for me to finish the jelly, bung on the Billy Joel and have a little dance. Who says we can't be free like kids from time to time?

Little Miranda rushes back in Actually, hang on. Kids aside, I've decided I need a little more explanation about this whole 'no husband, no serious relationship' business, if you please. And I'm sure your fabled reader chum is a tad curious as well—just what ON EARTH has been going on for you in that department?

deep breath Oh, all right then. I suppose it is time. Fasten your seatbelt, MDRC, and batten down the hatches as we bravely sail forth into the world of . . . DATING. We're in for a bumpy ride . . .

15

DATING

Clears throat Ahem. As you may or may not remember, MDRC, depending on what you've been doing between chapters (perhaps you've mown the lawn or knocked up a tart—if you'll pardon the expression), at the end of the previous chapter I warned you that we were in for a bumpy ride. Fasten your seatbelt, I recommended, buckle up and brace yourself and batten down the hatches (though maybe batten down the hatches first, because if you've already buckled up and braced yourself you might not be able to reach them to batten them down effectively. What do you mean I've gone too far with the analogy . . .?). I mentioned that we were going to be exploring the weird and wonderful, wild and wacky world of dating.

This is where it all kicks into gear. Let me be your Carrie Bradshaw, let me guide you through the saucy mysteries of ladies and men and shoes and rules and sexiness and banter and my own hilarious, marvellous, wicked and wonderful stories of romping through the world of dates. Yes, siree. Dates, second dates, the first kiss and all the subsequent shenanigans. *teeters on imaginary Manolo Blahniks, sips Cosmopolitan, adjusts Wonderbra* Except . . . umm . . . scratch that, as I'm afraid that's not going to happen. There's really no need for you to fasten your seatbelt (unless you happen to be driving a car and, if so, please put this book down immediately and FOR GOODNESS' SAKE FOCUS ON THE ROAD); you should also feel free to leave the hatches unbattened, for this, quite frankly, isn't going to be a very bumpy ride at all.

To be honest, and I know you'll be extraordinarily surprised to hear this: I am not an experienced 'dater'. I don't even *know* many people who are. At least, not in this country. I have a theory (the sort of well-thought-out theory that's concocted in the darkest reaches of the night, whilst eating drinking-chocolate powder with a spoon and pairing up my socks in a mad insomniac thought-binge), that the whole concept of dating is an elaborate trick played on British people by the makers of American television programmes. Because, really, who here *dates*?

MDRC, are *you* an experienced dater? Have you been known to sit elegantly on a bar stool on a week night, sipping a cocktail, awaiting a tall and handsome man? And, while we're sort of on the subject of cocktails, can we just take a moment to ponder the whole terrible business of cocktail-umbrella etiquette? Does one remove the umbrella and place it neatly on the bar, or is that offensive to the barman? And if it is, must you drink the cocktail with it still in, and risk being blinded by the little pokey stick? What's a girl to do? Sometimes the umbrella covers such a large portion of the drink that you have to sip at a very awkward angle in order to get any liquid near your mouth. And it's not a sexy angle, not at all. Boldly I say this: drink doesn't need an umbrella. It is already wet. I'm digressing a little, I can see, but I think it was, quite frankly, irresponsible of *Sex and the City* not to cover the whole cocktail-umbrella issue, and it's my duty—nay, pleasure—to bring it up now. You're welcome.

So, *do* you date? Have you ever found yourself in that rom-com datey moment at the end of an evening with a man you like, and suddenly you think 'Maybe I need to do something sexy; something that someone in a film would do,' so you opt for the swishing-your-hair-and-laughing move that Julia Roberts does so nicely? Ever done that? How did that work for you? A success? Or did a gust of wind suddenly fling your hair all over your face and make you look like a cave man? I tried it once, but with short hair it just looked as if I was having a small seizure. No kiss, but I did get a lift home from the paramedics.

Maybe you've been on a date, had a meal and then it ended with a nice romantic walk? Have you managed to elegantly teeter along in those high heels without getting them caught in something and leaving the shoe behind so you end up doing a few steps with a large limp? Or have you, like me, showed that you're a little bit cold of an evening—you know, revealed your feminine vulnerable side . . . only for it to backfire spectacularly as when your beau gallantly offers you his jacket, you take it and then realise you can't fit it on? That it simply won't go on over your upper arms? What does one do then? I went for the, 'Actually, I'm suddenly rather hot, don't worry,' thereby suggesting a pre-menopausal symptom. Not sexy.

Be honest, have you ever mastered any of these dating scenarios that this lovely life presents us, cruised adorably through them, to end up with the man of your dreams? Is it just me who's convinced that only a certain kind of woman from New York could do so—and perhaps only a fictional woman?

From what I can see, in this country, people just tend to sort of . . . bump into each other. Maybe in the pub, or in the office, or at the library. They then stare moodily at each other across the bar/desk/bookshelf for a bit, harbour wild romantic fantasies about the other for anything between five minutes and eighteen months, then eventually arrange it so that they'll bump into each other at a social event. Throughout said event they'll then make it abundantly clear that THIS IS NOT A DATE. WE ARE NOT ON A DATE. HA HA HA! IMAGINE IF WE WERE. THAT WOULD BE AWFUL. They'll then possibly get drunk

265

and snog each other, occasionally breaking off to reassure the other that this is an 'ironic' snog. Four years later, somehow, after one trip to the theatre, a couple of nights in watching the *X Factor* together and one BBQ where they meet each other's friends, they'll get married. That, according to my best observations, is How Dating Works In Britain.

You might think, 'Well, that's a bit depressing, Miranda. How unromantic.' But I'm just not sure that Brits are suited to the high stakes created by a formal dating ritual. A date, a proper date, is just a bit embarrassing, isn't it? A bit . . . staged. Is *anyone* really comfortable with the notion of sitting across from someone else in a quiet restaurant, so quiet that anything you say can—and will—be overheard by the surrounding diners? (Why doesn't anyone *talk* in those restaurants?) Then there's the end of the evening. You know the bit: you're going to have to say goodbye with that awkward peck on lips or cheeks, or someone's going to have to work up the confidence to ask someone into someone's house. I mean, really, what are we—Italian?

So I'm afraid I have very little advice to offer you as far as dating is concerned. I cheerfully wash my hands of the whole business.

uncharacteristically meek Er, hello.

Gosh, Little M. What on earth is wrong with you? You look terrified. Have you got a big lacrosse match on or something?

I wish I had a big lacrosse match on. Lacrosse is easy. You just run at people with a big stick and hit them in the teeth. No, this is far, far worse. I've got to

266

go out with . . . with . . . with a boy.

Oh dear, you poor frightened little poppet.

He goes to the local boys' school. We met at an inter-school choir-athon—

Sexy.

—and when Mr Selbourne the music teacher asked who wanted to come and sing the **Requiem** *next term, we were the only ones to put our hands up. And we smiled at each other. He's even taller than I am, and has intense eyes like David Hasselhoff in* **Baywatch.** *And he didn't mind that I was the only girl in the tenor section.*

Pretend you didn't hear that, MDRC.

He's asked me to meet him outside the corner shop. He said he'd buy me a Fanta and some white mice . . .

I hope he meant the sweets, not some actual small mammals, because that would be weird *laughing at her own joke*

This is no time for crappy jokes. Podge says that Clare-Bear says Twig says that Bella—who knows his sister's best friend's cousin—says he's never snogged anyone before and he'll probably try and lunge. I haven't kissed many boys before and I don't think I want him to lunge. I practised on my pillow last night, and Bella made a fake mouth from an orange but I was hungry, so I just ate it.

267

Listen, if you don't want to kiss him, you don't have to. If you see the lunge coming, then quickly bend down to 'tie your shoelaces'.

That's clever.

I am here to serve.

Bella says that usually if a boy's going to lunge he'll try and hold your hand first. But as Podge said, if we're eating white mice and drinking Fanta, we won't have any hands free.

If anyone knows what's achievable whilst holding sweets, it's Podge.

Please stop treating this lightly. I'm scared. What happens if he puts his tongue in my mouth?

Well, it does happen.

But it CAN'T. Bella says that if you kiss with tongues on the first date then you go on a 'slag register', and can't get married in the Church of England.

laughs so hard, inhales Diet Coke up nose Bella said that? And we all thought Bella was the cool one, the worldly one; the one with brothers who knew it all.

Oh, this is awful. I'm going to hide in the sports cupboard for a bit.

You do that, Little M. Pop out again when you're ready to chat.

MDRC, I imagine you might be a bit worried that my eighteen-year-old self is so shockingly naïve and unschooled as regards the ways of luuuurve. I was, as you may have a gathered, a bit of a late developer. Particularly in that sense. Ditto all my friends. I appreciate this might just be me, unless you were also at an all-girls school in the 80s.

You see, an all-girls school (worse for me too, with it being a boarding school) isn't terribly conducive to developing a particularly healthy attitude towards the opposite sex. Starved of actual living men, we lived off rumour. The first things that any boarding-school girl in the late 1980s would have heard about all that business were based entirely on something that the most hysterical/malevolent/imaginative girl in the school had said late one night.

Imagine the scene: it's midnight, and eight girls in Laura Ashley pyjamas are sitting cross-legged on a bed listening to Pandora, the head girl's younger sister, as she relays the ten love truths that have been passed round 300 girls of various ages and levels of hysteria, via a kind of faulty Chinese Whispers system. Here is what we were told:

1. 'If you kiss with tongues, you become legally French.'
2. 'You can get pregnant from sitting on a rugby ball which a boy has recently sat on.'
3. 'If you kiss a boy in a churchyard the dead people come out of their graves and scream.'
4. 'You can get pregnant if you hold hands and you've both got cuts on your hands.'
5. 'If you get off with a boy in your mum and dad's bed, it's the same as having sex with

your mum and dad.'

6. 'You can get pregnant from toilet seats.'
7. 'If a boy can still sing soprano in the choir after the third form it means he's a eunuch and you can use him as your servant.'
8. 'If you hold hands and jump in a river on May Day then you're legally married in Sussex.'
9. 'You can get STDs from shaking hands if both your hands are sweaty.'
10. 'English people can't get pregnant in Germany.' *(I believe this was originally said by someone trying to seduce a young man on a German exchange visit).*

As I say, it wasn't the best grounding. The only other source of information came via the odd 'trendy' teacher like Miss Manning. During class, she'd lower her voice conspiratorially and say things like, 'I've got quite a history in that department, you know; don't get me started on *men.*' We'd lean in expectantly, hungry for insights. 'If you learn only one thing from me, learn this . . .' she'd say. 'Wow,' we'd think. 'This teacher is *breathtakingly* saucy.' In *Sex and the City* terms, she was our Samantha. 'What *is* she going to reveal next?' Then with a faraway look in her eye, she'd say, '*Never* trust a man who's trying to sell you a second-hand refrigerator. Once the deal is done, he won't be calling you again.' We'd lean back in our chairs, certain that she'd just said something terribly profound and filthy. What did it mean? Was it euphemistic? Were we the refrigerator? Was *he*? Bella spun the rumour that 'The Refrigerator' was some kind of perverted sex move only done at orgies in nineteenth-century France. To this day, I can't look at an Currys catalogue without wincing.

A few years later, we realised this teacher wasn't quite who we thought she was. She wasn't our Samantha. It became clear that Miss Manning lived in a three-room bungalow with Miss Jenvey. They had three cats between them. Miss Manning taught Religious Education, and Miss Jenvey taught P.E. Furthermore, Miss Jenvey had a wardrobe consisting solely of 'weekday tracksuits' and 'weekend tracksuits' (the weekend ones had fluorescent stripes down the sides of the legs, and would sometimes be worn with Birkenstocks). The idols had fallen. We had no one—*no one*—who was in any way fit to teach us the mysterious and wonderful ways of luuurve. We remained heartily confused.

We did have sex education classes, of course. I understand that, in these enlightened times, Sex Ed is pretty comprehensively taught. Condoms on bananas, lengthy discussions about the emotional impact sex can have on a young lady, etc. But in 1987 in a deeply traditional girls' boarding school, Sex Ed was, if anything, more perplexing than frightening . . .

All 200 girls from ages fourteen to sixteen were summoned to sit in the school hall one morning, having heard from Milly in the fourth form that we were to be dealt a lesson of 'sheer, dirty filth'.

Miss Black the headmistress entered, looking embarrassed and hot. Miss Webb the biology teacher trotted in miserably behind her, and pinned a crude pencil-drawing of the human reproductive organs to the blackboard. All 200 girls tilted our heads to one side and squinted.

271

Miss Black then stepped up to the lectern, her gown billowing dramatically behind her, almost knocking the lectern over. She recovered and cleared her throat.

'Now—ahem—good morning. Today is your'—at this point Miss Black lowered her voice—'sex education lesson.' Her voice went back to its previous pitch. 'Please observe the posters behind me,' she said, indicating with a long stick, 'which show the basic layout of the'—again, the lowered voice—'*pubic* areas of the body.' Back to the normal level. 'Whether you know it or not, you yourself have such an area. Of course, during the *sexual* act, the male and female *pubic* areas join, which is a lovely and smashing thing to do of an evening if there's nothing good on the television. But know this, girls'—she put her shoulders back and looked authoritative. This is it, we thought.—'if there IS something good on the television and you DON'T want to do it, then you are well within your rights to JUST SAY NO. Do you hear me? JUST SAY NO. JUST. SAY. NO.'

The headmistress stopped, embarrassed, and muttered something that sounded like, 'Jolly good, that's that, then,' and scurried from the hall. It was only later that we learned that Miss Black occupied the third room in Miss Manning and Miss Jenvey's bungalow, and had recently been through a very nasty divorce.

We did have one teacher who was actually a Mrs, and seemingly happily married with two children. So, after prep one night, encouraged by Milly who'd just got an invitation to her first black-tie ball, a few of us gingerly approached her for much-needed advice on the subject of

272

flirting. She drew herself up to her full height and said, surprisingly, 'Girls, it's quite simple; it's all about the breasts. You need to enhance them: throw your shoulders back, consider a plunging neckline, pad your bra with jelly, whatever it takes. Once the breasts are in play, the whole game changes. They'll be putty in your hands.'

Well, this was a bit of a revelation (except to Twig, who was still size AA and had no need for a bra). The trouble was that that was really the only direct advice we'd ever been given. So we all acted upon it enthusiastically—a little too enthusiastically, perhaps.

A few terms later, at a Harvest Festival barn dance (oh yes), I spied a line dancer who rather took my fancy. I decided that now was the time to use that teacher's stunning advice: I was going to employ my breasts. I was finally going to make them work for me. This was their moment.

I approached the line dancer, took a deep breath, and tried to bring to mind an interesting fact about my breasts. I came up with the words that, if you know me well, you may be familiar with: 'Hi. When I'm naked in bed and I roll over, my breasts clap.'

He stared at me for a moment, and then line-danced gently away. Sex Education had failed me once again.

*   *   *

So is it any wonder Little M's so frightened right now, as she embarks on what is her first date? She hasn't got a clue what's about to happen to her. From my privileged position in the future, I *could* tell her that what's going to happen is this: she'll meet the boy outside the village shop at half past four. She'll be too nervous to speak, or make direct eye contact, so they'll nod at one another, like spies on a mission. In an attempt to pay Miranda a compliment, the boy will say, 'You're really tall, aren't you?' Miranda will blush girlishly, and respond, 'Yes. Jolly tall.' They will then go into the shop and buy some white mice and Fanta, which they'll silently consume whilst sitting on the verge outside the shop. Emboldened by sugar, the boy will lunge towards Miranda. She won't have time to bend down to 'tie her shoelaces' and he'll have grabbed the back of her head, mashing his face into hers until their mouths meet. Miranda and the boy will then separate. He'll pass back Miranda's white mouse that got wedged in his mouth at some point during the exchange. She'll throw it over her shoulder, and it'll hit a passer-by. They will then say a shy goodbye and return to their respective schools. Miranda will be red-faced and traumatised for a week, unable to talk about her experience, no matter how urgently and persistently her friends demand the details. The boy, however, will tell his entire dormitory that he and Miranda had 'full sex', which was 'brilliant'. Miranda will then be surprised and rather delighted by the attention she receives at the next inter-school disco. The rumour, of course, is that she 'puts out'. Which Miranda will think is a reference to putting out the bins at night. And she'll be thrilled to be thought such a useful and handy person who's willing to help with mundane domestic tasks. Which is why she'll keep talking about bin liners, to the confusion of all those around her.

But I think that it's best not to tell Little Miranda this. She'll find out soon enough. Let's keep Mum. *knocks on the door of the sports cupboard* Little M? It's twenty past four. Time to get out now. You're going to be late.

I can't go. I'm too scared. I don't know what we'll talk about. I've learnt the rules of football, so we could talk about those . . .

Um . . . well, I don't think you'll be doing too much talking.

WHAT?! D'you mean we'll . . . we'll be doing the thing that can't get you pregnant in Germany?

Oh! Well—I wouldn't want to ruin it for you. But—no. Don't you worry about *that*.

Right, but—OK, I'm NOT happy about what I'm about to do, but I am going to officially swallow my pride and ask you for some advice. Namely—what happens? What do people DO on dates?

Um—well—they—sometimes they have some food, and sometimes they talk about . . . stuff . . . and—um—

Come ON! I'm going to be late.

Um . . . oh, right, yes. Oh! I know. Here's a dating tip: 'Don't play hard to get with a man who's hard to get.' There.

That doesn't sound like something you'd say. Were

you quoting from something?

I was quoting from *Sex and the City*.

But what about your own life experiences? I mean, you're not married, so you must be out dating men all the time. Right? Am I right? Please tell me I'm right.

Um . . .

Oh God. This is a disaster. You don't know anything, do you? You're some kind of weird virgin nun loser.

No! And, RUDE. I have had relationships; they just didn't come about via this sort of . . . formal dating ritual thing.

Well, how did they come about, then?

One of them had a swimming pool. And, as you know, we love swimming, so I sort of stuck around. For five years, until I'd had enough of the smell of chlorine. And the other one worked in a bakery where I used to buy crumpets every day, and things just sort of . . . happened.

Two 'SORT OF' relationships? Is that it?

Well, then there was one man. I mean, we were kind of in a relationship. He'd come round, we'd have a meal, he'd often see me in my dressing gown, he was enigmatic, there was little conversation . . .

Wow. What was that all about?

Well, it was sort of . . . I suppose it was kind of more of a business relationship. He was sort of bringing the food round. And sometimes we'd share a keema naan if I'd over-ordered.

He was the TAKEAWAY MAN? You had a relationship with the takeaway man?

Um—well, it wasn't really a relationship, as such. He just sort of brought the food several times a week, and I ate it, and I paid him, then we went our separate ways.

Right. Because I don't think that actually counts as having a relationship. I think that's just 'ordering lots of takeaways from the same place'.

It's kind of intimate! And he gave me a birthday card once, so—

You used the takeaway place so much they knew your birthday? Mortificato. This really isn't what I want to hear. What about being taken out? Romantic dinners à deux? Restaurants and wine?

There have been quite a lot of restaurants and wine.

BY YOURSELF DOESN'T COUNT! Tell me, Big Miranda—am I about to go on our first and last date?

Yes. Sort of. Ooh—actually. Not quite. We do go on one more official, organised date. Although, it wasn't actually technically MY date. You see, nowadays there's a thing called 'internet dating'— it's like Lonely Hearts, but lots of people do it. You put all your details on the computer, and then if people like them they contact you, and you can go on dates to get to know each other.

But what's to stop people just lying to make people like them?

Absolutely nothing. That's the flaw and possibly the beauty of it. But it's not the only way. There's also 'speed dating', if you'd rather meet someone face to face before you decide whether or not you want to spend an evening with them.

Speed dating?

You know those police identity parades they use to catch criminals? It's a bit like that. Except instead of trying to pick a criminal out of a line-up, you're trying to pick a boyfriend. And instead of just looking at them you talk to them as well, for three minutes. And instead of being in a police station, you're in a bar. And instead of having to be sober, you pretty much have to be drunk.

This is Sodom and Gomorrah! This is how you meet people? Lying on the internet and drunken, three-minute identity parades? Maybe Miss Jenvey had the right idea after all. I'm off to buy a selection of weekend tracksuits and a cat—

No! Wait. I'm giving you the wrong impression. You don't HAVE to do internet dating or speed dating. I've only really done it by accident. There was a man who was waiting in a restaurant for his internet date. I was also there about to meet a friend, but she'd just called to cancel and I was feeling a bit sad. Then suddenly this man jumped up and said 'Hello!' and handed me a flower. And I was so surprised I took the flower and, before I knew it, he was sitting me down and offering me a glass of wine. I mean you would, wouldn't you, in that situation? You'd take the wine? And it was only when he said, 'You don't look very much like your profile picture' that I realised something was amiss and that he'd mistaken me for his internet date. But it was too late to back out by then: I'd already demolished half the bread basket. So I had to play along. It did mean pretending I was interested in homeopathy and batik, and had trekked the Inca Trail on my gap year, but it was worth it—at least, until his actual date turned up and threw a glass of wine in my face, obviously.

So you STOLE someone else's evening?

279

I wouldn't say that: I prefer 'borrowed'. Who knows, it could well have been the beginning of a beautiful relationship.

Was it?

No.

This is officially awful now. What about flirting? Tell me we've finally got that down pat.

No. No, siree. I refer you to the 'breast-clap' incident. Though I did try flirting one other time, at a party. We'd got onto the subject of our favourite childhood games and I found myself saying in a sexy whisper to a man from whom I was pretty sure I was getting all the 'Let's kiss later' signals, 'Do you like hide and seek? Meet me in that cupboard in five.' I winked, and then slipped into the cupboard when no one was looking. I thought that was amazingly brave and a pretty good chat-up line, to be honest.

I am impressed.

Well, thanking you very muchly. But please don't be.

Why? What happened?

After about half an hour in the cupboard, I realised he probably wasn't going to join me after all. So I sat there on my own in the dark, with the coats for company. And I could hear people saying 'Where's Miranda?' but I didn't want to open the cupboard door as it would look really weird. And the longer I was in there the weirder my appearance from it was going to look. So I just stayed there, until everyone had left the party, and the hosts had gone to bed. At about 4 a.m. I escaped, just as Dave, the host, came past to go to the loo. We stared at each other for a moment. What does one do in that scenario? Again, where's the life manual on this one? So I said, 'Lovely cupboard. Really lovely. One of the best. Thank you.' And left.

head in hands You're useless. What do I do now?

Well, you know. It doesn't really matter all that much.

Yes, it does! Love and sex and relationships are the most important things in the world. Everybody knows that. Even MISS HANDEL knows that.

I'm not sure that's entirely true.

What would YOU know?

Quite a lot, as it happens. I've been unattached for long periods in my twenties and thirties. And it's been fine. I've got to know myself, made some wonderful friends, worked, had fun, and learned to enjoy my own company. Most importantly, I get the bed to myself so I can sleep in the 'starfish' position at all times. I just live the life I want to live. And it's jolly nice.

PEGGY trots in, tail wagging.

PEGGY:

281

And you've got me!

Oh, hi Pegs, what have you been up to?

PEGGY:

Burying a bone in your pillows. Now settling down on your best cushion for a snooze. But before I nod off, I just wanted to tell Little M—I really am better than any human boyfriend Big Miranda could possibly have. I snuggle up to her for Saturday night TV, I stare at her lovingly and warm the cockles of her heart. I am a proper, old-fashioned stunner of a companion. Just a thought. Anyway, must sleep. Night night.

PEGGY TROTS OFF.

If you're genuinely happy, maybe I shouldn't go on my date.

No, you must go. Enjoy all that life has to offer. Gorge yourself on the buffet of existence. Just . . . don't get your hopes up. Not just yet.

sits down on a netball (you can't get pregnant from those) *I suppose I did always sort of hope I'd be spared all this dating and courting business. I knew it would never suit me. I just hoped that one day I'll meet someone, and we'll know instantly that we were meant to be together. Maybe someone famous; one of my crushes. Maybe I'll go to a Wham concert, be in the front row and George Michael will take one look at me and—*

Right, need to tell you something about George. One word: gay. Remember this. It'll spare you a lot of heartache.

Noooo! No WAY! I could never have seen that one coming! OK, well, maybe I'll be at another Band Aid and somehow get backstage passes and as Elton John comes off stage he'll look at me and—

Need to stop you there again.

SHUT UP. Oh. I know, I'll go to a studio recording of Fry and Laurie and . . .

Which one are you going for?

Fry.

Nope.

Oh.

Step away from the quirky creatives, Little M. We learn eventually (thanks to Will Young).

So, forget actors and musicians then—

Oh, definitely. Please do.

Goran Ivanisevic. Safe?

Safe. Good choice.

Whoever it is, I just hope I meet them at a party, or on the bus, and we lock eyes and maybe have a cup of tea. And that we . . . belong together. There'll be no embarrassment. It will be easy, natural, right. No stress.

That does happen. It's happened to friends of mine. It could well happen to us.

Do you really think it could?

I think that it almost definitely will. Because I for one will not be partaking in any formal nuanced dating dance. *takes Little Miranda's hand, as they both stare into the middle distance* The Universe has greater things planned for us, Little M. Now! Off you go! You're going to be late for this terrible date with the awful awkward boy, albeit with those Hasselhoff eyes.

OK, I'm off. Deep breath. Byeeee!

Bye! Have fun. And if he brings a rugby ball with him, FOR GOODNESS' SAKE DON'T SIT ON IT.

Phew. I think we dealt with that one very nicely, MDRC.

How are we all feeling? Tired? Emotional? Or more-than-ready to bound on together to the next stage? Time for an energy boost, methinks. How about this: whatever your relationship status—married, single, muddled, lonely, happy, thrilled, bored, or just plain gagging-for-it—I now invite you to put on the most romantic piece of music you can find (I personally favour Lionel Ritchie's 'Hello'), hold yourself, your partner, your dog, a cushion or a broom close, and dance. Be wooed (good word, 'woo') into a loved-up stupor.

Until there's something good on the telly, at which point JUST SAY 'NO'.

16

WEDDINGS

As I understand it, sitting here in my writing chair replete with sandwich (not plural—remember the diet book), if you're not careful, getting married can be the end result of dating. (Don't say you don't learn from me.)

Having put the dating world to rights, it would seem frankly remiss not to give at least a passing nod to the World of Weddings. Particularly as, for a lot of folk, the point of dating is indeed to end up wed. To have their 'Big Day'. And marriage is, as I see it, a fine and noble institution, leading to such wonderful things as homes, families and lifelong companionship. Yes, I am a huge fan o' marriage, even though I have yet to partake of it myself.

But as much as I think the notion of having a husband, and being a wife, is truly lovely-sounding—even, dare I say it, romantic—I am not sure I am ready. And I know it's not just me who hears themselves uttering that phrase, 'I'm just not ready.' But what is it, precisely, that we're not ready *for*? Well, MDRC, I can sum up all feelings of non-readiness for one's nuptials in three short points. Are you ready? Then please observe my points thus:

Firstly, we are not ready for conversations that go: 'Where are the keys, darling?'

'In the place they always are.'

'Where's that, then?'

'If you don't know, then I'm not going to tell

you.'

'Fine, we'll just have to miss the John Lewis sale then, won't we?'

'Yes, that's right, we'll have to just miss it.'

'Fine.'

'Fine.'

'Fine.'

Secondly, we are not ready for a 'present cupboard'.

And thirdly, we are not ready to hold a really quite serious conversation, nay summit meeting, about the pluses and minuses of getting an estate car.

That sums it all up for me. If one is not able to entertain the notion of these really quite simple things, one is not ready for the married life.

This is perhaps also a test of whether one has passed officially into adulthood or not (one, by the way, is currently enjoying the use of the word 'one'). One believes there should be a grading system, with badges, of the whole shebang. This would make it much easier when meeting people because if one of you has the 'I am an adult and ready for marriage' badge and the other one doesn't—STEP AWAY: it's never going to work. I know that might lead to a line of late-thirtysomething women in a bar with massive glittering badges, and only the odd older gay gentlemen with his, but at least we wouldn't run the risk of wasting five years with a man who was actually only ever masquerading as an adult. It can sometimes take that long to realise he never had the badge. (Bitter? Me?)

However, *I* wouldn't have the badge either. I'm not quite there yet (for which read 'still a child'). Well, who wouldn't rather try and beat their ski-jump Wii score than compare the prices of a Skoda and VW Estate?

But marriage has been on my mind lately. You see, I am at the stage in life where every other weekend seems to involve pouring myself into the car wearing an unnecessary hat, and driving to some obscure church/registry office/Buddhist Centre/ field in order to watch a couple of friends tie the knot. Now, delighted as I am for all these friends, is it just me who, having been to thirteen weddings a year for the last three years, would rather spend every weekend for the rest of my life locked in a caravan with Jedward than go to another bollocking wedding? That's not just me, is it? Tell me I'm not a mad, mean-spirited old hag.

For those of you who think I might be, please know that I have given this some serious thought and have noted below for your pleasure and perusal my reasons as to why weddings can get, shall we say, a little bit trying:

1. Hats

Yes, I'm kicking off with hats. What's that you say? 'That's a very petty thing to start your fine list with, Miranda. What's not to love about hats?' And quite right you'd be too; no sane person really hates hats. But I begrudge anyone who thinks their wedding day is so important that it forces me to look like a dowager duchess from the 1940s. You might say, 'Get a nicer hat, you're clearly not very good at shopping for hats, Miranda.' True, because *why* would I want to be good at shopping for hats? The only people who should be good at shopping for hats are people who wear them professionally, like Beefeaters,

288

builders, cyclists and aristocratic ladies of yesteryear. Bobble-hats aside, hats simply don't feature in a normal, run-of-the-mill twenty-first century life. FACT.

The only alternative to a hat at a wedding seems to be a fascinator. Which is like a sort of embryonic hat. A thing that is so flimsy and feeble it doesn't have the energy to turn itself into a full-on hat. Fascinators are indeed fascinating. Mainly because they appear to be just as expensive as a full-sized hat. Hats and their fascinator embryos get a big thumbs-down from me. Indeed, death to hats.

2. Presents

Now, I don't begrudge a friend a present; I assure you, I am no Scrooge. I adore present buying, actually. You know that thrill of giving someone you love something really well chosen and personal, something that truly reflects the depth and joy of your relationship. But you can't do that at weddings, can you? Because the WEDDING LIST kicks in. In no other scenario would it be acceptable to assume someone wants to buy you a gift and to specify exactly what to purchase from a very expensive website: present lists should begin and end with Santa.

Usually, the only thing that is vaguely affordable (no, I will NOT buy you a £350 coffee machine) is something called a sauce boat. You're buying your oldest friend a *sauce boat*. You have no idea what this woman is going to do with a sauce boat. She can't even cook a microwave pizza and regularly drinks condensed milk from the tin. But, suddenly, she's 'a bride', and she's decided that brides need sauce boats.

Death to wedding lists.

3. The Hen Night

Yes, the Hen Night. Where for one night only we are to find willies absolutely hilarious. Chocolate willies, willies on sticks, willies on hats which also, inexplicably, have boobs on them. We're expected to *shriek* with laughter at the hilarity of it all. But seriously—if any woman, in her day-to-day life, found willies as hilarious as people on hen nights are supposed to find them, then surely that would be noted down as a pretty serious problem? Symptomatic of some deep-rooted sexual dysfunction that would cause Freud himself to double-over in consternation. But on a hen night, fake male genitalia plus sambuca apparently equals the funniest thing you've ever seen in your life.

Still, at least the shrieking-and-sambuca hen nights have the advantage of being cheap. These days, we're subject to a far more monstrous phenomenon: the Destination Hen Night. This is where you pay £800 to go to Spain with a group of women you've only met vaguely twice before. There to pay homage to a woman who you were sort of friends with during your university Fresher's Week, who guilt-tripped you into coming by saying that 'No-one back at Bangor liked me very much—but you were always different. You *understood*.' Death to hen nights.

4. Driving

Why are weddings only ever in Suffolk, Devon, Northumberland or France. WHY? During the course of a 'wedding weekend' you will drive— scientists have proven—approximately four times the distance that a long-distance lorry driver travels in the course of a year. (All statistics and science facts contained in this book are entirely made up.) As a Londoner—Death to all weddings outside the M25.

5. Bridesmaiding

Uniformly horrendous. And brides, with your hat-wearing insistence, extreme wedding location and present list madness—what's with the asking someone over thirty-five to be a bridesmaid? What happened to you? Really? May I tell you this: it is NOT an honour to stand in the same outfits with a three year old, a nine year old and a fourteen-year-old supermodel. We, well, *I*, look RIDICULOUS. Why voluminous pink tulle? What's happened to your taste? Sure, on a three year old—adorable. On anyone vaguely 'strapping' you take on the proportions of a small gazebo. Death to older bridesmaids. Particularly as I end up with a crippling envy towards the proper bridesmaids, the adorable little child bridesmaids who get away with all the fun.

I'll explain this with a little 'list within a list' list. (Don't say I don't treat you right, MDRC.) Here we go:

Five Fun Things That Child Bridesmaids Can Do That Grown-Up Bridesmaids Really Want To Do But Definitely Cannot

i. Run up and down the aisle of the church singing songs of your choice in a high soprano voice whilst the bride and groom take their vows.

ii. When the bride and groom kiss at the altar shout, 'That's not who I saw him kissing this morning!'

iii. Smash your face down into the wedding cake, ' . . . because it looks yummy.' And be thought adorable for doing so.

iv. Shout 'Boring' at the father of the bride's speech, then 'Watch me!' and simply spin on your bum in the centre of the reception venue.

v. Look up strange men's kilts to see if they are wearing pants.

No, MDRC. Bridesmaiding definitely ain't what it used to be. Although I occasionally still do point v. (Why is there always one person at every wedding in a kilt?) And back to the master list . . .

6. Getting Stuck With An Uncle On The Dance Floor
I couldn't for the life of me tell you why, but the second the DJ starts up I seem to be a magnet for the obligatory-uncle-with-a-drinking-problem. His aim will be to Highland Fling me across the dance floor to 'Agadoo'. Death to uncles.

7. Marquee Etiquette
Definitely not something you'd have to contend with outside a wedding environment (unless you're part of a travelling circus and have taken to calling the Big Top a marquee). Here follows an example of the horrors that can come from ignoring Marquee Etiquette: I was once standing

around at a wedding reception (warm glass of wine, ham sandwich, casing the joint for drunken uncles) when I noticed it was getting rather chilly in there. 'Might be nice if someone closed the tent-flaps to trap the heat inside,' I thought. So I called out—over the music, which was pretty loud—to someone at the other end of the marquee: 'CLOSE THE FLAPS!' They couldn't quite hear me, so again I shouted, 'COULD YOU CLOSE THE—' at which point the music stopped and all you could see and hear was me in the middle of the marquee shouting furiously: *'FLAPS'*. The Drunken Uncle was immediately enamoured and introduced me for the rest of the night as 'The Flaps Lady'.

8. 'The Mother'

If you are unlucky, sorry, I mean, privileged, to know the bride well enough to stay at her parents' house the night before the nuptials, The Mother that we know and love from Christmas will very much rear her military head. There will be precision timings like you have never known: various sittings for breakfast (depending on your hierarchy in the wedding party); exactly when people are picking up flowers; dropping cakes off; delivering the young bridesmaids; when the father gets ready; when the make-up lady arrives; allotted times for the wedding video moments. Heaven forbid a video goes on or a photo goes off when we weren't expecting it. If it's not on the rota, IT IS STRICTLY FORBIDDEN.

If something does go wrong, here is what to expect in all pre-nuptial houses, moments before the family must present their serene happy faces as they walk down the aisle:

MOTHER:
Oh my God, oh my God, the lipstick doesn't match her flowers.

BRIDE:
[SCREAM!]

MOTHER:
This is a total disaster; her day is ruined. Darling, her day is ruined. The lipstick doesn't match her flowers.

DADDY:
Can't she put a different lipstick on?

BRIDE:
[SCREAM!]

MOTHER:
A DIFFERENT LIPSTICK?! We have been make-up testing every weekend for the last thirteen years in the lead-up to this day, and that is the lipstick that is right for her. This is the *only* one that complements her blusher, brings out her eyes and, more importantly, detracts from her ever-present upper-lip mole.

FATHER:
Are people really going to notice?

MOTHER:
I have spent six months choosing flowers to match ribbons, to match tablecloths, to match the invitations to match the lipstick. It all matches. OF COURSE PEOPLE WILL NOTICE.

It's a different coloured lipstick.

GAJ:
Who's lost their Pritt Stick?

MOTHER/FATHER/BRIDE:
[SCREAM!]

MIRANDA as OLDER BRIDESMAID:
Might I suggest that the most important
thing is that the bride and groom are in love,
about to show their nearest and dearest the
commitment they want to make to each other,
and a slightly different shade of lipstick really
doesn't matter? We will still all have a
lovely day.

EVERYONE TURNS TO STARE AT MIRANDA. A
PAUSE.

BRIDE:
[SCREAM!]

MOTHER:
Get her out of my house! She is no longer part
of this wedding.

BRIDE:
[TEARS!]

MOTHER:
[SCREAM!]

All right, so that might be the tiniest of
exaggerations to most wedding parties (outside

Essex). But seriously, what happens to brides? What happens to brides? I mean, what *happens* to them? What HAPPENS? Look, I'm spinning. I have gone into a confused spin. FLAPS! Frankly, death to brides.

Like the impromptu wedding speech of the drunkenest uncle at the drunkenest wedding in the drunkenest corner of Northumberland, I could go on and on and on. I could talk about the bride's 'going away' outfit, I could talk about the horrors of being put at the kids' table aged thirty-seven because you're the only single person there, or I could talk about the nightmare of being made to relive the whole thing a month later at the wedding video screening—a completely pointless exercise because I WAS THERE.

Little M rushes in, fresh from her first-ever date **Urh, urh, urh, he did lunge! He did! Urh! Snogging is revolting, and ends up with someone else nicking your sweets. Forget relationships. I am NEVER getting married.**

That's a relief, because you've just missed a big ranty list about the horrors of wedding days. Don't worry, Little M. Marriage isn't the be-all and end-all. You can get on with living your life.

I want to do something with my life. For me. On my own.

Good for you. But never say never. I feel the time might come very soon when we can accept the badge, when we'll be ready. But if I get married, know this: I'm going to do things differently.

There'll be none of this fancy-hen-night-big-formal-wedding malarkey at the Hart nuptials. I've got it all planned. I'm going to be the coolest, most laid-back, chilled-out bride ever. I'm going to have a registry office ceremony with four people as witnesses, and then a Hawaiian BBQ by a swimming pool where everyone can wear whatever they want.

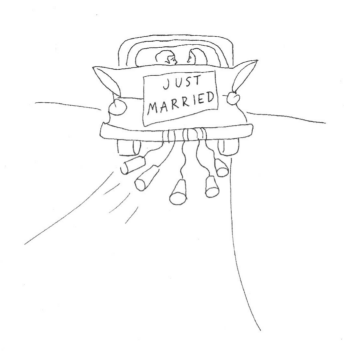

CUT TO:

EXT. ENORMOUS FLORAL-DRAPED MARQUEE. DAY.

MIRANDA at top table surrounded by three thirty-eight-year-old bridesmaids, wearing gazebos. Immediately behind her are

700 sauce boats. MIRANDA stands at the microphone, enjoying what is clearly the Biggest Day Ever in the history of Big Days.

MIRANDA:
ISN'T THIS JUST SUCH FUN! SUCH FUN! SUCH FUN! SUCH FUN! SUCH FUN!

What happens to brides? Seriously, what happens to them? I mean, what *happens*?

17

CULTURE

Now, MDRC, do you have a coffee table? Perhaps you're sitting in front of it right now? Perhaps your feet are artfully arranged on said table, resting on . . . what? The complete works of Shakespeare? A Wagner CD? A pile of Jonathan Franzens? The entire Booker Prize longlist? A delightfully squishy and yielding stack of *Economist*s and *New Statesman*s? (The magazines, obviously, not the professionals—however, if you're resting your feet on a stack of clever young men then I'll simply say well done and good for you.)

My coffee table tends to support nothing more than a hot beverage (and four old mugs from previous hot beverages), a *Radio Times,* an old *Take That* album, the *Complete Morecambe and Wise* box set, a packet of digestives and a copy of *Heat* magazine. You see—

Oh no—are we a cultural vacuum sitting around laughing at jokes on novelty mugs? Please say we get a bit clever? Do you have a library or something in another room?

I'll say this to you, my younger self, why *wouldn't* I be a cultural vacuum? You are. All you did yesterday was watch *Crocodile Dundee* and *Dallas,* and eat strange-looking sweets called UFOs (remember them, MDRC?).

I think you'll find I'm currently listening to Thomas Hardy's **The Mayor of Casterbridge** *on my Walkman.*

Yeah, but you're not actually reading it, are you? You're listening to it. You're passive.

I need to show off my Walkman! Walking around listening to something is cooler than sitting down and reading books like an old dweeb.

And is it really *The Mayor of Casterbridge* you're listening to?

Yes.

Really? What's happening in it? Right now?

Um . . . they're all having a big—uh—barn dance to celebrate the mayor becoming mayor. The whole of Casterbridge . . . it's hilaire, it's—oh, look, fine. I was listening to it but I got bored. I'm listening to the **Top Gun** *soundtrack. Bella let me borrow her Ray Bans for an hour, so I had to listen to it coz Tom Cruise wore Ray Bans in* **Top Gun** *all the time. I'm pretending to be Kelly McGillis in the bit where he comes up to her in the bar and starts singing 'You've Lost that Lovin' Feelin''. Maybe Goran Ivanisevic will do that to me one day . . .*

That would indeed be smashing (Pun!)
Look, Little M, the *Top Gun* fantasies only go to show that you are a dreamer, not a studier. You're deftly ignoring the pile of politics textbooks that you really need to read for your exams, and instead

300

of learning about the Cold War, you're lying on a bench in Ray Bans pretending you're Kelly McGillis. I think this categorically proves that you are in no way a scholar.

I could be. If I actually did stuff.

Possibly. But first, let's look at the facts. I'll remind you of the maths teacher asking you to define 'Pi' and you saying, 'It's different depending on which filling it is,' while in Politics you thought that the Cold War was in Iceland. If you're in no way learned or cultured now, then—

Excuse me? 'Not cultured'? I went to the British Museum last term to see the, um, Egyptians.

You see, you don't know what you saw: you spent the whole time deciding what to spend your £5 on in the gift shop. (Three bookmarks and a thimble, if I remember.)

Yeah, well, I have a print of Munch's **The Scream** *on my wall, I'll have you know.*

It's only because all the History of Art girls were talking about how they 'expressed themselves' through their pin boards. You got intimidated and ripped down your Wham posters so they'd think you were cool. It was nothing to do with cultural curiosity; it was peer pressure, pure and simple.

I still like that **Scream,** *though.*

I don't believe you.

OK, I find it really scary. It gives me bad dreams. Don't tell anyone.

I won't. And you see, Little M, all I am saying is—the girl becomes the woman. You're not culturally engaged now, and you won't be later.

I always thought I'd have some kind of amazing brain-explosion in my twenties and start going to the opera and buying modern art.

Nope. Unless by 'opera' you mean the *Smash Hits* Poll Winners Party, and by 'modern art' you mean McDonald's Happy Meals with drawings on the box. No, sorry, later in life you sink into the cheery cultural mire of Take That—

What are Take That?

Oh, just you wait. JUST. YOU. WAIT. They're a boy band—

Like Bros?

Like Bros. But brilliant. And there are five of them. Then four of them. Then five of them again. And they split up, but don't worry—they get back together and are weirdly even better. Basically, what I'm saying is—

You're an idiot. A moron. A tea-drinking, trash-reading, bucket of intellectual jelly.

RUDE!

I can easily turn myself into a bright, enlightened young woman. That's what I want to be. That's what I'm going to be. Oh, yes. I'm going off to read—to read—um—

You can't think of a single clever author, can you?

Uh . . . Freud. I'm going to read some Freud.

You only know who Freud is because he writes about men's rude parts.

giggles See ya, working very hard to make sure I never be ya!

That doesn't even make sense.

MDRC, now that Little Miranda's scampered off to try and find the dirty bits in the complete works of Freud and Kierkegaard, I can be completely open with you. Culturally, politically, 'brainiac-ally', I am something akin to a buffoon. At school, I was one of the funsters—fairly popular, very sporty— and it wasn't the done thing to be a brain box of any kind. Being a swot or a nerd or a geek was, well, swotty and nerdy and geeky, so I didn't bother. Then, at university, being fun and having fun were still far, far more important. I bought into this vibe wholeheartedly. I made sure I was always the first person to suggest hiring a bouncy castle or trying to invent a cocktail with cornflakes or hold a 'Make a David Hasselhoff out of Chocolate Buttons' competition (feel free to try that at home).

But now, at the age of thirty-eight, I'm coming to realise that my ignorance of all things cultural and 'newsy' (please note that even though I call myself a buffoon, I have just coined another brand-new word), can at times render me a little bit of an outsider. This marvellous, information-rich and enlightened society seems to be stuffed to the gills with single, professional, switched-on BlackBerry-wielding men and women who quite simply know stuff about stuff. Lots of stuff. Stuff that makes them sound, to me, as if they're speaking in Portuguese: 'Proportional representation' and 'New Deal-style economic stimulus packages' or 'Post-modernist architecture'. It's the done thing to crash through the door at a drinks party with the words 'So! Libya, eh? What a shower! Still, at least I've got that new Miro exhibition at the Tate to cheer me up and help me forget about that ghastly new sustainable farming policy. Ha ha ha.'

At some social events, this ignorance can prove tricky. I refer to the kind of events I wouldn't particularly want to be at anyway. Professional networking events, perhaps, where you're supposed to make a grand impression on a variety of fascinating new people, but more often than not find yourself spending the evening locked in the Ladies with a magazine and a packet of Kettle Chips, praying for home-time. I often come a conversational cropper at such events, simply because so many people have conversations that— MDRC, you're the first person I've ever shared this with—*I simply don't understand.* I don't know what they're talking about.

Now, if this one *isn't* just me—I dearly hope that it's not—then on this life conundrum I suggest you feel free to use any of the following conversational techniques in order to get things moving. Again, consider them my gift to you. You're very much welcome.

Firstly, if someone mentions something that you know nothing about (examples could easily include the Middle East, fisheries or land tax), and someone else responds, 'Don't get me started,' you must respond, 'Oh, I know! Don't get *me* started either.' If anyone then subsequently asks for your opinion you can respond with, 'No, I said *don't* get me started. Seriously—watch out. I will blow.' The people around you will then think that a) this woman knows exactly what she's talking about and b) she feels so passionately about it that'd we'd best not mess with her.

It really works. I know, just call me brilliant. As an addendum (good word, like 'kerfuffle', it keeps on giving) to this technique, you could then try saying, 'Let's be frivolous and discuss *Strictly Come Dancing* instead,' in the hope that someone bites. Alas, however, this approach rarely works. People tend to think you're being ironic and break into peals of drinks-party derisive laughter. You join in, but you know you'd like nothing more than to have a big larky chat about *Strictly*, ideally involving a series of demonstrations and some drawing of costumes on napkins. Ho hum.

Secondly, you could use 'The Repeating Trick'. Here's how it works: if you find yourself in a group of people discussing, say, economic stimulus packages and you simply can't join in, then just hit on an appropriate-sounding sentence you hear, and—repeat! For example:

Loud, intimidating person X: 'I mean, he's budgeted seven hundred and twenty billion over three fiscal years!'

Braying cultured person Y: 'Seven hundred and twenty billion?'

Sweaty-palmed YOU (eagerly): 'Yep. Seven hundred and twenty billion. Over three fiscal years. THREE!'

Of course, you don't know whether 'three' is good or bad, but by giving it emphasis it will work either way. Repeating things you don't understand will sound like you have a full grasp of this cultural and political issue. Again, if I may be so bold—brilliant. Consider me your ghastly-drinks-party manual. Your Miran-ual.

Your third nugget from the Miran-ual is: joining in with laughter. Now, this is key. There'll come a point in any conversation, however dull, when a big laugh will naturally occur. Of course, you'll have no idea that what they're laughing at is supposed to be a joke: as far as you're concerned, they might as well have said, 'FDRMMNNXXXXXQUYRABBIT', but you should join in the laugh anyway. Perhaps even laugh a little louder than the rest, allow yourself a small headshake and an 'Oh yes, jolly good, jolly good.' This will make it abundantly clear that you're extra plugged-in and absolutely on top of all the subjects being covered.

Finally, if none of the above works, pretend your phone is ringing and say 'Excuse me!', look at your phone and then say, 'Oh, I don't want to take this, but without my input now it will be total chaos in the office tomorrow morning—you know what it's like,' ending with a hearty laugh. Then walk quickly and professionally away doing fake important speaking in the phone, turn the corner, open the front door and RUN, run away, run away very fast indeed.

The worst time, I found, for trying to keep up with brainy conversations was during the whole Bank Crash thing. I couldn't cope. Suddenly everyone I knew—including friends who'd previously thought that Mrs Thatcher was still the prime minister—seemed to have a burning desire to discuss economics in great depth. Once, at a dinner party, somebody started talking about 'derivatives'. I misheard, and thought, 'Ooh, lovely, finally something I can join in with.' I duly piped up with, 'Well, they're alright I suppose, though to be honest I prefer chocolate derivatives. So much better to dunk in tea.' A stony silence fell upon the table. I made a mental note that from then on I should perhaps attend social functions in a big pointy dunce hat, to avoid confusion.

You might be thinking, 'At least it can't get worse, Miranda.' But I would say to you this: do you know me at all, MDRC? Of *course* it gets worse. My real intellectual trough came during a party being thrown by my then-boyfriend's new boss. It was all pretty high stakes: I wanted to do my man proud in front of his colleagues, play the erudite girlfriend and make a positive impression on all concerned. We were still at the relationship stage of 'Lying to Impress', so the boyfriend was yet to realise the level of my buffoonery. Things were going well. The conversation was about Saddam Hussein (at that time still on the run, as I remember it), and I was repeating sentences, joining in the laughter and shouting, 'Don't get me started!' like a pro. At which point the cheese-board was passed in my direction. I do love a good cheese-board and I picked up what appeared to be a curly, affected bit of Edam, and punctuated a hearty pretending-to-understand laugh by popping it in my mouth. Everyone fell silent and looked at me a little bemusedly. MDRC, what I had popped in my mouth wasn't curly Edam; it was a knob of butter! (Yes, I did just say knob—get over it, this is no time for jokes.) I had just stuffed a curly hunk of neat butter in my gob. Yet another of life's scenarios one isn't taught how to deal with.

I decided that the only way to move on was to ride it out: 'Oh, I do love butter,' I exclaimed. 'Who doesn't love butter? I mean, it's only one stage away from cheese, isn't it? It's *pre-cheese*, if you like! Anyone want to try some pre-cheese? No? Losers. You're all losers, ha ha!' The group remained silent and stared as I sat there chewing wildly, butter dribbling down my chin, feeling frankly sick as a dog. Then I remembered my Miran-ual. Out came the phone, cue the line about the office needing my help, then run, run, abort, abort.

Hello?

Oh, hello, eighteen-year-old me, how's the Freud going?

I might have got a bit distracted by some friends having a water-balloon fight.

Quite the little bluestocking, aren't we?

Oh, shut up. I'm eighteen. I'm allowed. You, on the other hand, have no excuse. You've not got children, your love life is a disaster, you don't do any exercise— SURELY you should have spent your free time (of which you clearly have lots) becoming a cultured and refined woman about town. It was my final hope: we'd be going to art galleries and book launches and having lunch on the South Bank with an Attenborough and pulling off a beret and a tweed waistcoat. You know, all chic.

Little M—time for your penultimate life lesson.

Do you remember in chapter two of this fine tome, when we discussed the issue of music? When I told you that you're simply not a trendy muso? That it's just not in your genes. It's not who you are.

Yes, and I thought that was OK until I auditioned for the school musical (because that's more my taste), and I was given the Waltzing MAN in Ballroom Scene.

Really, Little M, you HAVE to let that go.

Have you?

No, fair enough. But listen up, as with music, the same is true of culture. We're just not that into it. We're a bit more 'light entertainment', and we've pretty much accepted that about ourselves. Each to their own, I say. There are obviously enormous advantages to being really engaged, on every level, with the society you live in. I'm not dissing that; it's a healthy aspiration. If that's the way someone's wired, I would say to them gleefully—go for it. Become a friend of the Tate. Campaign for local government. Go on a protest march (if you're brave enough).

Wait—you've never been on a march? But we're

doing Politics A-Level. We must march!

Actually, I did accidentally go on one march. I was coming out of Peter Jones on Sloane Street, having just bought some very lovely new cushion covers. A vibrant floral fuchsia if I remember . . .

Not interested.

Soz. There was this big march going past outside, and I got caught up in it. I tried to duck out, but someone gave me a flask of tea, which was hard to refuse, and the next thing I knew, I'd marched all the way to Trafalgar Square. Exhausting.

I suppose that's better than nothing. What was the march in aid of?

I'm not entirely sure; it was definitely either pro-drugs or anti-drugs. And someone was waving a placard about not hurting mice in laboratories, but that could have been a metaphor for Palestine. It's very hard to say.

Oh, you DISGUST me!

I thought it better not to know. That way, when telling people anecdotes about 'my day at the march', I could change my story according to the company I was in: amongst Home Counties-types, it was the Countryside Alliance march; *Guardian*-reading metropolitan folk it was UK Uncut; the local dog show—PETA. It was perfect.

You are a massive dweeb and everything I never

want to be.

Hang on, I have a point to make. As I was saying before we veered off into march anecdotes (or 'marchecdotes', MDRC—another new word. I really am a linguistic pioneer), you're *not* Selina Scott, I'm afraid, however much you'd like to be. For now, you are socially The Silly One.

What, like The Stupid One?

My goodness, no, don't even think that. You're as smart as they come. You're just not especially serious-minded, which means that you're uniquely valuable to the world. It's brilliant being The Silly One. Once you fully accept this as your role and decide to make the most of it, you can relax and have fun.

What kind of fun?

At a dinner party you can initiate rowdy games of 'Would You Rather' at one end of the table, whilst people are earnestly discussing the new wave of young women playwrights at the other. So as they're asking, whilst leaning forward, glasses on nose, mouth puckered: 'But don't you think that the whole concept of a new wave constitutes a ghettoisation of female talent?' you'll be asking, leaning back in your chair, giggling, a bit pissed: 'Would you rather have an elbow on your ear, or an ear on your elbow?' Which is a question that does need asking, I rather strongly feel. Other questions in the 'Would You Rather' category might include: 'Would you rather have squirrels for feet or hamsters for hands? Or a face for an arse, or an arse for a face?' Fascinating stuff.

Oh God. We're the village idiot.

I've tried high-end culture. I tried ballet, but I just couldn't get along with it. That might have been because it spurned me as a teenager, but if I watch it now, it just makes me laugh. It's the men, if I'm honest. Call me ballerina-ist, but I'm not sure I can take a man seriously if he does those split-leg-run things for a living. So funny. And, bear with me, MDRC, but what about the 'ballet—how to put it—bulge'? The manly ballet bulge. Very hard not to remain focused solely on that area I find. Just me?

Do you remember when me and Sis put two eggs down our tights to pretend to be male ballet dancers?

Unnecessary information sharing. Shush now. I've tried opera too, but watching fat people warbling in Italian just isn't up my street. I mean, I'm sure there's more to it than that but, to be honest . . . snooze. And as for art galleries—

Oh, PLEASE say we drift knowingly about in art galleries. I'd love to become an Art Person.

You're just going through a phase of wanting to be one of those History of Art girls.

They are SO cool. Tallusha always wears a floaty bandana in her hair and looks brillo.

If you wore one, you'd look like Rambo. You

312

don't want to be one of those girls, Little M, you really don't. You don't want to be called names like Tallusha and Barrunka and Petrouchka and Candida and waft about talking rubbish about how Monet is really a case of the Emperor's New Clothes and how light influences beauty. We really aren't one of them.

When the laws of Miranda-Land come into effect, art galleries should legally only be used for the following:

i. Galloping. The wide, open spaces on those hard wooden floors are ripe for a gallop.
ii. Sliding. See above. In fact, sliding can often be an unexpected consequence of galloping.
iii. Ummm . . . nope that's it. Galloping and sliding.

In Miranda-Land, art galleries will be renamed Galloping Galleries and any paintings or sculptures present will be purely incidental.

What about all those people who really enjoy art galleries, and know about economics and stuff?

MDRC, I say this in hushed, I-may-be-wrong-so-please-don't-hate-me tones: I have a hunch that a lot of outwardly knowledgeable, plugged-in people don't *really* know what they're talking about. The whole 'Bank Crash' thing (actually, was it called the 'Bank Crash'? I'm not sure. You know, the scary thing when all the invisible money went wobbly) was, again, a good example of this. Everyone I knew had an opinion: 'Oh, it's all the greedy bankers' fault' or 'Out-of-control consumer debt' and 'People gambling with other people's cash. Terrible.' Then about eight months later, one by one, they sheepishly admitted that they hadn't had a clue what had been going on at all; it all looked a bit *Star Wars* to them. 'No, didn't understand a thing,' they said. 'Just felt I ought to say something. Pinched a few ideas from the papers. Seemed to work.' To which I thought, 'Hmm. I wonder if maybe *no one* knows quite as much as they claim they do, about *anything*? They all just don't want to look like The Ignorant One, so they blather on, stealing sentences from the *Guardian* higgledy-piggledy. *And*, maybe none of them actually *want* to go to the Vermeer exhibition at the Royal Academy. Perhaps they're dreading it. Maybe what they *really* want to do is lie around in pyjamas watching prime-time television and imbibing nibbles. Hmmm.'

Perhaps these people should, at least once in a while, give into their lower cultural urges. Musicals, farces, all manner of television—from sitcoms to Saturday night reality shows to escapist dramas.

They should stop seeing them as 'guilty pleasures'. To me, they're just pleasures. *Blood Brothers*, or Gilbert and George—it's all entertainment. Art is subjective and art as a form of entertainment escapism is as high art as any.

I hate to admit it, but what you're saying does sort of make a little bit of sense.

puffs self up to full height, smug and proud Oh, does it now? Have I *finally* got through to you, Little M? Have I *finally* convinced you that it's always best to be who you are? Are you now swayed by my most marvellous words?

No. I just thought that if it's OK to be an idiot, then I might not bother revising for my exams.

No, *no*. You absolutely must pass your exams. I insist. Without them, you might end up knowing literally nothing for the rest of your life, apart from every outfit that Jason Donovan ever wore in *Neighbours*. Please pass your exams. You need some basis of knowledge. It's very important, because at some point (in my case, I am thinking it will be aged around forty), you might start becoming interested in higher art. Classic novels, poetry, art—the whole thing. All I am saying is if you spend a lot of your adult life not interested, don't worry: other forms of art are justified. I reckon you are lucky if you come to the more learned stuff later in life. Just think, I have the joy of the Shakespeare sonnets all to come. I am the lucky one. So off you pop and revise, little one . . .

singing *'I've lost that loving feeling . . . whoa, whoa, whoa . . .'*

She's off. So, MDRC, how was that for you? How do you feel about the contents of your coffee table after that little romp-ette through the world of culture? Still happy with it? Or are you perhaps thinking that you might prefer a bumper *Take a Break* magazine to that Booker longlist? Hmm? Or maybe not. You're free to be whoever you want to be, and neither I, nor anyone else, should ever be able to judge you. On which note . . .

*boils kettle for jelly, cocks ear for arrival of like-minded friend, whacks on telly, shouts over the opening bars of the *Strictly Come Dancing* theme tune* It's time for my weekly dose of VERY HIGH CULTURE. Who'd rather be at the opera? NOT MEEEEEE!

PIT STOP!

Blimey, MDRC. That's what I have to say to you. Or maybe 'Gorblimey', if you're a Cockney builder from the Victorian era (never say that I don't make an effort to speak your language). Be it 'Blimey' or 'Gorblimey'—we've only gone and romped through very nearly a whole book together. Yes, we're now drawing our adventure to a close. Like a majestic galleon sailing into port, or a fine brass band reaching a climactic crescendo—we're damned nearly home. I think we all deserve a hearty pat on the back.

Please know, my dear chum, that it has been nothing but a pleasure and a joy to spend this time with you. There's no one for whom I'd rather have written. I do so hope you've enjoyed your stay in my literary mansion. But it's not quite goodbye. Not yet. Because our final Pit Stop wouldn't be complete without a farewell round of our most intriguing tick-box game. You know the drill; please tick if you have achieved any of the following:

☐ Had an imaginary conversation with a pet
☐ Sat on a rugby ball and worried about getting pregnant
☐ Discovered or re-discovered Arctic Roll
☐ Eaten the contents of someone's fridge whilst babysitting
☐ Let yourself be a child again
☐ Carried off a fascinator at a wedding
☐ Shouted 'FLAPS!' in a marquee
☐ Made a David Hasselhoff out of chocolate buttons
☐ Confessed to not understanding the bank crisis
☐ Galloped in an art gallery
☐ Reached a wonderful and almost Zen-like state of self-acceptance, possibly to the point of running up to strangers in the street, grabbing them by the shoulders and shouting, 'Hey! BE TRUE TO YOU!'

Obviously, MDRC, one of the above is a tad more important than the others. In fact, I'd venture it's the whole point of this book and it becomes your final task. Can you guess which one it is? Yes, well done. Obviously the whole point of this book is to teach you to:

Shout 'FLAPS!' at a wedding.

GOOD LUCK AND GOD SPEED

I've had a jolly interesting time here in my writing
chair. I'll miss tapping away at my tome. Amongst
other things, I've discovered that if you don't leave
the house for twenty-four days (my current record)
and the postman comes to the door, you will invite
the postman in for a chat. And then offer him the
mock Christmas dinner made out of cardboard,
which you knocked up while you were writing the
chapter on Christmas. Which will lead to him
asking another postman to do your street for the
foreseeable future, which will be very embarrassing
indeed. Sorry, Mr Postman—I was lonely, I meant
no harm.

But mainly, MDRC, I will really miss chatting
to you. So it's time to gather for a rather poignant
moment, as we turn the page into our very final
chapter. Now, please don't cry. Come on, you're
blotching the pages . . . or ruining your Kindle . . .
no, stop it now. On we go.

18

DREAMS

If you get to the end of this chapter, then you've only gone and read a whole and actual book. Wowzers. Well done. And if *I* finish this chapter then I've only gone and *written* a whole and actual book. Double wowzers. I never, in my short, young life thought I'd say that. 'I have written a book.' I can't say that it's a dream come true, because writing a book was never on the wish list. It wasn't on the wish list because I simply wouldn't have considered it an option. I wouldn't have considered it was something I could do, ever, not in a million years (you might think it still very much isn't, in which case, for the final time: RUDE). I'm not much of a 'words' person. At school, as we established, I didn't even read any of the set GCSE English books—I had all the audio-books on cassette. I once choreographed a rather natty dance routine to the final three chapters of *Jane Eyre* but I was not—as a wordsy person might put it—'literarily engifted'. But I'd like to take this opportunity to offer a giant 'NYANYANYAN*YANYAAAAAA*' to any teachers who might have suggested that my lack of word-er-ly talent could have prevented me from writing a book. (My GCSE English teacher, by the way, was called Mr Sentence. Honestly, not joking. True say. I mean, with a name like 'Sentence', what else could he do? Even if he'd dreamt since boyhood of becoming an astronaut, it was going to have to be either High Court Judging or English Teacher-y-ness.)

Anyway—MDRC. My beloved, my trusted reader, my faithful St Bernard of a chum. We have now addressed, confronted, lolloped through and gently probed (pardon) a number of important issues together. Like a contestant on a reality television show, we have been on a *journey*. Amongst other things, we now know how to break it to one's eighteen-year-old self that one doesn't ever develop a talent for dancing, prime-minister-ship or high culture, and that one doesn't get married in one's thirties; we've explored the murky depths of the relationship between a woman and her dog; we've learned of the dangers lurking deep within beauty parlours, hospitals, weddings and family holidays; and we're fully up to speed with how best to face down a band of pirates who've chosen to invade our cruise ship (NB: we may not actually have learned that last one, I can't remember).

I'd now like to lead you gently into our final subject: dreams.

I'm not talking about sleep-based dreams. I am not talking about the moment when your flatmate, uncle, partner or mum collars you in the kitchen of a morning, just when you're about to butter your toast, and says, 'Oh, I had the most amazing dream last night. Literally amazing. I was in this castle, right? Except it was our flat, but it was a castle, and Paul from my old office—well, it was sort of half him and half a unicorn, and he was playing backgammon with these old ladies who'd missed the bus to go on *A Question of Sport*— or maybe *Masterchef*? Anyway, Paul kept trying to make me toast a crumpet on his unicorn horn, but I wouldn't do it because his face wasn't hot enough. It was wicked.' SHUT UP, NO ONE BUT YOU IS INTERESTED IN YOUR FREAKY SUBCONSCIOUS.

We won't be talking about *those* kinds of dreams, thank you very much. I'm talking daydreams, goals, ambitions, childhood fantasies. Let's start with the latter. I love asking people what they wanted to be when they were children. We had such marvellous, quirky plans for ourselves, didn't we? I know it wasn't just me. No limits, no sense of what we thought other people might want us to be. Just our big, loopy, childish plans. Cowboy, ice-cream taster, pirate, pirate's moll, gardener, gardener's moll, official ice-cream taster to pirates. Whatever we wanted to be, we could be. I wanted to be a farmer's wife. That was my first encounter with the world of 'ambition'. Not a farmer, just a farmer's wife. Spatula in one arm, watering can in the other, a newborn lamb in my apron pocket bleating gently for its tea. No responsibilities, other than whacking a sturdy pie on the table at six o'clock. I built a lovely little dream-farm for myself. We had an Aga, a sheep that lived indoors, and our chickens would lay eggs on the doorstep before curling up at night with the border collie. The cows would live off buttercups. I'd make loaves from husks of wheat. The pigs would all be clean and friendly, and I would become some kind of farm-animal whisperer and know the every desire and whim of each animal we owned.

It's possible that I hadn't entirely grasped the challenges facing the modern agricultural family, but there you go. A dream's a dream.

As I matured into my teens, I stepped away from

Operation Farmer's Wife, and my fantasies mostly revolved around the meeting and befriending of famous people. I'd send myself to sleep with a major role-play involving me arriving at a swanky showbiz party in a posh hotel, causing a stir as people commented on my statuesque natural beauty. David Van Day, Tom Selleck, Kevin Bacon and Patrick Swayze would all fight over me. Emma Thompson and I would laugh about it over a cocktail (no umbrella). And then we'd all go back to Victoria Wood's for cake where Eric and Ernie would do a dance routine for us.

Fantasy-wise, I'm sorry to say this wasn't even the half of it. I did fake *Parkinson* interviews in my bedroom (I was always the last guest of the evening, always played in by T'Pau, and they installed a gold sparkly staircase especially for me). I'd have the audience in the palm of my hand, touching Parky's knee regularly, winking at Jason Donovan who was in the seat next to me. I would then find myself skating at glacial speed round the local roller rink, being hurled around in the manly arms of Christopher Dean. I stood atop my desk and played *Annie* to a packed Palladium, taking a lavish series of curtain calls as my rapt audience shrieked with joy. But alongside all the glitz, I made sure I left room for a bit of do-gooding, a bit of making a difference in the world. And how very *grand* I was about it all.

For your information and pleasure, I'd like to offer you an excerpt from the diary of fourteen-year-old Miranda (who is much like eighteen-year-old Miranda, except a tad shorter and pinker-faced, and wears dungarees):

322

17th JUNE, 1987.

*It's BLOODY HOT. And yes that is a swear
word, MUM, if you're reading this, MUM,
but if you're reading it then that's a major
BETRAYAL OF MY TRUST so you're just
going to have to cope with a swear word, aren't
you? Anyway, I'm thinking about how if it's
hot for me in my bedroom, then it must be
even hotter for the pandas in China who are
dying. Poor pandas. We did a thing on pandas
in Geography today, and the teacher said
that they're dying out and don't have enough
bamboo to eat so they can't make babies. Or
something. I said, 'Why don't you do something
about it?' And Milly said you can't; no one can,
it's global warming. So in the holidays I'm going
to set up a charity for pandas and rainforests. I'll
have to go to China so I'll miss the school trip to
Dungeness Power Station, but that won't matter
because I'll get famous from my panda charity
and I'll be able to go back there in the autumn
as a celebrity. I think that David Van Day will
be involved with my panda charity. And if we're
doing the pandas and rainforests then we might
as well do Africa as well. We can have a big
concert like Live Aid, David Van Day can sing a
song, and I can sing the bits I learnt for my choir
audition, and it can be at Wembley. I imagine
people will want to make a film about it, so I'll
have to be careful with contracts etc. If it wins
an Oscar I'll need to look nice for the Oscars,
so I must get Mum to buy me that purple shirt
from C&A. (If you're reading this, Mum, it's the
one with the military things on the shoulders—
though that might clash with the Oscar? Not*

323

sure.)

Do we ever stop dreaming? I know I haven't. I must have been at least twenty-five when the Spice Girls happened, and I distinctly remember imagining my way into the group. I was going to be the sixth Spice, 'Massive Spice', who, against all the odds, would become the most popular and lusted-after Spice. The Spice who sang the vast majority of solo numbers in the up-tempo tracks. The Spice who really went the distance. And I still haven't quite given up on the Wimbledon Ladies' Singles Championship. I mean, it can't be too late, can it? I've got a lovely clean T-shirt, and I've figured out *exactly* how I'd respond to winning the final point (lie on floor wailing, get up, do triumphant lap of the ring slapping crowd members' hands, then climb up to my family in the supporters' box).

It *can't* be just me who does this. I'm convinced that most adults, when travelling alone in a car, have a favourite driving CD of choice and sing along to it quite seriously, giving it as much attitude and effort as they can, due to believing—in that instant—that they're the latest rock or pop god playing to a packed Wembley stadium. And there must be at least one man, one poor beleaguered City worker, who likes to pop into a phone box then come out pretending he's Superman. Is there someone who does this? Anyone? If so, I'd like to meet you and we shall marry in the spring (unless you're really, really weird and the Superman thing is all you do, in which case BACK OFF).

Superman lunatics aside, I think it's sad when people stop dreaming, or start losing hope. Because holding onto the bonkers dream might just turn out to be the most marvellous thing you ever did.

MDRC, allow me to be your own personal Simon Cowell for a moment. Allow me to sit back, fold my arms, hoist my trousers northwards and say. 'YOU. *YOU* are the person this industry has been waiting for. YOU are what this competition is all about.'

If there's something you want to do, and you have any kind of basic skill or talent in that direction, please, please, please . . . *do it*. Begin. I feel that this is the only life advice I'm qualified to give—GO FOR IT. Keep plugging away. Heave yourself up the mountain, for there's bound to be a biscuit at the top. Someone's got to be the new X; someone's got to be the new Y. Or maybe you've got different kinds of dreams. Still not learned to knit? Do it! Fancy yoga? Bend over! Dreamed of walking the Pennine Way? Lace up your boots and BEGIN!

I was recently inspired by a little poem by Langston Hughes (check me getting all cultured in my old age):

> Hold fast to dreams
> For if dreams die
> Life is a broken-winged bird
> That cannot fly.
> Hold fast to dreams
> For when dreams go
> Life is a barren field
> Frozen with snow.

Big M, this all sounds very lovely and stuff, but it seems like most of my dreams haven't actually come

true.

That's because you haven't been honest about your dreams. You think right now that your dreams and aims are to get married, have children, play lacrosse at national level, perhaps be a PE teacher, do a politics degree and then become a politician. Don't you?

Those ARE my dreams, thank you.

They aren't really. They are the things you feel 'should' do. They are the things that other people want for you. They are the things that you know really aren't at the top of the list. What about those dreams that really make your heart sing? You have forgotten that one of our life-long dreams was to have a dog. You put it on every Christmas present list since you can remember, and now you have one. You have a dog.

But that's just a stupid little thing.

No, it's not. Those sorts of things really count. Because your heart singing is all that matters. But if you want a big example, just wait for this . . .

This had better be good, because I am a little down.

I think it's time you admitted your ultimate dream, Little M. You know, that dream you have of getting into comedy? Being a comedy actress . . .

SHUT UP! I haven't told anyone that. I am so embarrassed . . . who am I to think that I could do

326

that, for real? It sounds really arrogant to admit you think you could be on the telly.

Well, do you know, I rather wish you'd just have the confidence to admit it. Then maybe you would have done Drama and English for A-Level, done Theatre Studies at uni instead of Politics and focused on what you really wanted to do. It would have stood us in much better stead. Because here is the thing, Little Miranda: we never stop dreaming about getting into comedy. And at twenty-six, we finally started admitting it to people. Even though the dream seemed further and further away as I trundled through my twenties and early thirties in offices, I kept at it. I kept writing sketches in office stationery cupboards, kept trying them out in grotty London pubs, every summer went to the Edinburgh Festival and every September, when back in the office, would do another mail-merge to casting directors. And, get this—we are now a comedy actress. Professionally.

mouth falls open

Seriously, we are a comedian.

SHUT UP!

Are you bouncing up and down?

I am bouncing up and down.

Me too, although I have to hold on to my breasts to do so without damage.

I can't actually believe it. We get into comedy?

Yup.

I feel like crying.

Life may not be easy, Little M. Things do go wrong and it can be very tough. There isn't a road map for all the small but tricky issues in life. But if you follow your dream, you heart's desire, you will always be moving in the right direction, however much you may come a cropper on a beach, or in the hairdresser, or at a wedding.

The amazing thing is, for all that may not be quite right in my life, I do have my dream career. For how long, I don't know. The shelf-life for jobs like mine is pretty unreliable. But today I can call myself a comedy actress. I've gone from being the person hanging around the stage door for autographs, to the person being hung around for. This will never cease to amaze me. I did old sketches by heroes like The Two Ronnies, Victoria Wood and French and Saunders in village halls, and now I've actually met them.

Excuse me, hello, sorry? Did you just say . . . WE'VE MET FRENCH AND SAUNDERS?

Yup.

*No way. NO WAY. Shut up. SHUT UP! *shouts at her school friends, who are quietly putting on their gym kit* 'Guys, GUYS! I MEET FRENCH AND SAUNDERS WHEN I'M OLDER!'*

Calm down!

Calm down? CALM DOWN? This is BEYOND amazing. I mean, I've just watched them on the TV and dreamt about perhaps one day doing a sketch with them or being in a play with them and them being my best friends and we all sit around and have tea and scones together and laugh and laugh and laugh and you—you've actually . . . I mean . . . how did it go? When you met them?

Not too shabby, actually.

Oh, phew.

Well . . .

Oh, no. WHAT did we do?

No, no. It's fine. It's just . . . there was sweat involved. Meeting heroes is sweaty-making. There was so much sweat, in fact, that it seemed as if all the moisture in my body, and a good portion of the Dead Sea, had gathered on my upper lip.

YOU HAD A SWEAT MOUSTACHE WHEN YOU MET FRENCH AND SAUNDERS? I'm cringing.

It wasn't that bad. But actually there was a moment when a bead of sweat rolled its merry way off my lip and landed on my breast, which I dealt with by declaring loudly, in the middle of the conversation, 'Don't worry, that was a sweat-dribble; my breast isn't leaking.' Which turned out to be entirely unnecessary as they hadn't noticed the dribble in the first place.

You might as well have 'carried a watermelon'. I am revolted and ashamed.

Well, if it helps, my attitude was, 'Sod it, I've just met French and Saunders.'

True. Wow. WOW. I am going to have a celebratory box of Flumps.

You do that, Little Miranda, go—chill out, eat, eat your Flumps, and live in hope. Because things do happen. Things do change. Worry really is futile. Don't fear the future. Dreams do come true, and I have the sweat-spattered shirt to prove it. I may not (yet) have become the Wimbledon Ladies' Singles Champion, but I have briefly met Goran Ivanisevic. He isn't (yet) my husband BUT . . . I did shake his hand and emit an inaudible, high-pitched cross between a laugh and a cry, which I'm hoping might have been interpreted as a sophisticated Croatian mating call.

You see, you may not be a muso, you may have spent what sounds like dull years working in an office, you may be worried we aren't married yet, you may be depressed that we are culturally still a bit of a vacuum, that we are old before our time when it comes to adventure holidays and that we no longer do organised sport. But, firstly, some of those things that don't seem ideal at the time inform the future and, secondly, so much *is* good, and I have a hunch that there's so much good still to come.

*Thanks, Big M! *sits back, happy, looking forward to the future for the first time**

330

Now, MDRC, back to you for a final flourish. I hope your dreams have come or will come true. Or you feel inspired to down tools on what you wrongly thought was making you happy and follow the real dream. I feel happy and lucky and blessed to have had so many dream moments come true. And there is so much more that I hope I will tell you about some day. Oh, so much. But, for now, the time has come for me to bid you *au revoir*—definitely, I hope, not goodbye, my lovely, lovely chum. Right, well, off I pop. But I shall leave you with this last story. I think it sums it all up pretty well . . .

I was once on a very jolly Christmas chat show. Also on the bill was a massive star of small and large screen. A multi-millionaire, a respected international legend, someone for whom all dreams have supposedly come true, and who, on paper, has a 'perfect life'.

However, at thirty-eight, when I finally feel my life is beginning and that I might be able to start doing things my way, I know that even that star regularly feels like an idiot. To varying degrees, we all feel awkward. Whether we hide it with arrogance, shyness, modesty; whether we play the clown or the trendsetter, everyone struggles.

At the end of the show, we all had to sing along to a naff (and therefore very much to my taste) Christmas song. Fake snow was falling in the studio, the audience was clapping, there were dancers wearing Santa hats: it was a joyous, camp romp. I forgot I was on television and, as I lustily sang and bopped along, feeling wholly content, I glanced along to the other end of the sofa, at the star. They were looking pained and a little nervous. Out of place. They looked at me. They saw me

331

freely camping it up with my truly marvellous 'sitting-down hand-and-shoulder dancing,' and said, not meanly—I believe searchingly and perhaps with envy—'You just don't care, do you?'

I could have thought, 'Help, I must look like an idiot: I am on telly, doing sitting-down hand-and-shoulder dancing, while this person is playing it cool and I most definitely am not.'

The eighteen-year-old me would have stopped immediately, crushed by the peer pressure and pretended it was all ironic, but *I* carried on. And with total confidence, I said, 'No. I really don't.'

Life, eh?